Finding the Virgin Mary

Finding the Virgin Mary

*Her Evolving Stories
from Early Christianity to Today*

JUDITH M. DAVIS

McFarland & Company, Inc., Publishers
Jefferson, North Carolina

ISBN (print) 978-1-4766-9373-6
ISBN (ebook) 978-1-4766-5489-8

LIBRARY OF CONGRESS AND BRITISH LIBRARY
CATALOGUING DATA ARE AVAILABLE

Library of Congress Control Number 2024038640

© 2024 Judith M. Davis. All rights reserved

No part of this book may be reproduced or transmitted in any form or by any means, electronic or mechanical, including photocopying or recording, or by any information storage and retrieval system, without permission in writing from the publisher.

Front cover: (clockwise, from top left) Enthroned Virgin statuette, c.1490–1500 (Metropolitan Museum of Art); stained glass from the Cathedral of Saint Mary of the Immaculate Conception, Peoria, Illinois; *Madonna del Rosario,* c. 6th century; *The Immaculate Conception* by Diego Velázquez, 1618 (National Gallery, London); Head of the Madonna, 1920s mezzotint after painting by Sandro Botticelli (Library of Congress); *Our Lady of Guadalupe* (Shutterstock); *The Mother of God of Tenderness Towards Evil Hearts* by Kuzma Petrov-Vodkin, 1914; *Maria Santissima* by Andrea Fossombrone, 1956 (private collection); *Madonna della Pietà* by Michelangelo, 1488–1499, Saint Peter's Basilica, Vatican City; *Surfing Madonna* mosaic by Mark Patterson, 2011, Encinitas, California; Virgin Mary with Child icon (Shutterstock); *Maria Immaculata* by Carl Faust, 1917; *Virgin and Child in Majesty* sculpture, c. 1175–1200 (Metropolitan Museum of Art); religious postcard featuring Mary, early 20th century; *Madonna and Child,* late 6th century, Saint Catherine's Monastery, Sinai, Egypt; *Aranjuez Immaculate Conception* by Bartolomé Esteban Murillo, c. 1675 (Museo del Prado, Madrid); *Vierge de Gloire* by Richard Brunck de Freundeck, 1945 (Strasbourg Museum of Modern and Contemporary Art); *Immaculate Heart of Mary* chromolithograph, c. 1900 (Library of Congress)

Printed in the United States of America

*McFarland & Company, Inc., Publishers
Box 611, Jefferson, North Carolina 28640
www.mcfarlandpub.com*

To all the daughters of Mary, called to minister as she did:
May she and her son affirm your calls and enable your vocations!

Contents

Acknowledgments	xiii
Preface	1
Introduction	5

1. Gospels Real and Imagined: First to Seventh Centuries — 9

The "Real" Gospels — 9
Biblical Backstories: The Extracanonical Gospels — 12
  Mary in the *Protogospel of James* 13 • The Earliest Devotion to Mary? 15 • Mary as Minister in the Temple of Jerusalem: The Earliest Image? 16 • Mary in the *Gospel of Pseudo-Matthew* 16 • Mary in the Qur'an 18
Mary's Early Reputation as a Miracle Worker — 20
The Narrative Theology of Gospels Real and Imagined — 20

2. Mary's "Life Stories": Fourth to Twelfth Centuries — 22

Mary's Voice Heard Loud and Clear: Romanos the Melodist — 23
Epiphanios the Monk and the First Life of Mary — 25
Later Marian Biographers and the Development of Mary's Story — 26
  John Geometres: Mary's Life as Sermon 27 • Euthymios the Athonite: Mary's Life as Biography with Embellishments 28 • The "Holy Theft" of Mary's Clothing 32 • Mary's Life Foreshortened: Symeon Metaphrastes 33
Mary as Protector of the Faithful — 34
Mary's Death and Entry into Heaven — 34
Mary in the Afterlife: Queen of Heaven and Hell — 38
What Does the Narrative Theology of the Lives of Mary *Say to Us?* — 38

3. Mary in the Early Middle Ages: Devotions, Churches, Shrines, and Books of Praise (Sixth to Twelfth Centuries) — 40

Sixth-Century Marian Miracle Stories: Gregory of Tours — 41
   Mary, Master Builder 41 • Mary, Provider 41
The Most Famous Marian Hymn — 42
Paul the Deacon's Classic Marian Tale — 42
Two Early Shrine Collections — 43
   Saragossa, Spain 43 • Chartres 43
Mary in the "Dark Ages" — 44
Later Shrine Collections — 45
Early English Selections from the Mariales — 47
Little Left Unsaid: Early Books of Praise for Mary — 49
What Is the Narrative Theology of These Writings? — 50

4. The Long Twelfth Century I: Miracles in the Age of Faith and Feudalism — 52

The Age of Faith — 52
Genesis 3 Fulfilled: Mary and the Devil — 53
The Feudal World — 54
Mary's Competition: The Noble Lady of "Courtly Love" — 55
The Noblest Lady of Them All: Medieval Marian Lyrics — 56
The Mary of the Medieval Miracle Stories — 57
Vincent of Beauvais, an Author in the Latin Tradition — 58
Seafarers Menaced by a Storm Saved by Mary, Star of the Sea — 59
Adgar and the First Vernacular French Marian Miracle Collection — 60
   A Cleric Cured by Mary in a Field of Flowers 61 • Enlarging a Country Church 62
Wace and an Early Vernacular "Life of Mary" — 63
Best-Selling Author Gautier de Coinci (1177–1236) — 65
   Mary as Chess Queen 65 • The Miracle of the Abbess Whom Our Lady Delivered from Great Distress 66 • The Miracle of the Young Nun 70 • The Miracle of the Hanged Thief 75 • The Knight of 150 Hail Marys 77 • The Miracle of the Misplaced Engagement Ring 80 • The Miracle of Théophile, or the Devil's Charter 81 • The Miracle of the Rich Man and the Widow 86 • The Miracle of the Priest Who Knew Only One Mass 88 • The Miracle of the Peasant Who Could Learn Only Half of the Hail Mary 89 • The Miracle of the Candle That Came Down to the Jongleur 90

A Narrative Theology of Subversion: Mercy, Not Judgment, Prevails	92
Another Thirteenth-Century Miracle? The Holy House of Loreto	94

5. The Long Twelfth Century II: Marian Tales from the Continent and England — 95

About Gondrée and How Our Lady Came to Be Called Notre Dame de Chartres	95
The Miracle of the Knight Saved from Death by the Undergarments He Wore That Had Touched the Chemise of Chartres	97
Mary's Royal Troubadour, King Alfonso X of Spain	98
Gonazalo de Berceo, a People's Poet	100
The Pregnant Woman Saved by the Virgin 101	
The Miracle of the Artisan Monk and the Ugly Devil	102
The Miracle of Our Lady's Tumbler	105
The Miracle of Our Lady at the Tournament	109
The German Novice Master's Masterwork	111
Sir Walter of Birbeck, the Tardy Knight and Saintly Monk 111	
Jacobus of Voragine: Mary's Life, Mary's Stories in the Calendar of the Church	113
The Feast of Mary's Nativity and Marian Genealogies 114 • A Son Restored to His Mother 114 • The Monk Who Could Learn Only Two Words of the "Ave Maria" 115 • Mary's Hand on the Scale 116 • The Knight Who Sold His Wife to the Devil 117	
Mary at the Apex of Paradise in Dante's Divine Comedy	118
Mary Tales and Poems in Middle English	119
The Widow's Candle for the Feast 120	
Geoffrey Chaucer: Mixed Messages About Mary	121
The Monk and Our Lady's Sleeves	122
Anonymous Marian Lyrics in Middle English	123
What is the Narrative/Poetic Theology of These Works?	125
François Villon's Ballade of Prayer to Notre Dame	126

6. From Story to Drama to Anecdote: The Miracle Tales Evolve — 128

The Holy Kinship as Romance	128
The Romance of Saint Fanuel and Saint Anne 128	
The Shrine-Madonnas	130

Contents

Affective Piety Dramatized: The Miracles of Our Lady Performed   134
    A Baby Restored to Life 134 • The Miracle of the Child Promised to the Devil 135 • The Devil in Disguise: The Miracle of Saint John the Hermit 139

A Prescient Trend   140
    Our Lady's Day in Court, or Why She Is Called Our Advocate 141 • A Dramatic "Life of Mary" in the Middle English N-Town Plays 143

A Marian Lament/Lament for Mary   146
Mary in the Passion Plays of France   147
Our Lady of the Sermon: Marian Devotion as a Guarantee of Heaven   149
What Is the Narrative Theology of the Waning Middle Ages?   150

7. What Happened to the Stories? That's Another Story   152

Between Devotion and Reform: Erasmus of Rotterdam (1469–1517)   152
Renaissance and Reform   154
Apparitions I: Our Lady of Guadalupe   156
The Counter-Reformation: Mary and the Church Militant   158
A Cover-Up and a Revelation: Mary as Bishop—or Pope   159
    The Cover-Up 159 • The Revelation 159

Defenders of Mary I   161
Defenders of Mary II: The "French School"   162
A Response to the Enlightenment: The Glories of Mary   164
Apparitions II: Mary and the Miraculous Medal   165
The Pope and the Dogma: Pius IX and the Immaculate Conception   166
Apparitions III: Mary and Lourdes   167
Other Nineteenth-Century Visions of Mary: Priest and Goddess   168
Feminists, Philologists, and Mary   169
Mary Stories and the Medievalism Phenomenon   171
What Are the Narrative Theologies of the Post–Reform Era?   172

8. A Tale of Four Stories from Then to Now   174

A Life of Mary from the Byzantine Tradition, Medieval Version   174
A Life of Mary from the Byzantine Tradition, Modern Version   175
Theophilus: From the Seventh Century to the Twenty-First   178
Sister Beatrice, Perennial Penitent   178
The Grain Miracle Legend   180
    From Story to Ballad 181 • From Ballad to Folk Tale 182 • A Nineteenth-Century Grain Miracle in the Upper Midwest 184

From Tumbler to Juggler, Converso *to Child: Our Lady's Minstrel*	185
Pseudo-Matthew at Christmastide: The Cherry Tree Carol	187
Narratives and Theologies Across the Centuries	188

9. End of Stories, End of Story? Where Is Mary in Modernity?   190

Mary as Messenger I	190
Midcentury Mary: A New Dogma	191
Mary the Subject of Debate in Vatican II	192
Mary at Mid–Century: Another Denial	194
Mary as Countersign: Her Presence in the Twenty-First Century	194
Mary as Messenger II	195
Gladys and the Glowing Rosary	196
Finding Mary Past and Present, There and Here	200
Chapter Notes	203
Bibliography	221
Index	233

Acknowledgments

The act of writing might be a solitary enterprise, but the activity of making a book takes a community. I've been privileged to have the help of an especially diverse community to compose this tribute to Mary.

Standouts in the community: my family, beginning with my spouse, Bill Davis, who has encouraged and edited my writing (his is the Ph.D. in English) for the many years of our marriage. Together with him, my sisters Roberta and Margaret Felker and my brother Bill Felker have been steadfast critics, editors, cheerleaders, and sources of inspiration throughout. They speak from their own experience as storytellers. Roberta preaches regularly at Holy Wisdom Monastery in Middleton, Wisconsin. Margaret told folk tales for many years at different venues in Madison. Brother Bill publishes his stories in the *Yellow Springs* [Ohio] *News* and in a series of books.

Holy Wisdom Monastery, an ecumenical community in Middleton, Wisconsin, has been a source of support and inspiration as well. Oblates (associates) of that community have been important companions on my journey, especially my friend Kathy Woytych and my coach, the Rev. Lisa L. Nelson, as well as my incomparable editor Leora Weitzman. Almost 20 years ago I gave a retreat on Mary at the monastery, and I thank all of the people who participated for their questions, affirmations, and challenges.

At a 2013 conference on "Mary in Mennonite Dress" sponsored by the Associated Mennonite Biblical Seminaries in Elkhart, Indiana, I presented my first findings about Mary in extracanonical works. Afterward, some friends asked if we could meet to talk about Mary. We did indeed meet for several months at a local restaurant, calling ourselves "Mary Panera." I thank Joyce Hostetler, Alice Roth, and Becky Tyson for their questions and perceptions about Mary.

The Sisters of the Order of Saint Benedict in St. Joseph, Minnesota, provide an environment of personal and academic support for writers and others who need space for creativity. Many thanks to Sister Ann Marie

Biermeier and her colleagues for their more-than-Benedictine hospitality and encouragement of my work in their Studium program and beyond.

The Goshen College Library has been a source of information and vital assistance for many, many years. I especially appreciate the interlibrary loan librarians Abby Nafziger and Esther Gudea for their steady competence in obtaining whatever I needed for my work.

I am grateful to Future Church, a progressive Catholic organization that promotes equality in the Church, sponsoring presentations and producing reading materials on subjects ranging from women in the early Church to seminars on Scripture. A few years ago, former executive director Deborah Rose asked me to organize a "Mary Project" based on Marian doctrines and feast days. Many thanks to Deb for publishing the work of Elizabeth Johnson and Mary Catherine Athans as well as mine. It was a privilege to be in such inspiring Marian company.

Since beginning this journey, I have become what I call a "radically reformed" Catholic. I am grateful to my Mennonite community, especially members of my small group, Mary and Glenn Gilbert, Marna and Bill Mateer, Anita Boyle and Jerry Lapp, Merle and Jane Baker, and Maribeth and Arden Shank, for their penetrating questions and wonderful skepticism, especially regarding extracanonical works.

Many joy-filled thanks to my publishing editor, Layla Milholen, for her affirmation and willingness to consider yet another book on Mary; and to Natasha Bolger, who took charge of the technical aspects of imagery and send-off.

And yes, thanks to the Mother Most Powerful whose mantle has surrounded this work. I could not have done it without the help of all the above communities as well as the Communion of Saints.

Preface

Finding the Virgin Mary retells stories about Mary from the Second Testament through Christian antiquity and the Middle Ages to the twenty-first century, showing her evolution from the strong "partner of God" described in a number of early Christian commentaries and medieval writers to the silent, obedient handmaid of the Church after Vatican II. My aim is to show how the images of Mary created and reflected in the stories about her have evolved throughout the ages and to challenge the reader to see Mary anew, reframed by those images. The narrative or story theology of these tales reflects woman as the image of God, an image the Church has often professed but seldom if ever recognized in practice. My intent is to exchange the concept of the Divine Feminine for reverence for, and acknowledgment of, the Feminine Divine.

Finding and telling Mary stories has been my part-time project for the past 30 years. Born a cradle Catholic, I cherish an early memory of my mother's light blue novena book and rosary as well as a vigil candle burning at the feet of a white-robed statue of Mary. Mama's prayers were most fervent for my father, a Marine in World War II. His "miraculous" survival of a direct mortar hit made the St. Paul papers, and our family knew why: Mary's power defied mortar shells and wave attacks, storms at sea, and bombs on land. The vigil light continued to burn in thanksgiving even after he arrived home.

Lessons in church and school, however, presented pallid, perfect images of Mary in statues and paintings, along with exhortations to imitate her silence, humility, and acquiescence. As a child, I felt that Mary was more than a little unreal, too good to be true. As an adolescent, I saw her as someone whose perfection (to say nothing of virgin motherhood) I could never achieve. As a college student, I tended to forget her entirely.

Later, however, as a single parent I came to appreciate Mary, seeing her for the first time as a strong woman who was almost solely responsible for the upbringing of her son, and I began to count on her for support. She never failed me.

When Vatican II began, I was hopeful that it would bring Mary into a more realistic and accessible perspective, but although it declared her the "Mother of the Church," it also reduced her titles and roles; edited her out of the Mass except for brief mentions in the Confession of Sin, the Creed, and the Canon; and eliminated many Marian prayers. I joined the crowd of people who, like author Charlene Spretnak, felt ourselves to be "Missing Mary."[1]

I had a glimpse of the missing Mary in graduate school, where I encountered her in some of the writings of the Middle Ages, and I was hooked. I ended up becoming a medievalist, concentrating on French romance, a more acceptable genre at the time, but the stories about Mary stayed in the back of my mind. In a poem to Mary by the fifteenth-century poet and outlaw François Villon, I found a reference to the romance of Mary stories. After years of teaching and administration, I followed their allure.

A Summer Fellowship from the Indiana Committee for the Humanities gave me the opportunity to revisit France, this time to explore medieval works that dramatized Marian miracles. In the Parisian Center for Research and History of Texts I found literally hundreds of references to Mary's stories. I visited her churches, cathedrals, and shrines in Paris, Chartres, Rocamadour, Lourdes, and Poitiers, returning home with a staggering list of stories to explore.

The fellowship required that I present my findings to the "general public." In order to engage my audience, I commissioned a costume that resembled the dress of a fourteenth-century French matron whom I called Marie de la Fère, my persona for reminiscences of a pilgrimage from northern France to Chartres by way of Paris. In the course of her journey, Marie hears tales about Mary's miracles from other pilgrims; in Paris, she and some of her company attend two plays about Mary's dramatic interventions in human affairs. She shares these stories with her audience.

In translating some of the tales that my pilgrim heard, I found that the authors showed Mary to be both familiarly winsome and enormously powerful, a partner with God in the work of salvation. I also found that this Mary has a message for people today. As I recounted the tales of her love and compassion, admonishment and support, demands and rewards, the responses surprised and moved me. Protestants and Catholics, women and men, reacted warmly, often emotionally, to the idea of Mary as a strong, capable, wise, and affectionate mother who never stops looking after her children, even the most wayward. Women, in particular, surprised and moved by the autonomy and vigor of the medieval Mary, expressed a "sense of empowerment" in hearing her stories.

Those Mary fans and I were not alone. Books on the Mother of Jesus have appeared regularly over the past 30 years, beginning with Marina Warner's *Alone of All Her Sex* in 1976. Jaroslav Pelikan presents a historical and cultural description of Mary, her importance and influence—political, social, religious, artistic—in *Mary Through the Centuries* (1996). Elizabeth Johnson's *Truly Our Sister* (2003) offers a scholarly theological and historical appreciation of Marian interpretations through the ages. Miri Rubin's *Mother of God: A History of the Virgin Mary* (2009) presents an engaging, encyclopedic history of Mary. Mary Christine Athans' *In Quest of the Jewish Mary* (2013) situates Mary historically and theologically, concentrating on the Jewish background of her story. Stephen Shoemaker's *Mary in Early Christian Faith and Devotion* (2016) presents a comprehensive scholarly account of the development of Marian teachings and devotion from the second century forward. Rachel Fulton Brown's *Mary and the Art of Prayer: The Hours of the Virgin in Medieval Christian Life and Thought* (2018) situates her comprehensive research on all things Marian in the context of daily prayer. Ally Kateusz's *Mary and Early Christian Women* (2019) is notable for her coverage of early Christianity, illustrated with artifacts as well as depictions of Mary.

Impressive as they are, these Marian works don't engage the development of Marian *stories* from their origins to the present. The more I read, the more I wondered: How did stories about Mary begin to appear in the Middle Ages? Were they products of the medieval imagination, inspired by popular devotion? Or, like much medieval literature, did they originate in the ancient world? If so, where did they come from, and when? I began delving into the past, finding evidence of a Marian tradition that dates back to the beginnings of the Christian church.

Following that tradition, I began my own collection of stories about Mary that date from the second century onward, translating from Latin and French, Anglo-Norman and Middle English, summarizing scholarship and researching history. Like my medieval forbears, I make no special claim to originality; as an *amateur*, literally a lover of this material, I rely on old collections as well as scholars and other collectors of tales. Also like them, I have chosen those tales that may appeal to a contemporary audience; this book—intended to be both scholarly and accessible—brings the strength of the Marian tradition from its beginnings to the twenty-first century.

In working with this tradition, I had to face a problem that has shadowed the stories since their inception. The problem is apparent in the following personal story.

Some years ago I lived in Strasbourg, France, for a time, often attending Mass in the magnificent red sandstone cathedral that dominates the city. Known for its splendid rose window and intricately carved façade, the Cathedral of Our Lady of Strasbourg is a masterpiece of Romanesque and Gothic artistry. Two of its most famous sculptures frame the portal of the south transept: Ecclesia (Church) and Synagoga (Synagogue). Wearing a crown, Ecclesia holds her head high; her left hand holds a chalice, her right a staff topped by a cross with an empty shroud, symbolizing Christ's triumph over death. Opposite Ecclesia, on the other side of the door, Synagoga stands listlessly, head bowed, eyes blindfolded. Her left hand touches the tablet of the First Testament; her right hand lifts up half of a broken spear. The symbolism is obvious: Christianity has triumphed over Judaism.

The statues literally embody anti–Judaism or anti–Semitism, a prejudice that permeated Christian writings from the second century on. What began as a rivalry between two belief systems hardened into bitter opposition and polemic, with prominent Christian churchmen accusing first-century Jews of killing God. The undercurrent of antisemitism in the Gospels, particularly in John, became mainstream and tainted nearly every tale about Mary, beginning with the very first extracanonical work, the *Protogospel of James*, and continuing into modern times.

In retelling Mary's stories, I have edited out that antisemitism, acting from a deep concern about its resurgence in the twenty-first century. May religious prejudice of every kind be edited out of our world as well!

Introduction

Stories about Mary began to appear in the second century, a spring of tradition that branched off from the mainstream of teaching based on the canonical gospels, becoming a torrent of texts about Mary, her relationship with God, and her motherhood not only of Jesus but of all members of the Christian church. These texts, known as apocrypha, or extracanonical writing,[1] supplied additional information about the lives of both Jesus and Mary, supplementing and sometimes supplanting orthodoxy with imagination.

Responding to controversies surrounding Jesus' parents and birth but also reflecting popular devotion, stories of Mary's life portrayed her as an exceptionally pure and holy woman, worthy to be the mother of God. Extracanonical writings describe her life as resembling or even paralleling that of her son; they establish her as a person uniquely gifted by God in her life, in her motherhood, in her death, and in her role as perpetual partner with God. Both the extracanonical texts and other Marian stories reflect orthodox depictions of Mary as extraordinarily pure and holy; however, many also portray her as a strong and powerful woman in her own right with her own following of women, one who—in partnership with her son—continues the work of salvation after her death. These stories show the valiant Mary, the active Mary, the Mary who takes the part of sinners and turns them into, as Pope Francis called them, "everyday saints," which is, after all, the enterprise of her son.

I believe that stories about Mary and the "signs and wonders" or miracles that she performed respond to a deep psychological need for an image of the feminine divine. All Christian churches, and especially the Catholic church, project and promote predominantly masculine ideas of Godhead that are deeply rooted in a patriarchal and often misogynistic tradition. Only men can be priests. Women may read only the First Testament and the Epistles at Mass, never the Gospel, the Word reserved for a male presider who alone can bring Jesus to the altar. This, of course, is because women are daughters of Eve and subject to male authority for that very reason. The Son of God was born in the person of Jesus Christ; women cannot image God as Jesus did—only men can.

The ancient and medieval Mary can be seen as a counter-sign to that exclusivist theology. Interpretations of her life, dating from the second through the thirteenth centuries, show her descended from a priestly family on both her mother's and her father's side, active in Jesus' ministry, prominent in the early days of the Christian church. Mary is God's partner: Her *fiat* in response to Gabriel's proposal—"let it be done"—echoes the *fiat* that resounded in God's creation of the universe; her body co-creates the body and blood of Jesus, the Son of God. These stories about Mary reflect a profoundly incarnational theology in which images of divinity are revealed in both mother and son.

Narrative or "story" theology isn't new. We may look at the entire Bible, for example, as a frame tale for a series of stories that unfold, from the First to the Second Testament, concerning the relationship between God and God's creatures, beginning with the Spirit moving over the face of the earth and continuing with that same Spirit's animating a small group of frightened people who would leave their place of refuge and go out to change the world. Jesus of Nazareth was adept at story theology. With their characters and settings drawn from everyday life, his parables delivered the good news of God's care for people in terms they could understand: a woman searching for a lost coin, a spendthrift, wayward son, a widow and a judge. Folks hearing Jesus' stories could understand that God searches everywhere to find those who have abandoned their divine home; that God seeks out the lost, seeing the smallest as precious; that God welcomes back the sinner, no matter how contrived that sinner's repentance might be; and that God hears the prayers of the persistent.

From the earliest days of the Christian church, stories formed the basis for tradition and belief. Four writers set down the story that Jesus lived and the parables he told. Very early on, tales of the martyrs, ultimate witnesses to the faith, inspired a tradition of writing about the lives of holy ones as examples for their contemporaries and beacons for their spiritual descendants. Prayers to the holy ones, or saints, often spoken in the presence of their relics—physical remnants of their lives on earth such as bones, ashes, or scraps of clothing—were answered, often dramatically. The sick recovered; the blind regained their sight; the paralyzed walked again with their neighbors. These events were called *miraculi* (from the Latin *miror*, to wonder at) or miracles, indicating something marvelous and beyond natural causation, worked by God through the agency of holy people.[2] Marian miracle stories follow this pattern, and the message of their narrative theology is clear: Mary is God's partner as well as God's servant in salvation history.

Introduction

This book includes four kinds of stories: first-century Biblical (canonical) episodes; early extracanonical biographies or "Lives of Mary"; medieval miracle tales; and later retellings that survive in legends, drama, songs, and folklore as well as modern story collections.

Chapter 1 takes in stories about Mary from the Second Testament to the early Middle Ages, beginning with biblical episodes and continuing with extracanonical "gospels." Chapter 2 includes her exceptional childhood, her adult years with Jesus, and her leadership of the early church as well as accounts of her death and entry into the afterlife, concluding with assurances that she will intercede for her family on earth. Chapter 3 lays the groundwork for the extravagance of devotional collections that began early in the Middle Ages, embracing liturgies, hymns, and books of poetry and praise as well as stories.

An important and little-known aspect of these early works is that they describe Mary's priestly ancestry and her sacrificial role in the Passion of her son. Individual genealogies trace her family's descent from the priestly tribes of Aaron and Levi. Early biographies depict her as participating in the Last Supper, taking part in the events of the Passion, and continuing the legacy of Jesus as an ecclesial leader.

Chapters 4 and 5 contain miracle stories from France, Spain, and Italy. These tales are only a fraction of the hundreds of Marian tales that spread from the East throughout Europe and beyond. Miracle stories focus on her power and intimate relationships with those devoted to her; visual evidence of these relationships appears in statues, frescoes, paintings, and manuscript illuminations.

Chapter 6 begins the evolution of Mary's stories through the influence of Church councils, the rise of the middle class, and the phenomenon of affective piety. Legends and biblical tales alike take the form of drama; at first Mary appears on stage as the royal Mother of God, but with time her role diminishes. By the fifteenth century, Passion plays show Mary most memorably as the helpless, tearful mother at the foot of the cross. From appearing as the subject of her own story, Mary evolves to become an object of devotion—and pity.

Chapter 7 recounts the circumstances surrounding the decline of miracle stories and the paradoxical emergence of depictions of Mary as priest. In art, we see the Renaissance preference for the humanistic depiction of religious figures; in church history, we observe the Reformers' "demotion" of Mary to the status of a humble housewife beloved of God. Paradoxically, theologians begin to engage in speculation about Mary's role in salvation history, some of them suggesting a "priestly" interpretation of that role.

Chapter 8 follows four major miracle stories as they are transformed into ballad, folk tale, Christmas carol, opera, radio show, and film, to say nothing of countless collections and adaptations. The trajectory of these retellings tends toward what I call a "pedestalization" of Mary, making her into a distant if uplifting presence rather than an actor in her own story. A possible exception is a modern Greek Orthodox *Life of Mary*, compiled from ancient and medieval sources and containing additional material about her evangelizing journeys.

Chapter 9 suggests some answers to the question "Where is Mary today?" The Vatican speaks of her in terms of the "Marian Principle," the complement to the dominant "Petrine Principle" (not to be confused with the Peter Principle, no matter how tempting) that is identified with the church. More realistic voices call her "Friend of God and Prophet."[3] They emphasize her role in Jesus' upbringing as well as his ministry. They point out the history of her depiction as priest, fully appreciating her as a model and icon of women's ordination.

While the Bible suggests some of Mary's qualities and capabilities, the extracanonical stories—and especially the medieval tales—attribute activities and influence to Mary beyond what is recorded by the four evangelists: They go farther than Scripture, asserting and reassuring us that Mary is indeed the image of God, that the female is also divine. Like the Creator's *ruach*, or breath, she brings a new world into being. Like Jesus, she invites sinners to repent and saves them—repeatedly—from the powers of evil. Like the Holy Spirit, she hovers over a sinful world, ready and able to make its denizens holy, eminently capable of serving as an advocate for humanity. When she functions in the more traditional role of mediator, it is as a supremely powerful one: Her requests are always granted because she is intimately related to the divine grantor as well as to the human grantees. This book is an introduction to the Mary we have been missing.

Chapter 1

Gospels Real and Imagined
First to Seventh Centuries

The "Real" Gospels

Conventional wisdom has it that Mary is mentioned only a few times in the Second Testament. With a scriptural background limited to liturgy and childhood "Bible Stories," I had to study and reconsider the passages in which Mary appears. I've found that the Gospel writers identify her either by name or as "the mother of Jesus" more than 150 times; they assign her 17 names and titles.[1] Although she doesn't speak often, her words are memorable (momentous in John, when she instructs the servants to do whatever Jesus tells them). The "real" Gospel authors provided just enough information about the mother of Jesus to inspire stories of how Mary got to be that mother: her parents, her upbringing, how Joseph became her fiancé, the life that brought her to the moment of Gabriel's invitation and led her to the foot of the cross.

In Luke 1:34, we find Mary daring to ask Gabriel, "How can this be?" There she was, in the presence of the one who stood in the presence of God, posing a logical and pointed question to a divine messenger. "How can this be?" She was only engaged, not married. Mary Anne Case speaks of Mary's response as "…her cross-examination of the angel of the Annunciation, … Note also that … she speaks of not having known a man rather than of a man not having known her, thus taking on for herself the active description of the sex act as knowledge usually ascribed to males."[2]

Questioning authority was a trait that Mary would pass on to her son. Gabriel replies to her with the news about her cousin's pregnancy, "for nothing is impossible with God." Mary's response is immediate. "I am the Lord's servant." Traditionally, her answer has been interpreted as an act of supreme humility and passive obedience to the Will of God. Actually, however, "I am the Lord's servant" echoes an address to God made by her illustrious ancestors in faith over the centuries. Abraham calls himself the servant of the Lord (Gen. 18:3). David is the Lord's servant in Psalm 36; and Samuel responds to the voice he hears in the night, "Speak, Lord, for your servant is listening" (1 Sam. 3). As Isaiah had prophesied, Mary's son would also be the servant of the Lord.

Far from being passively acquiescent, Mary's obedience resonates with agency and power. The word "obedience" comes from two Latin roots that mean "listen to" and "hear." Mary's obedience is literally the result of listening actively to Gabriel, questioning respectfully, and responding fervently. She has listened to and heard the Word of God, which has taken form and life within her. She has become God's partner in the salvation of the world.

Mary's partnership is reflected in her prophetic response to Elizabeth's blessing: her soul "magnifies the Lord" and foresees a world in which the powerful give way to the lowly and the hungry are fed while the rich go hungry. She makes a revolutionary call for peace and justice that foreshadows her son's message and her witness to that message throughout his life and beyond. Reflecting divine mercy and strength, Mary's actions mirror God's both in Scripture and in many of the later stories that are told about her.

Early icons of the Eastern Church and later Western paintings depict Mary's presentation of the baby Jesus in the Temple of Jerusalem (Luke 2:32–38). Many of these scenes take place in front of an altar. In one striking icon, Mary is a high priest with Simeon, their hands covered by her veil and the sleeves of his robe (a sign of respect and humility) as she offers and he accepts Jesus, the Son of God. In the words of Dorian Llewelyn, this is the place "[o]f the greatest and final encounter between the divine and human that occurs in the one person of Christ. Both temple and [Mary the God-bearer] also point forward to the Eucharist, the extension of the offering of Christ into all places and times.... In this icon, Mary is shown as assuming a sacerdotal role which will be consummated at the sacrifice of Calvary."[3]

Mary's priestly role is one of service and accompaniment as well as sacrifice, one that will continue beyond the death of her son for ages to come.

We find the next mention of Mary in Luke 2:41–51, twelve years later. The evangelist may have been charitable in his description of Mary's address to Jesus: "Child, why have you treated us like this?" Think of her being reunited with her boy after three harrowing days of hunting for him everywhere, and hearing him respond to her (justifiable) reproach by saying, with more-than-adolescent wisdom, "Didn't you know that I must be in my Father's house?" After that, Jesus turns from challenging his elders in the Temple to obedience in his parents' home, but Mary continues to think about her son's begetting and his time in the Temple, "treasuring all these things in her heart." Although Jesus is a model son in Nazareth, perhaps the "things in her heart" tell her that her precocious son will leave home to learn from his cousin John and go his own way on his Father's business.

Mary was Jesus' first—and maybe, initially, most perplexed—disciple. When Jesus chose to be baptized and then went off into the desert for more than a month and came back to begin his mission, she could only trust and imagine.

But imagine she did. John's Gospel (2:1–11) shows us that, knowing her son as she did, she had also come to guess at—if not yet fully appreciate—his mission and his power to achieve it, and she exercised her own unique powers of faith and persuasion to convince him that it was time to begin. All she had to say to Jesus was, "They have no wine." Not a statement, it was a request made in full confidence that he could, and would, do something about it. Even though Jesus rebuffed her, she believed and persisted, serenely turning to the servants and saying, "Do whatever he tells you."

The result: an extravagant "2,400 glasses of phenomenal wine.... And it is Mary ... who throws open the door to the proclamation of the gospel and the public life of Jesus—and she walks through the door with him. She reminds us that all miracles need is willing participation in the unfolding of the mystery, ... and that vessels—that we—are better filled with the wine of wholehearted joy than with empty rituals."[4]

Mary's words remind Jesus—the Word—of what he has come for, and she will continue to remind him in story and song through the ages.

But first she must suffer through her son's arrest, trial, condemnation, torture, and execution. The Passion of Jesus takes up two chapters—18 and 19—in the Gospel of John. His death is described in two verses. Mary, her sister, and Mary Magdalene are standing close to the cross with the apostle John. Jesus' next-to-last act on earth is to see that his mother is taken care of (John 19:26–27). Joseph is dead; without a male relative to provide for her, Mary would be left without resources, a virtual outcast in society.

Jesus' words, poignant in their brevity, would inspire pages and chapters and treatises on Mary as the sorrowful mother, overshadowing Mary the disciple, faithful to the end.

After Jesus' ascension, Mary was there when the Holy Spirit swept through the upper room in wind and fire, as described so vividly in Acts 1:8–14 and 2:1–4. She surely recognized the One who had visited her so many years ago as the tongue of fire appeared above her head. With the other women and men in that room, she received the Holy Spirit's power, making her a witness to Jesus "[i]n Jerusalem, in all Judea and Samaria, and to the ends of the earth."

Mary isn't mentioned again in the history of the early church. It will be the task of later writers to follow her as she not only accompanies her son on his earthly mission but carries the Word out into the world. She will be his ambassador, his interpreter, his companion and partner in other gospels through the ages.

Biblical Backstories: The Extracanonical Gospels

The stories that follow circulated among Christians during the second through the tenth centuries, a time of political and ecclesiastical turbulence. After a period of both expansion and persecution of the early church, the Roman Emperor Constantine I recognized Christianity in 313. He established the city of Constantinople as his "new Rome" in 330, the capital city for the Eastern empire known as Byzantium. Christianity was made the state religion scarcely 50 years later. In 476, Rome fell to invading barbarian hordes; the ensuing chaos left the Church as the principal source of what order there was, making it a secular as well as an ecclesiastical power in the West.

In the East, violence erupted over the use of icons in worship during the eighth and ninth centuries. As the turmoil over icons increased, and as East and West drew further apart in custom and governance during the ninth and tenth centuries, a significant number of Byzantine clerics fled to the West, finding refuge in the monasteries of Italy and France. As the flow of scholars and monks to the West continued, early Eastern stories of the Blessed Mother were translated into Latin, supplementing and enriching a growing Marian tradition in the West.

Early in this same period, the second through the tenth centuries, the biblical canon developed into 27 books that were proclaimed to be authentic Christian writing. At the Council of Nicaea in 325, the canon was discussed, but the most important action of the Council was the declaration that Jesus was both divine and human, with its implication that Mary was the Mother of God. The first prayer to Mary was composed sometime in the third or fourth century. The fourth century saw the establishment of the biblical canon at the Council of Rome in 380, and during the fifth century, the Council of Ephesus (431) proclaimed Mary to be the *Theotokos*, God-bearer, Mother of God.

The two extracanonical gospels below were written by authors who "borrowed" the familiar names of James and Matthew to lend authenticity to their accounts. They focus on specific aspects of Mary's person and life because each one was written to respond to the religious or cultural or dogmatic concerns of the time. These stories are not widely known, due to a fifth-century papal decree that listed the acceptable or "canonical" 27 books of the Second Testament, declaring others to be "apocryphal" or extracanonical.

Biblical scholar J.K. Elliott observes that "Christians from the second and third centuries onwards seem to have been avid readers.... The curiosity of pious Christians about the origins of their faith was increasingly satisfied by a growing number of Gospels, Acts, and other types of literature."[5] If some of the details in these extracanonical tales seem exaggerated or fantastic, it's because their authors were believers competing with the more sensational secular romances of the times.

Mary in the *Protogospel of James*

The *Protogospel of James* dates from the middle of the second century.[6] From this text, we learn about Mary's birth, education, and marriage; we can see the origin of traditional Christian motifs depicted in paintings, sculpture, and sermons from that time forward. We also can see details important to the audience of the time, such as Mary's weaving of the Temple veil in the royal and priestly colors of purple and scarlet, symbolic of Jesus' heritage and mission.

Mary's father, Joachim, is a very wealthy man, grieved that his wife, Anna, and he have had no children during their 20 years of marriage. Sorrowfully, he leaves her alone and goes away to fast and pray, vowing not to eat or drink until God visits him. Anna, equally grieved, begs God to help her as God had helped the childless Sara (Abraham's spouse who conceived Isaac in her old age). In answer to her prayer, an angel appears to her, saying, "Anna, Anna, the Lord has heard your prayer, and you shall conceive and bear, and your child shall be spoken of throughout the world." Elated, Anna promises to give the child to God. About this time, Joachim returns to the city. Informed of his coming by two angelic messengers, Anna greets him at the city gate with her good news. In fulfillment of Anna's vow, Mary's parents put her three-year-old self in the custody of the Temple priests, and during her stay in the Temple she receives all her food from an angel.

When she reaches the age of 12, Mary can no longer remain at the Temple and must be married. The high priest, Zacharias, assembles the widowers of the area,[7] asking each to bring a staff that Zacharias takes into the temple with him. When the high priest returns Joseph's staff to him, a dove flies out of it and perches on Joseph's head, a sign of his being chosen as Mary's spouse. Joseph demurs because of his age; Zacharias berates him for his hesitancy and Joseph agrees to take Mary into his house, where he leaves her to continue his work in another city.

The continuing narrative includes details such as Mary's weaving of the Temple veil in the royal and priestly colors of purple and scarlet to shroud the Holy of Holies. Pausing in this work, Mary hears an angel's voice. She is depicted as asking herself, "Shall I verily conceive of the living God and bring forth after the manner of all women?" This musing prepares the ground for later church tradition that Mary bore Jesus without the labor and pain of ordinary childbirth.

Mary gives her assent and visits her cousin Elizabeth. When she returns to Joseph's house, he learns that she is six months pregnant. At first, he berates her, but his fear and anger are allayed by the vision of an angel. Although Joseph is reassured, Annas, the scribe, is scandalized when he visits Joseph and sees the visibly pregnant Mary. Annas accuses them both of sin, and despite their declaration of innocence, Mary and Joseph must submit to an ordeal called the "test of bitter waters,"[8] which is supposed to expose their sin. (According to the book of Numbers, the "water of bitterness" consists of holy water mixed with dirt from the floor of the Temple tabernacle and brings a curse on the woman if she is unfaithful. In this case, because Joseph is accused of secretly consummating their relationship and lying about it, he must undergo the test as well. If they can drink the "water of bitterness" without becoming ill, they are considered innocent.) When the two are called before the community, people marvel that they appear to be unharmed and, therefore, sinless.

As in the Gospel of Luke, the Roman Emperor Augustus issues a decree requiring all citizens of the empire to be counted; at this point, however, the narrative diverges from Luke's account. As Mary and Joseph are traveling to Bethlehem, Mary's time comes, and Joseph leaves her in a cave with his sons while he looks for a midwife near Bethlehem. When he meets a woman, he tells her he seeks a midwife for his betrothed—"She is not my wife but has conceived by the Holy Spirit." "Can this be true?" asks the woman, and as they approach the cave, they see a brilliant cloud around it. The woman declares that salvation has been born to Israel, and a great light envelops Mary and the child Jesus.

As she leaves the cave, the woman encounters her friend Salome, and tells her excitedly that a virgin has given birth. The disbelieving Salome offers to prove her wrong. When Salome goes to examine Mary, however, her hand is consumed with fire; only when she worships Jesus is she healed.

As in Matthew's Gospel, the Magi present their gifts, and Herod orders the massacre of all male children two years old or younger. The *Protogospel* does not say how the Holy Family escapes, but Mary's cousin Elizabeth and her baby John flee to the hill country, where a mountain opens up to hide them. The *Protogospel* concludes by describing the death of Zacharias at the hands of Herod's soldiers. Simeon, who succeeds

Zacharias as the high priest of the Temple, is told by the Holy Spirit that he will not die until he sees the Christ.

The *Protogospel of James* ends at this point. The theology implicit in this narrative, emphasizing Mary's virginity before, during, and after the birth of Christ, has endured for two thousand years.

An account of Jesus' birth from around the same time in the *Odes of Solomon*, a collection of hymns, contrasts boldly with the *Protogospel* and the *Pseudo-Matthew* below, offering another perspective on Mary as a powerful virgin mother:

> And the Virgin became a Mother
> With great mercies.
> And she labored and bore the Son without pain
> Because it did not occur without purpose.
> And she did not seek a midwife.
> Because He allowed her to give life.
> She bore with desire as a strong man.
> And she bore according to the manifestation.
> And she possessed with great power.
> And she loved with salvation.
> And she guarded with kindness.
> And she declared with greatness.
> Hallelujah.[9]

Unorthodox as it may be, this poetic tribute to Mary celebrates the strength and partnership with her son that was suggested in Scripture and will eventually emerge in stories of the Middle Ages.

The Earliest Devotion to Mary?

It seems only natural that early Christian women might have seen Mary as a role model and even as a liturgical leader. As we will see in later writings, women had been present at the Passover meal, and Mary had offered bread and wine to them as Jesus had to the apostles. In a practice that probably began much earlier than the fourth-century record, women showed their devotion to her by baking small cakes or loaves of bread and offering them to her, a practice condemned by Epiphanios, the bishop of Salamis, Greece (d. 403). In his *Panarion,* or "breadbasket" of remedies against heresy, Epiphanios describes them as "Collyridians" (from *collyris* or "bread"). He claims that "[t]hey attempt an excess and undertake a forbidden and blasphemous act in the holy Virgin's name, celebrating offices in her name with women officiants." He considers them heretics, saying that the women "prepare a certain carriage with a square seat and spread out fine linens over it on a special day of the year, and they put forth bread and offer it in the name of Mary, and they all partake of the bread."[10]

Like Paul and others before and after him, Epiphanios disapproved of women's taking roles of leadership in worship; Stephen Shoemaker observes that "[t]he practices he attacks under their name, female leadership and the veneration of Mary, were quite clearly a part of his late fourth century religious milieu."[11] And if the Collyridians were indeed participants in a service devoted to Mary, how old was the practice? Given the custom of separating women and men in religious services and other venues, it's possible that the Collyridian homage dates back to the early days of Christianity.

Mary as Minister in the Temple of Jerusalem: The Earliest Image?

The lower level of the Basilica of Saint Mary Magdalene in Saint-Maximin-la-Sainte-Baume in southern France contains a number of stone sarcophagi, or coffins, as well as stone slabs that are etched with images of Christian saints and First Testament figures. Among them is a slab showing a young woman with her arms upraised in prayer. Above her is the inscription "Virgo Maria Ministra in Tempulo Gerusale" ("Virgin Mary Minister of the Temple in Jerusalem"). Dating from c. 375–500,[12] this may be the earliest portrayal of Mary in priestly robes, offering prayer in the Temple of Jerusalem. Scholars agree that the image shows the young Mary and attribute its origin to extracanonical sources.[13] The image itself appears on p. 17.

This portrayal recalls the *Protogospel of James* assertion that Mary spent her youth in the Temple. The presence and authenticity of this Marian image suggest that her intercessory power was recognized very early—indeed, engraved in stone.

Mary in the *Gospel of Pseudo-Matthew*

Between 600 and 800, elements of Mary's life were woven into another extracanonical text: the *Gospel of Pseudo-Matthew*.[14] This story continues to emphasize Mary's virginity, influenced by the writings of early church fathers as well as some statements associated with the Council of Ephesus portraying Mary as an ideal Christian virgin: "Mary never saw the face of a strange man, that was why she was confused when she heard the voice of the angel Gabriel.... She sat always with her face turned towards the East, because she prayed continually.... When she put on a garment she used to shut her eyes...."[15] This ascetic ideal would influence Church teaching for centuries to come, infused into stories as well as prayers, hymns, liturgies, and other devotions.

The initial chapters of *Pseudo-Matthew* tell of Mary's birth and early life, adding details to the earlier *Protogospel*. The author portrays Mary's Temple stay as a quasi-monastic retreat of prayer and study. In this work, Mary defends herself against accusations of impurity, saying, "From my childhood, when I made a vow to God, I have remained as pure as when God created me."[16] This seems to be the first mention of a vow of chastity attributed to Mary, which would become a prominent feature in later stories and teachings.

Pseudo-Matthew continues the *Protogospel* story, with one addition: Two days after the birth of Jesus, Mary leaves the cave, finds a stable, and places Jesus in a manger in the company of an ox and an ass, details that have become part of the Christian Christmas tradition.

Pseudo-Matthew tends toward the extraordinary and the marvelous in recounting

Fifth-century image of Mary as minister in the Temple of Jerusalem, her hands upraised in prayer. Stone slab in the lower level of the Basilica of Sainte-Marie-Madelene in Saint-Maximin-La-Sante-Baume, France. Edmond-Frédéric LeBlant, *Sarcophages chrétiennes de la Gaule* (1886), pl. 57.1

the flight into Egypt. When the Holy Family finds a cave in which to rest, dragons bar their way. Jesus climbs down from his mother's lap and stands before the dragons, which kneel and adore him. Lions and leopards escort the Holy Family through the desert, pausing to bow to him in homage and mingling with the oxen, asses, and sheep the family brought with them. On the third day of their journey, Mary wishes to rest in the shade of a date palm tree; looking up at its fruit, she says to Joseph that she would like to have some. Joseph is surprised; he was thinking of water, since they have so little left. Jesus tells the palm tree to bend down and give his mother some fruit; it obeys him, and then he asks the tree to rise and give them some of the water below its roots. A spring bubbles up from the roots, and they drink.

Another extracanonical text tells of the family's capture on the way to Egypt by two thieves, Titus and Dumachus. Titus bribes Dumachus not to harm the family, and Jesus foretells that in thirty years they will be crucified with him.[17]

When the Holy Family reaches Heropolis, a city in Middle Egypt, they must stay in a temple that honors more than 300 gods. As mother and son enter the temple, all of the idols topple to the earth, shattering into smithereens; the city's inhabitants convert on the spot.

The rest of *Pseudo-Matthew* tells stories of Christ's infancy and young manhood, recounting his precocious miracles and learned teachings.

Mary in the *Qur'an*

Along with Christian stories about Mary that were circulating in the seventh century, another account of her life appeared in the foundational text of Islam.[18] The Qur'an—literally, a book, a reading, or a recitation—contains a series of revelations received by the prophet Muhammad between 610 and 632. In this text, Mary "is the only woman referred to by her proper name. She is known for her own person and is called upon on many occasions by her personal name … [S]he has a story of her own and she is part of the dialogue that forms an important element of Qur'anic storytelling."[19]

Mary first appears in Sura (Chapter) 3 of the Qur'an.[20] This passage describes her mother, the unnamed wife of Imram (Joachim), as she dedicates her exceptional child to the Lord. Fulfilling her vow, she gives Mary to the care of Zaccarius, the Temple high priest. The Qur'an scholar Hosn Abboud finds Mary's presence in the Temple to be "like an icon for women: God accepted Maryam graciously in the temple as a manner of admitting that the notion of the feminine is fundamental in terms of serving God."[21]

As in the *Pseudo-Matthew* text, Mary is given provisions from God during her time in the Temple, and Zaccarius is told he will father a child. The parallel with the *Pseudo-Matthew* text continues: Angels say to Mary, "God gives you news of a Word from him whose name will be the Messiah, Jesus, son of Mary, who will be held in honor in this world and the next, and who will be one of those brought near to God. He will speak to people in his infancy and his adulthood. He will be one of the righteous." Mary responds, "My Lord, how can I have a son when no man has touched me?" The angel replies: "This is how God creates what He will: When He has ordained something, he only says, 'Be,' and it is."[22]

Sura 19 returns to Mary's story and tells it in another way. Here, Mary has secluded herself from her family when God sends a spirit, usually interpreted as the Archangel Gabriel, to "[a]nnounce ... the gift of a pure son." Mary asks how this could happen, and the angel answers, "This is what your Lord said: 'It is easy for me. We shall make him a sign to all people, a blessing from us.'" When the time comes for Mary to deliver her child, she retreats "to a distant place," and, "[w]hen the pains of childbirth drove her to cling to the trunk of a palm tree, she exclaimed, 'I wish I had been dead and forgotten long before this!' But a voice called out to her from below, 'Your Lord has provided a stream at your feet and if you shake the trunk of the palm tree toward you, it will deliver fresh ripe dates for you, so eat, drink, and be glad....'"[23] Jesus does not appear in his own nativity story.

When Mary returns with her baby to her people, they shame her: "Mary! You have done something terrible!" She points to Jesus, indicating that he will defend her. When her relatives scoff, saying, "How can we converse with an infant?" Jesus speaks up. "'I am a servant of God. He has granted me the Scripture, made me a prophet; made me blessed wherever I may be. He commanded me to pray, to give alms as long as I live, to cherish my mother.... Peace was on me the day I was born and will be on me the day I die and the day I am raised to life again.' Such was Jesus, son of Mary."[24] The baby Jesus speaking in his mother's defense is a miracle to which the Qur'an refers more than once; this miracle, more than others recounted in the Qur'an, has captured the imagination of Muslim believers.[25]

In describing himself as a servant of God, Jesus defends Mary and places himself in the company of prophets. The remainder of Sura 19 emphasizes the importance of prophets, but also insists that "...it would not befit God to have a child. He is far above that."[26] Mary's human nature seems to have posed an insurmountable barrier to perceiving Jesus as the Son of God. Be that as it may, both Mary and Jesus are praised in other contexts as "signs for all people" and witnesses to faith (Suras 21, 91, and 23:50). Throughout the Qur'an, Jesus is called "Mary's son" because although he is one of the great prophets, he is not divine: Only Allah is God, and God is one; Islam does not recognize the Trinity.

One of the *hadith*, or collected sayings attributed to Muhammad, affirms that all children are touched by the devil as soon as they are born and that this contact makes them cry, but "[e]xcepted are Mary and her son."[27] Other *hadith* characterize Mary as "the best woman of her time." Mary is numbered among the elite of the universe, along with Khadija, Muhammad's spouse, and Fatima, his beloved daughter. Even Fatima, however, cannot compete with Mary, who is "the chief lady among the inhabitants of Paradise."[28]

In The Qur'an, Mary appears prominently as the exalted figure described by the *Protogospel* and emphasized by early church fathers: chosen by God, placed above all women for her virtue. She has her own story, one that is excluded from the canonical scriptures but "demonstrates the continuation of the Marianic tradition (and vision) from Christianity to Islam."[29]

Mary's Early Reputation as a Miracle Worker

Stories of Mary's intercession and miracle-working date back to the third and fourth centuries. During this period, the first known prayer to Mary circulated throughout the Christian world. Known in Latin as the *Sub Tuum Praesidium*, "Under Your Patronage," it addresses Mary directly: "We fly to thy patronage, O Holy Mother of God! Do not despise our petitions in our necessities, but deliver us always from all dangers, O glorious and blessed Virgin."[30] In the early Christian-Roman world, patronage involved a relationship between a powerful person and a client: In return for homage, the patron would protect the client. This early prayer reflects the confident, confiding attitude of the petitioner in asking for Mary's protection.

Testimony of Mary's miracle-working power comes from Saint Cyril, Archbishop of Jerusalem (313–386), who stated in a homily that Mary "[u]sed to do many mighty works, and perform healings among the people, which were like unto those that were wrought by Jesus our God, but she never permitted the Apostles to know [about them], for she fled from the praise of men. And the Apostles were closely associated with her all those times when they were preaching."[31]

Chapter 6 of *Pseudo-Matthew* states that "[t]he angels of God were often seen speaking with her, and they most diligently obeyed her. If anyone who was unwell touched her, the same hour he went home cured."[32] In a similar vein, the sixth-century *Arabic Infancy Gospel* describes a woman possessed by a demon who stood in the road throwing stones at people, much to the distress of her friends. "And when Lady Mary saw her, she pitied her, and upon this Satan immediately left her," and the woman "was cured of her torment."[33]

The Narrative Theology of Gospels Real and Imagined

What do these early writings say to us about Mary?
The canonical gospels offer glimpses of a woman strong enough to

risk her reputation on the word of a messenger; a prophetic woman who foretells the mission of her son; a woman so confident in her faith that she has the *chutzpah* to ignore her son's brush-off and order the servants to obey him; a woman who has the courage to accompany her child on his mission and the bravery to stand by him as he dies in agony and disgrace; a woman touched again by the Spirit when it confirms the leaders of the early church with tongues of fire. The Scriptural narrative about Mary shows her strength and valor.

In contrast, early extracanonical works, while still attentive to Mary, tend to downplay the power she shows in the canonical gospels. Instead, influenced even in the first two centuries by the writings of church fathers, they offer what had already become more "traditional" interpretations of her. Mary's extraordinary purity is guarded from birth; Joseph is an elderly caretaker and guide. We see little or nothing of her actions as described by the evangelists. Although the Qur'an devotes an entire sura to Mary, it too emphasizes her purity, carefully preserved.

These early stories may work best as an introduction to the idea of Mary as the focus of a story; even when they are notably theologically conservative, they are also (sometimes wildly) imaginative, offering hints of what is to come. And we catch glimpses of Mary's miracle-working, which we will be able to see more clearly in the next few centuries.

Chapter 2

Mary's "Life Stories"
Fourth to Twelfth Centuries

Marian stories, along with Marian devotions, took early root in the Eastern (Byzantine) Church. Emperors of the Byzantine Empire—and their consorts—built and patronized churches, three of which were dedicated to Mary: the Church of the Theotokos (God-Bearer) in Chalkoprateia, the Church of the Hodegetria (The One Who Shows the Way), and the Church of the Panagia (The All-Holy) in Blachernai. Each claimed relics of Mary.

Eastern theologians had influenced the two church councils of Ephesus and Nicaea that proclaimed Mary to be the Mother of God. Christians celebrated the feast of the Presentation of Jesus to Simeon on February 14, under the rubric of the *Hypapante* or Encounter,[1] that momentous occasion when Jesus met the prophet who foretold his mission while his mother recognized the import of the meeting but said nothing. Mary, the "all-holy," was the subject of writings that exalted her virginity and proclaimed her life of prayer and seclusion from the world—removing her, in an echo of *Pseudo-Matthew*, from scriptural and actual reality.

Justin Martyr (c. 100–c. 165) had been the first to establish a parallel between Eve and Mary, coining the "Eva-Ave" dichotomy ("Ave" coming from the first Latin word, "Hail," of Gabriel's greeting) to stress Mary's obedience in contrast to Eve's disobedience, salvation versus sin.[2] From Ephrem of Syria (c. 306–373) we learn that Jesus was conceived though Mary's hearing the words of Gabriel, a description inspiring artists to portray the Annunciation quite literally as a beam of light entering Mary's ear. Ephrem's writings stress the virgin birth of Jesus and may be the first to identify Mary as a symbol of the church.[3] Epiphanius of Salamis (d. 403), already famous for his tirade about the Collyridians, also emphasized Mary's virginity, extending it to continue after Jesus' birth.[4]

It's not too much to say that these early Eastern theologians established the "ground rules" for speculation about Mary for the next fifteen centuries, influencing hymnody and liturgies as well as stories about Mary.

Byzantine (now Eastern Orthodox) liturgies were—and remain—elaborate, embellished with *kontakia* or "sermons in verse, accompanied by music."[5] One of the best-known series of *kontakia* is found in the sixth-century *Akathistos Hymn*, so named because it was recited and sung standing up. This series of verses alternating between praise and narrative takes Mary from the Annunciation to the birth of Jesus with a series of greetings that list her titles and describe her virtues and accomplishments. Many of these greetings go on to become commonplaces of Western poetry and liturgy from late antiquity to the present: Mary is hailed as the star that causes the sun to shine, bridge from earth to Heaven, key to the gate of Paradise, downfall of demons, conciliation of the Righteous Judge, haven for the seafarers of life, immovable tower of the church. Each series of salutations ends with "Hail, bride unwedded!"[6]

The custom of addressing Mary with a series of titles both metaphorical and literal continued in both Byzantine and Latin churches with litanies and hymns of praise.

Mary's Voice Heard Loud and Clear: Romanos the Melodist

I believe that later biographies of Mary were influenced by one of the most revered interpreters of Mary's maternity and power, the sixth-century monk and writer of elaborate hymns on biblical themes known as Romanos the Melodist (c. 490–c. 560). Romanos comes with his own Marian miracle legend: As a young monk, he was known for his lack of musical ability. Not only was his voice unpleasant to hear, but he was also tone-deaf. After a religious retreat, he fell asleep and dreamed that he was visited by Mary, who appeared to him holding a scroll. "Take it and eat," she said, and he did as he was told. When he awoke, it was Christmas Day, and Romanos was chosen by the Patriarch of Constantinople to sing the principal hymn. His fellow monks cringed at the prospect of another rasping and off-key performance, but after he stood in the pulpit and opened his mouth in a splendid poem of praise, everyone in the church was swept away by the glory of his voice and the beauty of his rhetoric.

Romanos' writings about Mary indicate a unique appreciation of her personality and her power—perhaps as a result of that Christmas Eve encounter:

> He reveals a developed fascination with Mary's personal qualities, and he takes interest in various aspects and stages of her life, her psychology, and her emotions.... [In his works,] [i]nstead of merely pointing to her son, [Mary]

stands next to him and cooperates with him. [Romanos' works] urge the audience to relate to the mother of God as a sovereign being.[7]

Not only that, but Mary's voice is strong and familiar when she speaks out in intercession for sinners: "Mary is able to say whatever she likes to God."[8]

Perhaps the most influential and enduring of Romanos' sermons in song is "Mary at the Cross," written in the form of a dialogue between Mary and Christ. It begins with a description of Mary and the other women who followed Jesus after he was arrested. She cries out to him "in torment,"

> "Where do you rush, my Son? Why this haste to finish your course?
> There isn't another wedding at Cana;
> You can't be hurrying to change water into wine now;
> Should I come with you, my Son? Or better, wait for you somewhere?"[9]

She describes the road, "still strewn with palm branches," testimony to the approbation of the crowd that has since rejected him, asking why they have turned to hatred. She asks where Peter is, with all his bravado, all the companions and disciples—not one of them visible. She cries, "In the face of their neglect, / you have redeemed everyone, you have denied yourself to no one, / my son and my God."

Jesus answers,

> "If I do not suffer, do not die, how shall I redeem Adam?
> If I do not enter the tomb, how shall I harrow Hell?
> As you know well, I am being unjustly crucified.
> So why weep, my Mother? Rather proclaim to all:
> 'He has freely accepted his suffering,
> my son and my God.'"[10]

The dialogue continues with Jesus telling his mother that she should not be like the other women who weep, not understanding that he is dying for the salvation of the world. Mary reproaches him, asking how she should not cry out at the injustice done to him. She points out that Jesus has cured the sick and raised the dead during his lifetime; why must he die now? Patiently, her son describes the sin of Adam and Eve, asking her not to grieve but to "cry out, 'Have mercy on Adam, / show pity to Eve, / my son and my God.'"[11]

When Mary asks if she will ever see her son again, Jesus assures her that she will be the first to see him when he rises from the dead. He asks her to remain calm at his death, when the heavens darken and the Temple veil is torn. She responds by proclaiming that his sacrifice "redeemed all those who were dead…. You saved by dying! You gave your holy Mother / the privilege of faith to cry out to you, / 'My son and my God.'"[12]

This passionate, compassionate exchange between Mary and Jesus—even though it incorporates church doctrine—characterizes Mary's role in the life of Jesus as one of faithful accompaniment and frank conversation. "The couple never parts, after all; she is with him in the beginning and the end, and then again at the new beginning of the Resurrection."[13]

Romanos' liturgical emphasis on Mary's strength, her influential voice, and her partnership with her son—reflected in his many works—undoubtedly influenced the most dramatic Marian works of early Christianity, the *Lives of Mary* written by four Byzantine monastics.

Epiphanios the Monk and the First *Life of Mary*

Although the Roman world venerated Mary in church-building, liturgical devotion, and song, the Eastern church produced the first accounts of Mary's life, furnishing details that would color medieval commentaries, sermons, and miracle tales.

At the end of the eighth or beginning of the ninth century, a cleric associated with the monastery of Kallistratos, Epiphanios the Monk, produced his work *Concerning the Conduct of the Supremely Holy Theotokos and the Years of her Life*.[14] Beginning with an extensive genealogy, Epiphanios describes Mary as descended from the line of David and being of royal blood; her Levite ancestors make her a member of a priestly line. The monk follows the *Protogospel* and other extracanonical texts in describing her childhood and life in the Temple, ascribing her withdrawal from ordinary life to sorrow at the death of her mother Anna, but emphasizing her devotion to the scriptures and her love of learning.[15] Epiphanios seems to be the first author to describe Mary's appearance. He says that she was "of medium stature," fair-haired and light-complexioned, with dark brows and "a prominent nose." Her face was narrow "and filled with divine grace."[16] According to Epiphanios' description, Jesus looked like his mother, almost feature for feature: Their physical resemblance embodies their spiritual connection.[17]

Like Marian biographers after him, Epiphanios recounts the life of Christ in tandem with his mother's and often in ways that overshadow it. We see his birth (emphasizing Mary's perpetual virginity), the visit of the Magi, the family's five years in Egypt, and the moment Mary and Joseph find him in the Temple. Mary is not mentioned in the monk's account of Cana, where the bridegroom leaves to follow Jesus. Joseph dies at the age of 110.

Unlike later biographers, Epiphanios does not describe Christ's

Passion at length but emphasizes his mother Mary and disciple John at the foot of the cross. Of particular importance during the Passion are the seven "myrrh-bearing women" of Scripture, each one named, in a radical departure from tradition. Among them are Mary Magdalene; Salome, mother of the sons of Zebedee; and Joanna. After his death, Jesus appears first to his mother in the house of the apostle John, then to the others.

After her son's ascension, Mary becomes an ascetic once again. She leads an active life, however, healing the sick, casting out evil spirits, and caring for the poor, widows, and orphans. Some of the women she cures, including the wife of Paul, come to live with her.[18]

According to Epiphanios, Mary lived to be 72.[19] In his description of her passing, Mary predicts, and Gabriel announces, her coming death; the apostles gather, along with Mary Magdalene and some of Mary's relatives. Mary delivers a final address to them, speaking of "fearful mysteries." Christ arrives and receives her spirit, and she is buried. Later, when the apostles are together at her tomb, they see her body taken up. Epiphanios ends with Saint James commissioning the apostles to evangelize throughout the world.[20]

The monk's brief account shows Mary in the light of a priestly heritage, in a constant and loving relationship with her son, in companionship with other women, and in privileged witness to her son's resurrection. Her own ministry continues Jesus' work of healing, exorcism, and caring for the poor. In comparison with some of the more florid extracanonical renderings of Mary's days on earth, Epiphanios' *Life* is brief and relatively undramatic; his work, however, took on a life of its own, enlarged and embellished over the course of centuries.

Later Marian Biographers and the Development of Mary's Story

During the eighth and ninth centuries, extracanonical stories about Mary circulated both on the European continent and in England.[21] Byzantium, however, was riven by conflict over the role of icons (images of Christ, Mary, and the saints) in worship. During this time and into the tenth century, many iconophiles (supporters of the images) left for the West, while others stayed and rode out the two periods of iconoclasm that damaged or destroyed sacred art. During the tenth century, three such iconophiles contributed to the growing body of literature about Mary: John Geometres (c. 935–c. 1000), Euthymios the Athonite (c. 955–1065),[22] and Symeon Metaphrastes (d. c. 1000). All three were metaphrasts: writers who edited, abridged, translated, or rewrote the works of others for their audiences, both religious and lay people. John and Euthymios produced full-length *Lives of Mary*; Symeon's shorter account was a reading for the feast of her Assumption on August 15.

John Geometres: Mary's Life as Sermon

John the Geometre, a nobleman and military officer who retired to a monastery, was "a leading member of an elite religious confraternity associated with the church of the Mother of God" in Constantinople, the same church where Mary appeared to Romanos the Melodist.[23] Written to honor Mary on the feast of her Assumption, his *Life of Mary* drew on biblical and extracanonical sources as well as historical and theological elements. Described as "a sequence of homilies," "a treatise," and "a panegyric in praise of the Virgin's heroic contests and her array of unsurpassable qualities and virtues,"[24] Geometres' work is perhaps most notable for its depiction of Mary as a constant companion and partner of Jesus in his miracles and ministry.

Geometres describes Mary as physically, spiritually, and intellectually exceptional: beautiful, socially reserved but friendly, and graceful in every sense of the word. At the wedding feast in Cana, the bridegroom cuts short the celebration to follow Jesus; his bride joins him to follow Mary. Soon after Cana, Joseph dies; his sons follow Jesus, and his daughters, Mary. As Jesus traveled, "…all these men and women accompanied him…. At this time, his mother led them all, and was protector, mediator, and sovereign."[25] Geometres emphasizes her extraordinary leadership and authority among her son's disciples as she accompanies Jesus, performing miracles as he does. She also participates in Christ's Passion "…in a unique and intimate way, mingling her maternal suffering with the sacrifice of her son."[26]

After a final meal with Jesus and their companions (Geometres omits the blessing of the bread and wine), Mary begins her own journey as she listens to the trial, following Jesus to the cross where she shares his sufferings. Her words to Jesus reverberate with anguish for his pain; in response to her question, "What will become of me?" Jesus gives her into the keeping of the apostle John. She herself finds the tomb for his burial and advises Joseph of Arimathea about asking for Jesus' body, accompanying him in spirit as he seeks out Pilate.

Mary is the first witness of all the events of Jesus' resurrection, and he appears first to her (although she keeps the knowledge to herself, thinking that her testimony might be suspect). Geometres describes Mary as the center of the Christian community after Christ's ascension, praising her leadership and teaching. She is portrayed as traveling for a time with the apostle John, directing the other apostles' activities, sending them out on missions, inspiring preachers, supporting their evangelical efforts, and pardoning and converting their enemies.

According to Geometres, Mary is in her eighties when she dies, known as the "mother of mercy." His depiction of her passing follows the now-familiar pattern of the angel bearing a palm of victory, a gathering of the apostles, Jesus' appearance, and Mary's falling asleep gently, entrusting her spirit to her son. During her funeral, miracles abound, and all nature celebrates her life. Three days later, Thomas arrives and is shown her tomb: It is empty. Her body has been taken up.[27]

John Geometres is an eloquent advocate for the concept that Mary, in giving birth to Jesus, bore the Trinity, a belief that would be embodied—literally—in medieval shrine-madonnas, those sculptures of Mary that opened to reveal Father, Son, and Holy Spirit within her body. Geometres emphasizes that she is as close to Jesus as Jesus' human and divine natures are to each other—as daring a concept in the twenty-first century as in the tenth. Geometres paved the way for an equally daring version of Mary's life that was nearly contemporaneous with his.

Euthymios the Athonite: Mary's Life as Biography with Embellishments

Another tenth-century *Life of Mary* was formerly believed to be the work of Saint Maximos the Confessor.[28] Recent scholarship, however, reveals it to be a translation and rewriting of Geometres' text by Euthymios the Athonite into Georgian, one of the Eastern languages used in the monasteries of Mount Athos in Greece.[29] Born into a wealthy family, Euthymios (c. 955–1028) spent time at the imperial court as an adolescent and visited Constantinople often as an adult. Educated in both Greek and Georgian, he was diffident about his command of the latter. He was encouraged to write in Georgian by Mary, who appeared to him as a queen who spoke Georgian. In his vision, Euthymios must have looked pale or sickly, and Mary asked him what was wrong. He replied that he was dying, but Mary told him not to be afraid, taking him by the hand and telling him to get up and speak Georgian fluently from that time on. And from Mary's visit onward, so he did.[30] He produced more than 50 translations and adaptations of other works, often abbreviating or simplifying them for less learned readers. It appears that Euthymios used texts from both Geometres and Symeon Metaphrastes to fashion his Marian biography.[31]

This text, like that of Geometres, emphasizes Mary's active participation in Jesus' ministry, the company of her women followers, and her

Chapter 2. Mary's "Life Stories" 29

leadership in the life of the early Jesus movement. Euthymios, however, assigns her in addition a priestly role in Christ's passion as she offers her son to God.[32]

The work begins with Mary's priestly genealogy: In Joachim and Anna, "the houses of Judah and Levi are united, that is, the royal branch and the priestly branch intertwine."[33] Of Mary's time in the Temple, he notes that she was taught as well as fed by an angel: "[S]he loved to learn and was a good student, retaining all that was good, reflecting at length on the divine scriptures with all wisdom, for she would become the mother of the Word and the wisdom of God."[34] At about the age of 12, Mary experiences a "great mystery." From the light-filled sanctuary in which she is standing comes a voice: "Mary, from you my Son will be born."[35] Although she is amazed by this message, she says nothing to anyone.

The temple priests are hesitant to find a husband for Mary because of her vow of chastity but finally decide on an engagement rather than a marriage. At 70-plus years, Joseph is the perfect candidate. The matter is decided when his staff blossoms and he accepts her as "the queen and leader of his house." Mary becomes the "director, instructor, and ruler of all his household"[36] and takes charge of Joseph's daughters.

At the Annunciation, Mary is not startled at the angel Gabriel's appearance, for the angel was one of those who had brought her nourishment in the temple. As Euthymios interprets this scene, the archangel's words, "The Lord is with you," abolish the curse of Eve: God's invitation to Mary means that women should no longer be subordinate to men.[37]

In another reversal of the punishment of Eve, Mary's childbirth is painless. Jesus "did not let his mother know the manner of his birth, and instantly he appeared outside her womb and sat on the throne of her arms."[38] The author describes the visit of the Magi and Herod's jealousy, the presentation of Jesus in the Temple, and the slaughter of male babies under the age of two throughout Judea. It is the child Jesus himself, according to the author, who arranges the details of the family's flight into Egypt.[39]

Jesus grows to adulthood. "From that time on, the Holy Mother became a disciple of her sweet son ... for she no longer saw him as a mere man but she served him reverently as God and received his words as the words of God."[40] After Cana with its canceled wedding and the beginning of Jesus' public life, Mary accompanies Jesus; Joseph remains at home and dies there at the age of 110.

Mary has her own coterie of disciples, including the mother of James and John, the biblical Johanna (the wife of Herod's steward), and Mary Magdalene. Magdalene appears as "a disciple and a servant, a good companion, obedient to the Queen ... and she was made worthy of the ultimate grace of being an apostle" to Jesus.[41] Euthymios portrays Magdalene as the equal of Peter in zeal and prominence.[42]

The most impressive and radical aspect of Euthymios' biography is his account of Mary's participation—with other women—in the Last Supper.[43] (Like Geometres, he describes her constant presence during Christ's Passion and her active leadership of the small believers' community.) At the Last Supper, "as Jesus directed the apostles and disciples, so did Mary direct and instruct the women who accompanied him. That is why, when during the dinner, the Great Mystery unfolded, *she offered the sacrifice herself as the priest and she was sacrificed; she offered and she was offered.*"[44] This is the first and perhaps the only mention that we have of women's presence at the institution of the Eucharist, although they must have been there; the Passover meal seems always to have been a family celebration. Mary's role here is momentous: She acts in direct parallel with Jesus to share the Eucharist. In a true imitation of Christ, as Jesus offers himself and is offered, his mother offers herself and is offered as both priest and sacrifice. At the conclusion of the meal, Jesus gives the women into her keeping, as his "substitute" directing their work and service.

After Jesus' arrest, Mary shows both courage and wisdom, remaining as close as she can to her son throughout his ordeal. She stands outside while Annas and Caiphas judge Jesus, questioning the people who are entering and leaving the court, asking them to tell her the truth about what is happening. She joins Jesus in his suffering as she had joined him in his ministry.

Mary's soul is pierced by pain as her son is crucified, fulfilling the high priest Simeon's prophecy at Jesus' presentation in Luke 2:29–32, but she prays for his tormentors even as she laments, "as in a night beyond time … surrounded by sadness and mourning."[45] Anguished, she begs God and Jesus to tell her why her son's death could be allowed. After the sword pierces her son's side, however, she laments only briefly; her immediate concern is an appropriate burial, and she searches for a suitable tomb herself. Finding one, and learning that it belongs to Joseph of Arimathea, she goes to him, urging and emboldening him to ask Pilate for the body. She herself helps Joseph to take Jesus from the cross and, with Joseph and Nicodemus, prepares Jesus' body for burial.

In a meditation on the presence of women at the foot of the cross, Euthymios says that "the men were not their equal in audacity and fearlessness nor in excellence over the others. That is why some evangelists did not give their names and some evangelists did not recall any of their names."[46] Euthymios mentions all the women's names he knows, emphasizing Mary's courage and care for them during the Passion.

Mary stays at the tomb, keeping watch and witnessing the great earthquake that rolls the stone from the door of the tomb. The author states that she "was the eyewitness of all … that is why, before everyone, she received the announcement of the resurrection … and she brought the news to the disciples and the myrrh-bearing women."[47] He observes that the evangelists did not include this information because no one would believe Christ's resurrection solely on the word of his mother—a logical enough assumption.

Between his resurrection and ascension, Jesus appears many times to Mary, "whenever it seems good to him." And, of course, she is present when he ascends to Heaven. Afterward, she takes charge of her son's followers, both male and female, instructing the apostles in fasting and prayer and joining them in their vigils. Mary actively prepares the apostles for Pentecost.[48] Euthymios emphasizes that she had been filled with the Holy Spirit and "clothed with power from above"[49] since the archangel Gabriel's visit.

During her ministry after Pentecost, Mary directs the apostles and disciples, serving as a model for members of the growing Christian community. "Gracious and merciful to everyone," she does so many good deeds that—as the evangelist John (21:24) described Christ's life—it would take an "enormous amount of writing" to do her justice. She is the steward of Jesus' message, and she takes her son's place as a comfort and inspiration to his followers. As a co-minister with the disciples, she preaches and commissions the apostles to go into the countries that, the author suggests, she chooses for them.

Mary's active ministry begins as she prepares to leave Jerusalem in the company of the apostle John and Mary Magdalene. Jesus, however, has other plans for her, ordering her to return so that she might "…lead the believers and take charge of the church in Jerusalem with James, the brother of the Lord [Joseph's son] … and every care or work of the Christians was entrusted to the all-immaculate one."[50] Teaching, preaching, leading, counseling, directing, interceding for the new community, Mary is at its center: The apostles report to her their successes and failures, and every year they return to Jerusalem to celebrate the feast of the Resurrection with her. Despite opposition from unbelievers, Mary works miracles through her "grace and intercession." She casts out demons and cures incurable diseases, among the many "wonders and miracles" attributed to her.[51]

Euthymios' account of Mary's passing includes numerous elements of previous accounts of her death, adding details. When Jesus visits Mary on her deathbed, she asks him to bless every soul that calls upon him in commemoration of her. As her funeral bier is carried through the city, all the sick are cured. Her assumption is not directly described but is implied when the apostle Thomas arrives three days late and is shown an empty tomb by the rest of the apostles. With Mary in Heaven, the author asserts, the world continues to see miracles and other proofs of her care.[52]

The "Holy Theft" of Mary's Clothing

This anecdote is included, rather like a postscript, in both Geometres'[53] and Euthymios' biographies; the Athonite's version is more interesting, and I recount it here as one of the first "holy thefts" of a relic in church history,[54] directly associating a remnant of Mary's clothing with miraculous events.

In the time of the Byzantine Emperor Leo (r. 457–474), two brothers undertake a pilgrimage to the Holy Land. In Galilee, they lodge with an elderly Jewish virgin and notice a room in her home that is filled with incense and a crowd of people suffering from a variety of illnesses. Their hostess tells them that the room contains a coffer that conceals one of Mary's garments, left to the woman's family in antiquity. Handed down from generation to generation, always guarded by a virgin in the family, the garment—which Mary wore at the annunciation, at the nativity, and when she nursed the infant Jesus—has become the source of countless miracles.

Awed, the brothers ask to spend the night in the room with those who sought healing; they receive permission to do so. After the last person in the room has fallen asleep, the brothers measure the coffer and carefully observe its design. The next day, they continue on to Jerusalem after promising to bring the elderly woman anything she might need. Once there, they commission a replica of the coffer and on their way home they stay again in the holy room, where they exchange the replica for the genuine article containing Mary's garment. The brothers then return to Constantinople where they plan to build a church to house the relic, but Mary "move[s] their hearts" to tell the emperor, who builds a magnificent shrine for the garment.

At the conclusion of the brothers' story, which ends his work, Euthymios lists 79 of Mary's graces and accomplishments, echoing the praises of the Akathistos Hymn. Among them are some of the most prominent themes of Marian literature: Mary converts the lost and conducts those who have strayed back to the straight path. She is the help and deliverance of those in dire straits, a pleader for the enslaved and those in trouble. In addition, "[s]he is our intercessor before the just judge. / She is the destroyer of the records of our sins. / She is the downfall of demons."[55]

This *Life of the Virgin* may leave the reader with some ambivalence, particularly with regard to the example Mary sets for other women. The vow of chastity, the painless childbirth, and the exaltation of perpetual virginity can have an alienating effect. Yet in other ways, this portrait of her is empowering as her authority and centrality shine forth. This text and—to some extent—that of John Geometres challenge received ecclesiastical wisdom with their witness to Mary's own disciples, her presence and priestly offering at the Last Supper, her following of Jesus in every moment of his Passion and death, his appearance first to her, and his commissioning of her as a leader in the early church. As such a leader or presbyter, she might—must—have presided at commemorations of the Last Supper, perhaps with one of the Twelve, perhaps with Mary Magdalene, sharing bread and wine as her son had commanded.

Both biographies offer us the portrait of a strong and powerful woman, a partner with God in the conception of her son, a partner with Jesus in his earthly enterprise, and a partner with the Holy Spirit in the leadership and nurture of the nascent church.

Mary's Life Foreshortened: Symeon Metaphrastes

Images of Mary's strength and participation in the life of her son, vivid and compelling in the biographies of John Geometres and Euthymios the Athonite, disappear almost entirely in the work of Symeon the Metaphrast, whose *Metalogion* became an ecclesiastical favorite. Symeon used the church calendar as his organizing principle, assigning to each feast day a tale of the corresponding saint. His relatively brief account of Mary's life was assigned to August 15, the date traditionally associated with her death and assumption.[56]

After recapitulating Gospel stories of Jesus' birth and avoiding any mention of Mary's co-ministry with Jesus, Symeon briefly mentions Cana and then moves into Jesus' Passion. He says that Mary is "with her son," especially during the time when his disciples abandon him. Writing about Mary's participation in the events leading up to Jesus' death, Symeon focuses on her suffering at the foot of the cross, elaborating on the dramatic exchange between Jesus and Mary begun by Romanos and developed by theologians and preachers through the centuries.

For Symeon, Mary is the first and only witness of Christ's resurrection. Symeon briefly mentions her presence at Pentecost. After Christ's ascension, the apostles disperse to preach and teach, but Mary lives in the apostle John's house on Mount Zion.

Symeon draws on the *Protogospel* for a reference to Mary's childhood in the Temple and the choice of Joseph as her guardian. He takes some elements of his *Life* from Euthymios (or Geometres) but omits any reference to her participation in Jesus' ministry and her leadership after his death. He emphasizes Mary's brokenness and loss as she stands at the foot of the cross, describing her memories of her son's childhood, her wish to bury him in her heart, and her desire to be buried with him. There is no mention of her priestly heritage, nor any intimation of a deeper significance to her sufferings such as participating in the agony of her son. Symeon describes her reproaches, questions, and expressions of grief at great length and in dramatic detail. His drawn-out representation of Mary's sorrow will pass into poetry and drama in the Middle Ages as "The Marian Lament,"[57] inspiring enduring devotion to Mary's sorrows. Stories of her agency and her power, her love for and partnership with Jesus, seemingly disappear for a century or two, only to take more vigorous form in miracle tales.

Mary as Protector of the Faithful

The stolen Marian garment preserved as a relic—her voluminous veil, or *maphorion*—was cherished by the Church in Constantinople. Two other relics were housed and displayed there as well: her sash (presumably retrieved from Thomas, according to a tale recounted below) and a portrait of her ascribed to the Gospel writer Luke.[58] During a siege of the city in 626, an icon of Mary as well as her *maphorion* were carried in procession around the city. "[W]e are told that at the crucial moment of the battle, the [invaders] saw the figure of a woman in dignified garments running alone along the walls of the city."[59] Another source testified to the "…appearances of the Virgin herself to her people, as a veiled lady or as a warrior maiden fighting in the very battle."[60] The vision so startled and daunted the attackers that they retreated, and the city was saved. Although this episode seems to be the first instance of Mary's protecting "her" people, it will not be the last. Mary not only intercedes—she actively intervenes on behalf of her own.

Mary's Death and Entry into Heaven

Alongside these *Lives of Mary* is another series of extracanonical stories, focused solely on the circumstances of Mary's death. During the fifth and sixth centuries, a multitude of separate but similar accounts of Mary's passing and the disposition of her body emerged in both the East and the West. In Byzantium, the story was known as the *Dormition of the Theotokos* and comprised two major threads. The Palm Tradition contains stories in which Mary receives a palm branch from an angel before her

Chapter 2. Mary's "Life Stories"

passing. The Six Books Tradition is a more liturgically oriented account of her passing in six brief segments, or "books." In the West, Mary's death was called the *Transitus Mariae (The Passing of Mary)* and contained elements of both traditions. (Epiphanios, John the Geometer, and Euthymios used both traditions in their accounts of her passing; all three featured the angel with the palm.)

Written between 400 and 500, the *Transitus* enjoyed the greatest popularity and dissemination.[61] This narrative begins some years after Christ's death, when Mary learns from an angel that she will be "taken up out of the body in three days." She asks that the apostles witness her passing; the angel assures her that they will all be there and gives her a brightly shining palm branch, symbol of immortality and victory over death.

Saint John is preaching at Ephesus when a cloud envelops him and takes him to Mary's house, where she shows him the palm and her burial garments. The other apostles join them, having been transported from the far-flung places where they had been preaching; some have been raised from the dead after being martyred. Together, they await Mary's final hours. At the third hour of the third day of their vigil, Jesus arrives in a blaze of light, accompanied by angels. Jesus invites Mary to enter into the "treasury of eternal life," and Mary asks Jesus to deliver her from the power of darkness and the dominion of Satan. After Jesus reassures her that he will be with her, Mary lies down on her bed and the apostles see Jesus give her soul to the archangels Michael and Gabriel. Jesus accompanies Mary's soul with them into Heaven.

Three virgins prepare Mary's body for burial; it shines with a brilliant light and smells like lilies. The apostles lay her body upon the bier, and John is chosen to lead the funeral procession, bearing the palm. As they walk to the sepulcher, a huge moonlit cloud spreads over the bier, and an angelic host sings a melody of surpassing sweetness. Nearly 15,000 people gather, marveling at the sight and sound. One of them, an unbeliever, rushes up and tries to overturn the bier, but his hands shrivel up to the elbows and stick to the bier.[62] The man begs Peter to help him, but Peter says that only if he becomes a believer in Christ will his hands be free. The man then confesses his belief in God and Jesus Christ; as he kisses the bier, his hands are restored. He thanks God and praises Christ; Peter gives him the shining palm, telling him to take it into the city and lay it on the eyes of the blind, who have only to confess belief in Jesus to have their sight restored.

The apostles proceed to the valley of Josaphat, as directed by Jesus, and find a new tomb, where they lay Mary's body. After they close the sepulcher, Jesus and the angels return. Jesus wishes them peace and asks what he should do with her body. Peter and the other apostles reply that as Jesus overcame death, so should he take his mother's body with him into Heaven. Jesus says to them, "Be it done according to your will." The archangel Michael rolls away the stone from the door of the sepulcher and Jesus says, "Rise up, my love ... you who did not suffer corruption by union of the flesh will not suffer decay and corruption now."[63]

Mary rises from her grave and thanks her son; Jesus kisses her and gives her to the angels to be borne bodily into Paradise. Jesus ascends into Heaven accompanied by Mary and the angels; the apostles are taken up into clouds and returned to the places where they had been preaching (or to their tombs).

A later extracanonical text[64] depicts Thomas as being brought late to the events surrounding Mary's passing. Arriving at the Mount of Olives just in time to see Mary's body being taken up, he cries out to her, "In your mercy, make your servant glad as you go to Heaven!" Mary sends down her sash to him; he takes it to the site of her burial in the valley of Josaphat, where Peter tells him, "You were always late to believe, so the Lord has not permitted you to be at his mother's burial." Thomas asks to see Mary's body, and the apostles point to the sepulcher. Thomas tells them that the body is not there; refusing to believe him, they remove the stone and find the tomb empty. Thomas then shows them the sash, and they rejoice together.

The second thread of Mary's dormition story, the *Six Books*, dates from as early as the fourth century[65] and comes from the East as a tale with liturgical elements. Each "book" is relatively brief—four or five pages in English translation. Like many Marian stories, it traveled to the West. In Book One, the anonymous author announces that Saint John made the work known "in order that there may be a commemoration of my Lady Mary three times in the year, because if mankind [sic] celebrate her memory, they may be delivered from wrath."[66]

In Book Two, Mary prepares to go to Bethlehem, saying, "...I place my trust in my Master whom I have in heaven, who, whenever I cry to him, hears me." She asks Jesus to send the apostles to her, emphasizing that Jesus hears her prayers.[67] The apostles assemble, some brought back from the dead. Book Three describes the cures Mary performs before her death: cases of diabolical possession, leprosy, and cystitis, among others. In all, "the virtue of help went forth from my Lady Mary upon the afflicted, and straightaway 2,600 souls were healed, men and women and children," as well as the judge of Jerusalem and his family. Jesus himself comes to "gather his mother out of this world."[68]

Book Four describes Mary's passing. Standing beside her deathbed, the apostles ask her for a blessing, which she gives in a series of requests to Jesus. She asks that "bad times cease from the earth when people hold a commemoration to my body and spirit, which have quitted the earth." She asks that pestilence, war, and famine cease in the land where she is revered and that the land itself be spared locusts, blight, mildew, and hail. She asks that

> "everyone who is sick be healed; and who is afflicted be relieved; and who is hungry, be satisfied; and whoever is captive through violence, let his bonds be loosed; and if any are sailing on the sea, and storms arise against them and they call on the name of the Lord, let them be preserved from injury; and let those too who are in distant lands, and call upon my name, come [home] in safety. Let the fields, too, from which offerings are offered in honor of me, be blessed and bring forth the seeds which are concealed in the furrows; and let the vines, from which wine is pressed in my name, bear good bunches [of grapes]; and let there be concord and peace on all created beings that call on Thee...."
>
> Then our Lord, Jesus, said to his mother: "Everything thou hast said to me, Mary, will I do to please thee; and I will show mercy to everyone who calls upon my name."[69]

Mary is transported—seemingly body and soul—to Paradise in a "chariot of light," and the apostles return to their graves or their preaching.

Books Five and Six describe an "apocalypse" (revelation) to Mary of the rewards and punishments reserved for souls after their death, with her son affirming her influence in Heaven and the nether regions as well as on earth. She passes through all twelve gates of the heavenly Jerusalem, entering the realm of the Trinity. In the sixth book, Mary is shown Gehenna (Hell), with sinners standing outside it waiting for the final day of judgment, when they will be damned. She prays for them, and Jesus assures her that "because afflictions shall abound unto men, ... those who call on thy name shall be delivered from destruction."[70]

In the *Six Books* dormition story, we have, in essence, very early testimony[71] to Mary's power to aid those who call on her and her son for help. Her assurances of the healing of the sick, the release of captives from imprisonment, the abating of storms at sea, the preservation of sailors from harm, and the safe return of travelers to their homes would emerge centuries later in miracle stories. Her promises of abundant harvests in fields blessed in her name would be remembered by farmers for fifteen hundred years. (Sometime in the 1950s, my uncle, Father Bill Keefe, was asked to bless a farmer's field in northern Minnesota that was threatened by an invasion of army worms. Uncle Bill put on his vestments, took his holy water bottle, and blessed the property. The farmer later reported that his field was safe: The pests had stopped at the edge of his land.)

Like Mary herself, these stories did not die but simply slept for a few centuries before emerging in sermons and songs, liturgies and devotions.

Mary in the Afterlife:
Queen of Heaven and Hell

A more sensational "apocalypse" shows Mary's power dramatically in both Heaven and Hell. In the later Greek *Apocalypse of the Theotokos*, dated after the ninth century,[72] Mary appears as a formidable presence. This much darker narrative, which describes a tour only of the nether regions, begins with Mary's royal command: "In the name of the Father and the Son and the Holy Spirit, let the archangel Michael come, so that he may tell me about the punishments and about the things in heaven and on the earth and below the earth."[73] As Jane Baum comments, "Her command is couched as a prayer, but rings out grandly in the text, especially since the myriad angels who arrive to do her bidding immediately launch into a series of acclamations such as might greet an empress."[74]

With the archangel Michael as her guide, Mary tours the underworld, weeping with compassion at the punishments meted out by God. In this afterlife, sinners suffer from fire, the fangs and claws of wild beasts, darkness, and despair. Although all sinners implore her to help, she intercedes only for Christians, saying, "Look on their punishments, for every creature calls upon me, your servant, saying, 'Holy Mistress, Virgin, help us!'" Then the Lord says to her, "Listen, Holy of Holies, All-Holy Virgin, if anyone calls upon your name, I will not forsake him, either in heaven or on earth."

After Mary continues to beg Jesus to have mercy on Christian sinners, Jesus grants them respite for the 40 days of Pentecost.[75]

This version of Mary's tour of the regions beyond the earth became "one of the most popular apocrypha of the Christian tradition ... widely diffused throughout the eastern Christian world"[76] and carried into the West, where Mary's intercession would be preached and illustrated for centuries. The tours of regions beyond the earth, of course, found their most elaborate interpretation in Dante's *Divine Comedy*.

What Does the Narrative Theology
of the *Lives of Mary* Say to Us?

Mary's story seems to have been important, perhaps even essential, to the people of the early church. For the church fathers, it was vital that she be seen as all-pure, all-holy, a woman worthy to bear the Son of God. Stories such as the *Protogospel* established her royal and priestly lineage and even suggested that she was conceived without the sexual union of her parents. They "proved" that she gave birth to Jesus without losing her

Chapter 2. Mary's "Life Stories"

virginity and reinforced a growing number of church doctrines about her, beginning with the pronouncement that she was the *Theotokos*, the Mother of God. Expanding that view of Mary, a number of writers—liturgists, homilists, and others—wrote about her as a strong, serious, and reflective voice (Romanos) as well as a partner with her son in his life and in the life of the early church (John Geometres and Euthymios). Although later "biographers" tended to ignore her voice and pass over her accomplishments, accounts of her death, especially the Six Books versions, highlighted her miracles as well as her promises to protect and sustain her followers from her position in Heaven. Marian "apocalypses" reflected her image as the regent for her son, Queen of Heaven, Mother of Mercy, and Empress of Hell.

CHAPTER 3

Mary in the Early Middle Ages

*Devotions, Churches,
Shrines, and Books of Praise
(Sixth to Twelfth Centuries)*

A rapidly increasing number of church buildings named for Mary—from small chapels to parish churches, cathedrals, and basilicas—as well as liturgies, feast days, and songs attests to an increase in Marian devotion during the early Middle Ages. The third-century prayer appealing for Mary's protection sowed the seeds of a superabundance of devotional works.

The earliest liturgy of the Virgin was composed in Syria in the fourth century. The fifth century saw the establishment of two major "feasts," or liturgical celebrations, of Mary. In Jerusalem, her presentation in the Temple was celebrated as a feast on November 21. Meanwhile, as mentioned earlier, the Feast of the Memory of Mary (her passing) was set on August 15 and first celebrated at the *Kathisma*, or "seat" of the Theotokos, a church located on the way to Bethlehem where the *Protogospel* says Mary rested during the journey.

During the sixth century, Rome saw work begin on the Church of Santa Maria Maggiore, where an icon of Mary holding the infant Jesus (attributed by legend to Saint Luke) was said to deliver the city from an outbreak of plague. In Soissons, France, a former temple of Isis was dedicated to Virgin Mary, while the site of a former temple to Diana was repurposed and named in honor of Mary.[1]

During that century, also, the Eastern church established the Feast of the Annunciation on March 25; the Feast of the Nativity of the Virgin on September 8; the Presentation of Christ in the Temple on February 2; and the Dormition of Mary on August 15. The *Akathistos Hymn* entered the Byzantine liturgy.

Sixth-Century Marian Miracle Stories: Gregory of Tours

One of the most influential western bishops, Gregory of Tours (538–594), included four Marian miracle stories in his *Glory of the Martyrs*.[2] Gregory's tales, two of which are related below, contain many of the elements that would satisfy the Christian imagination for centuries: an intractable problem (such as physical illness or danger, poverty, moral failings, or grave sin); anguish and prayer; Mary's miraculous intervention; and resolution of the problem.

Mary, Master Builder

The first tale is set in Constantinople in the sixth century, where the Emperor has ordered the construction of a church in Mary's honor. Scores of workers are exhausted by their efforts—all in vain—to raise the gigantic columns, 16 feet in diameter, intended to support the roof. Finally, Mary appears to the architect and shows him the kind of scaffolding he needs, as well as how to set up a system of ropes and pulleys. "Then you can raise them with three schoolboys," Our Lady says. The architect does as he is told, and people marvel at the sight of three young boys actually raising the columns that so many strong men had failed to move.

Mary, Provider

Gregory also tells of a monastery dedicated to Mary that fell upon hard times. Impoverished and hungry, the monks complain to their abbot: "Give us some food or let us leave—we will starve if we stay here." The abbot reassures them that Mary would not let her monastics perish, and they keep an all-night vigil in prayer. At dawn they find their granary stuffed with wheat, so much that they can scarcely open the bulging door.

Many years later, they face famine again; once more, they pray all night; and after their pre-dawn prayer, when they have fallen asleep from hunger and weariness, an angel comes and leaves an enormous pile of gold on the altar. Amazed, the abbot wonders who has been able to carry the gold into the church, which had been locked and bolted shut. When none of his monks can answer him, the abbot realizes that the riches have been a gift from Heaven. "But it is not surprising that the Blessed Virgin, who conceived without intercourse with a man and who remained a virgin even after the birth [of Christ], effortlessly supplied the monks."[3]

The Most Famous Marian Hymn

During the eighth century, an oratory, or small chapel, was dedicated to Mary at the papal church of St. Peter's in Rome. One of the most famous Marian hymns was composed: the "Ave Maris Stella," or "Hail, Star of the Sea." The metaphor of Mary as "Star of the Sea" came from Jerome's fourth-century etymology for Mary's name, which he took to mean "a drop of water from the sea [*stilla maris*]." A later copyist mistakenly rendered the words as "*stella maris*,"[4] "star of the sea," and the title became permanent, borne out by Mary's reputation for rescuing sailors from storms and shipwreck. The hymn calls on her as "kind mother and ever Virgin, happy gate of heaven" to "break the chains of sinners, give light to the blind.... Show yourself to be a mother; may the One who was born for us hear our prayers through you."[5] The hymn is still sung as part of the monastic daily prayer service.

Paul the Deacon's Classic Marian Tale

One of the most influential Marian stories of all time was set down by a Benedictine monk/historian known as Paul the Deacon (c. 720–c. 799), who translated the now-classic account of Theophilus from Greek into Latin. In this tale, Mary rescues a cleric who had sold his soul to the devil in return for ecclesiastical advancement. After the cleric repents and appeals to Mary, she snatches the bill of sale from the Evil One and returns it to her servant, who burns it and sings her praises. The story of this cleric, later called Theophilus, would become one of the most popular and enduring Marian tales of the Middle Ages, sculpted into the façades of cathedrals, depicted in stained glass windows, and told and retold throughout the continent and beyond in prose and poetry, narrative and drama.

Hrotsvitha of Gandersheim (c. 935–c. 1000), a convent-bred dramatist, brought out a brief (903 lines) *Life of Mary* as well as a 455-line account of Theophilus' pact with the Devil.[6] Based on the *Protogospel* and *Pseudo-Matthew*, her Marian *Life* is written in the Latin hexameters of a classically educated noblewoman of the Ottonian empire. Hrotsvitha emphasizes Joachim's nobility of spirit and Anna's patience in the face of the scorn faced by Mary's parents for their infertility. Mary runs up the fifteen Temple steps at the age of two, flourishing there and performing miracles of healing: "And anyone sick or having failing limbs / Who only touched her instantly was cured."[7] Jesus is born in an underground cave that glows with dazzling light at his birth. The Holy Family's journey to Egypt ends Hrotsvitha's account, as idols fall and the Egyptian ruler pleads with Mary for "favour [sic] from the Boy / who lay in his happy mother's loving lap."[8]

Brief as it is, Hrotsvitha's *Life* is significant for its author's classical learning as well as her unusual familiarity with extracanonical sources. To my knowledge, she is the only medieval woman to write about Mary's life—a distinction indeed.

Two Early Shrine Collections

Saragossa, Spain

In the early days of the church—about the year 40, according to legend—Saint James was striving to convert the pagan tribes in what is now Spain. Discouraged at his lack of success, he was sitting dejectedly, head in hands, when Mary appeared to him, standing on a pillar of jasper (a semiprecious stone). She reassured him, saying that because of his preaching, the inhabitants of Spain would become as firm in their faith as the stone of her pillar. She encouraged him to build a church there and vanished, leaving the pillar behind. Inspired by his vision, James continued preaching, finally achieving the conversion of many. He had a small chapel built, with a wooden image of Mary placed on the pillar. Over the centuries the chapel became a church, then a basilica known as Our Lady of the Pillar.[9]

Mary's appearance to Saint James—a bilocation, since she was supposedly living in Jerusalem at the time—marks the first of what would be many apparitions in places that would become shrines, each with its own legends about her intercession or intervention.

Chartres

While other stories made the rounds of monasteries during the ninth and tenth centuries, certain popular tales featured Mary's tunic (or chemise) and sometimes her *maphorion* or veil, according to narratives preserved by the Cathedral of Chartres in France. One story has it that Mary's chemise—which she wore at the birth of Jesus—had been given to the Holy Roman Emperor Charlemagne by the Empress Irene of Byzantium. Charlemagne's grandson, Charles the Bald, was said to have given it to the cathedral in 876.[10] Like its Byzantine counterpart (see "The 'Holy Theft' of Mary's Clothing" in Chapter 2), the cloth was displayed in a splendid golden setting, the Holy Reliquary or *Sainte Chasse*, and placed on the main altar.[11]

In 911, Chartres and the cathedral were besieged by the Viking Rollo and his hordes. Calling the Count of Poitiers and the Duke of Burgundy to his aid, Bishop Gantelmus not only supplied the citizens of Chartres with arms but also brought out "[t]he interior tunic [chemise] of the Mother of God," placing it over the main entrance to the city. The chronicle states that the invaders were blinded and defeated by the Christians under Mary's banner and protection.[12] Bishop Fulbert of Chartres (c. 960–1028) encouraged the cult of Mary's tunic, composed homilies featuring her miracles, and commissioned Marian liturgies.

The city of Chartres became an important pilgrimage site, its cathedral considered one of the Virgin's many royal residences. Other sites included the Cathedral of Notre Dame at Laon, said to possess some of her hair, and Notre Dame de Soissons, which claimed one of Mary's slippers. The Sainte Chapelle in Paris also had strands of her hair; the royal church of Saint Denis, just outside of Paris, had some of her "nail parings, which were kept in a red satin purse at Poitou."[13] The twelfth century saw no fewer than five major collections of miracle stories in England and France alone, and vernacular versions of the life of Mary circulated widely. We—modern and post-modern readers—who are tempted to dismiss a catalogue of Marian items as kitsch should think about our baseball and football museums, our sports halls of fame, our assortment of stars and footprints in front of Grauman's Chinese Theater in Hollywood, and our pilgrimages to the homes of stars such as Elvis Presley. All of us cherish tangible reminders of those we care about—in Marina Warner's words, "commonplaces of the heart."

Mary in the "Dark Ages"

The tenth and eleventh centuries saw the strife-filled beginnings of the Holy Roman Empire in the secular world. In the spiritual realm, the Great Schism of 1054 divided Christianity into two churches, Roman Catholic and Eastern Orthodox. Largely sheltered from these political and theological storms, local bishops continued to consecrate new churches, many of them to Mary; monks continued their work of preserving both secular and religious learning. Books called *Mariales*—collections of Marian devotions and miracle stories—were compiled in monastic communities. These *Mariales* furnished the material for individual collections all over the world, beginning with England and the Continent. In France alone, three major collections recounted miracles associated with Mary in the shrines of Laon, Soissons, and Rocamadour.[14]

Other miracle collections, not necessarily associated with Mary or her shrines but often containing Marian miracles, were designed to be read to monks at meals and were called legendaries, from the Latin *legere*, "to read." Because both *Mariales* and legendaries were written in Latin, their audiences were necessarily clerical; some of their subject matter, however, was designed to appeal in sermons to laypeople whose knowledge of their faith was minimal. Even in these brief, early stories, we hear of the restoration of fully functioning faculties to Deaf people, to people whose speech or vision was impaired, and to people who had difficulty walking; we hear of arduous childbirths aided; of paralysis, fevers, sterility, and sciatica cured. Sailors and passengers alike are rescued from ships foundering in violent storms. Bitterly quarrelling brothers are reconciled, prisoners released from their chains, even the dead restored to life, all through Mary's intervention.

Later Shrine Collections

A story in Latin associated with the Cathedral of Notre Dame de Laon[15] shows Mary in a different light: that of a mother insulted and offended whose son punishes the offender. The text shows us a group of monks and priests, led by their abbot, carrying relics of Mary in procession from town to town. Everywhere they were received with great honor, and in many places miracles of healing occurred. In one place, however, not far from the city of Tours, the resident monk refused to let them place Our Lady's reliquary on the high altar, directing them instead to a side altar in a dark corner of the church. (He was afraid of losing out on the usual feast-day collection, which might be diverted to the reliquary collection and thus would not benefit the local church.) But the people of Tours who had been following the relics told the arriving pilgrims about the miracles they had witnessed, directing the pilgrims to take their offerings to Mary's altar. Livid with jealousy, the monk ordered the reliquary and all of the relics out of the church.

Chastising the monk, the lord of the region put his own personal tent at the service of the reliquary group; the women of the group brought splendid wall hangings to decorate it and lamps to illuminate it through the night. But, says the author, "the just King Jesus did not tolerate the insult to his mother. At vespers, the offending monk was seized with an epileptic fit and fell to the ground in front of everyone, terrifying the crowd with his contortions. The bell tower of the church shook and cracked from the top down, and the largest bell plunged to the ground and broke. Deeply regretting his actions, the monk threw himself face down before the reliquary to beg forgiveness of the Queen of Heaven. He then asked that the reliquary be brought to the main altar, but his request was not granted."

We hear no more of the monk and his ruined church; some of these early stories end abruptly, perhaps to let the storyteller add interpretations and warnings about failing to give Mary the honor that is her due.

Another brief miracle story, from Soissons,[16] tells of the man named Boso, a knight's servant, who visited that shrine with friends. He refused, however, to honor Our Lady's slipper, making fun of his friends and their devotion. "A real slipper," he said scornfully, "would have rotted away in the centuries since Mary's assumption into heaven." The punishment for his rash words was immediate and harsh. He was seized with excruciating pain; his mouth twisted and his eyes almost popped from his head. Disfigured and contorted in agony, he groped his way into the shrine and threw himself down in front of the altar, writhing there in torment. Moved by his ordeal, the abbess of the sanctuary and her sisters helped him to the altar. When he was blessed with Mary's slipper and other relics, he began to recover.

The magnificent Marian shrine of Rocamadour, in southwest France, produced a collection of 126 miracle stories, divided into three "books," or sections. Rocamadour is home to a famous statue of Mary, darkened by candle smoke and time into a "Black Madonna." The shrine was and continues to be a stop on the Camino de Santiago as well as one of the most popular Marian shrines in the world. As varied as they are numerous, the miracles in this collection feature cures of diseases including fever, epilepsy, paralysis, cancer, and blindness. Mary saves pilgrims from robbers, rescues sailors from tumultuous seas, frees prisoners from their chains, and restores the goods of robbery victims. She even cares for the creatures of her devotees—a bull is returned to its herd, doves are saved from predators, a favorite hunting hawk is cured of a fatal wound.

A relatively unusual miracle beneficiary, a peasant, receives help from Mary in Book 2 of the Rocamadour stories. Through labor and cultivation, this peasant, Bernard, has acquired a prosperous holding, complete with a herd of cattle. Alas, he has attracted the attention of a group of vandals who attack his land and set fire to the house he occupies with his family. Seeing himself and his loved ones in an impossible situation, Bernard promises to present a wax model of his house to Our Lady's shrine in Rocamadour if he and his family are spared. Immediately "the evil ones" flee the property, and Bernard puts out the fire and saves the rest of his goods.[17]

We can assume that Bernard donated that wax model—known as an *ex-voto*, or fulfilment of a promise—to the shrine. (Many shrines, medieval and modern, display ex-votos in the form of plaques, paintings, or replicas of the body part that was cured, together with an acknowledgment of the favor received. Successful childbirths are represented by tiny babies.)

Chapter 3. Mary in the Early Middle Ages

The miracle stories above benefit specific shrines. Other Marian tales, whether in anonymous collections or in the works of individual authors, are situated in locations which would have seemed exotic to their audiences—Rome, Constantinople, Cologne, Compostela, Pisa—satisfying a taste for miraculous deeds in faraway settings as well as wonders closer to home.

Early English Selections from the *Mariales*

Anselm, abbot of Canterbury (d. 1109), addressed these words to Mary in a sermon:

> Lady, full and overflowing with grace, all creation receives new life from your abundance. Virgin, blessed above all creatures, through your blessing all creation is blessed, not only creation from its Creator, but the Creator himself has been blessed by creation.... The whole universe was created by God, and God was born of Mary. God created all things, and Mary gave birth to God. The God who made all things gave himself form through Mary, and thus he made his own creation.... Mary [is] the mother of the re-created world ... the mother through whom all things were given new life.... Without God's Son, nothing could exist; without Mary's son, nothing could be redeemed.[18]

Anselm's encomium to Mary exhibits the fervor that permeated the religious world of the twelfth century. A century earlier, in 1066, the French had invaded England, imposing their governance and their language on the conquered land. Thanks to a long-established network of Benedictine monasteries in both countries, a number of Marian miracle stories circulated in both England and France. No matter their country of origin, clerical authors used many of the same sources for their miracle collections, choosing narrative details that reflected their personal preferences as well as their religious convictions. Most early authors wrote in Latin, including Eadmer (c. 1060–c. 1126), an early advocate of the teaching that Mary was born free from original sin (a teaching known as her Immaculate Conception). Another Latinist was Dominic of Evesham (?1077–c. 1143). Some English authors, however, wrote in Anglo-Norman, a variant of northern French that prevailed in England after the invasion.

One of the most important English Marian writers is William of Malmesbury (c. 1090–c. 1143), whose spiritual and intellectual contemporaries were similarly devoted to Our Lady. English writers began to compile Marian stories in the 1120s, and William's work "marks the culmination of this first creative impulse, before its spread to the Continent and incorporation in much larger collections, from the late twelfth century onward."[19] Drawing from at least four different sources that were available to clerics in the West, William wrote some 53 miracle tales, situated in locales ranging from England and France to Germany, Italy, and Spain as well as Egypt, Turkey, Constantinople, and Jerusalem.

William seems particularly fond of Ebbo the thief, who batters down every obstacle to his illegal entries, slithers into the smallest corners in which something might be hidden, covets everything, and steals as much as he can. Growing older, he loses his touch and is caught and condemned. Because he has honored Mary all his life, giving a tithe of his takings to the poor, Mary protects him from the gibbet, and he becomes a monk.[20] The story of Ebbo becomes a Marian classic, a staple of collections for the next 200 years, together with William's tales of the priest who knew only one mass, the peasant who moved boundary stones, and the pregnant abbess.

Like other clerical authors of Marian stories, William points out the foibles of those vowed to the monastic life. His account of "The Drowned Sacristan" shames a monk who, despite his devotion to "the queen of the world," falls in love with a woman who lives across the river from his monastery. This monk greets Mary every time he passes her image, even on the way to visit his paramour. One evening as he is crossing the river his foot slips; falling into deep water, he drowns. The next morning, his brother monks look for their companion, who was supposed to be in charge of the church; they find his body washed up on the riverbank. Interrupting their lamentations, the body returns to life and tells the story of his rescue.

He had died, the sacristan says, and angels and demons had arrived to quarrel over his soul. The angels were losing the argument when the Mother of God appeared and asked the devils what right they had to his soul; they replied that he had died without confessing his many sins. Mary threatened to take his case to her son for judgment, and suddenly the sacristan found himself on the riverbank with his fellow monks.[21]

In the Prologue to his stories, William echoes much older perceptions of Mary. After ascribing to her the four essential virtues of prudence, justice, courage, and temperance, he alludes to her vow of chastity as well as her extraordinary understanding and memory of her son's mission and describes her as "...pondering [these things] in her heart. It is for this reason that the whole world owes to her the full knowledge of its salvation, *for she did not begrudge the apostles the knowledge she so fully commanded ... she is rightly called the apostle of apostles and evangelist of evangelists; for it was thanks to her that the foundational doctrine shone forth on the very founders of the faith.*"[22]

Little Left Unsaid:
Early Books of Praise for Mary

From the earliest days of the Church, sermons on Mary influenced both the clergy and the faithful. Two major religious orders fostered and spread Marian stories and devotion to the Mother of God throughout the Middle Ages. Benedictines, founded in Italy by Benedict of Nursia in the sixth century, followed a Rule that divided the day into periods of work and prayer. Named for the city of Cistercium (Cîteaux) in France, the Cistercians were founded in 1098 to follow a more stringent form of the Benedictine rule. Both Benedictines and Cistercians were headed by men devoted to Mary; the daily routines of their monasteries included numerous prayers to the Virgin, and some of their monastic libraries housed collections of Marian stories and books of praise. Bernard of Clairvaux (1090–1163) and Amadeus of Lausanne (c. 1109–1159) were two of the most influential Cistercians of their time.

Nicknamed "Our Lady's Troubadour," Bernard wrote volumes about Mary, including four homilies of praise.[23] Using Luke's account of the Annunciation as the source of his inspiration, Bernard launches into a series of laudatory descriptions of Mary's encounter with the angel Gabriel. I find it intriguing that although he insists on the virgin birth of Jesus, Bernard considers Mary's humility (a virtue which he regards as a lack of pride) more important than her virginity: "It seems evident that she conceived by the Holy Spirit because, as she herself said, God 'regarded the humility of his handmaiden' rather than her virginity."[24]

Bernard's second homily on the Annunciation concludes with a series of exhortations to anyone and everyone facing the headwinds of life, whether spiritual or material:

> In dangers, in hardships, in every doubt, think of Mary, call out to Mary. Keep her in your mouth, keep her in your heart. Follow the example of her life and you will obtain the favor of her prayer. Following her, you will never go astray. Asking her help, you will never despair. Keeping her in your thoughts, you will never wander away. With your hand in hers, you will never stumble. With her protecting you, you will not be afraid. With her leading you, you will never tire. Her kindness will see you through to the end.[25]

Nine hundred years later, a "holy card" with Bernard's good counsel on it nestles in my childhood book of readings for worship.

Amadeus of Lausanne (c. 1109–1159) was a member of the Abbey of Clairvaux before becoming an abbot and then a bishop. Author of eight Marian homilies, he invites his audience to "the banquet of the Mother of God."[26] The "banquet" consists of these eight sermons, beginning with an introduction and following the life of Jesus as it is lived in the company of Mary. The fifth homily reflects on Mary's compassion at the death of Christ; the sixth depicts her participation in her son's resurrection and ascension. The final two homilies describe Mary's death and assumption into Heaven, where she continues to look after her devotees.

Amadeus' final two homilies bear traces of the Six Books tradition, traces which we will find throughout the major miracle collections of the following centuries. In Sermon VII, he observes that Jesus left his disciples to be taught by his mother: "Though indeed they had been taught by the Spirit, yet they could be taught by her who put forth to the world the Sun of Righteousness."[27]

As she had healed and delivered people during her lifetime, Amadeus says, she continues after her death: "For those who sail upon the sea ... and call upon her with complete faith she rescues from the breath of the storm and the raging of the winds." She saves souls from the Devil, and "[i]n the places dedicated to her holy memory she wins movement for the lame, sight for the blind, hearing for the deaf, speech for the dumb, curing every kind of weakness and affording countless gifts of healing." She lights up the world with her miracles, helping her own as a generous, beneficent mother.[28]

Later writers were even more extravagant in their descriptions of Mary, ascribing to her all virtues and human knowledge. A monastic now known as Pseudo-Albert, for example, wrote a scholarly work known as the *Mariale or 230 Questions on the Annunciation*.[29] In it he discusses Mary's age (twelve), her physical appearance (beautiful), and what she was doing at the time (contemplating). In addition to possessing all virtues, she has knowledge of the entire university course of study for a master's degree. Because she possesses every grace, she has received the gift of all seven sacraments; however, in the case of holy orders, she has the grace and privileges of the priesthood, *without having received the sacrament of holy orders itself*.

Pseudo-Albert thus excuses himself from the dangerous discussion of Mary's priesthood, respecting church tradition with the facile implication that she was not ordained.[30] He raises the issue, however, and it would be discussed for hundreds of years.

What Is the Narrative Theology of These Writings?

Echoing its Eastern beginnings in sermon and devotion, the Marian tradition in the West expanded in song, liturgy, and story during the early

Chapter 3. Mary in the Early Middle Ages 51

Middle Ages. As churches and shrines to Mary dominated the cities and the lives of their inhabitants, the body of tales about her traveled from country to country, from monastery to monastery, collected and preserved by monks. In these early tales, Mary speaks with the voice of authority to command as master builder; she provides for her servants, punishes those who doubt her or her son, rescues souls from the Devil. Although she speaks relatively rarely in these early tales, her voice carries the authority of Heaven, and her power is unquestioned. She is the mover of the action, the decider of the outcome of the narrative. Even the physical remnants of her life on earth can influence the course of a battle or effect a cure.

It's also very clear from the stories and the books of praise devoted to her that Mary acts in Heaven as she did on earth: in partnership with Jesus. Every author emphasizes the extraordinary cooperation between mother and son that derives from the equally extraordinary relationship between the human and the divine. Mary works incessantly to connect and reconcile earth and Heaven, God and humanity. She is altogether deserving of the praise so lavished upon her by her faithful ones, who have begun to call her "Our Lady."

CHAPTER 4

The Long Twelfth Century I
Miracles in the Age of Faith and Feudalism

The Age of Faith

Saint Anselm, theologian and prince of the Church, epitomized the Marian spirit of what is called "the long twelfth century," that period from about 1100 to 1300 during which France—as well as England and much of Europe—knew relative peace. The great University of Paris vied for spiritual splendor and intellectual achievement with the Cathedral of Notre Dame as it rose to ever greater prominence, protected by the river Seine from the riotous living of its scholars. Writers both secular and sacred throughout the country—together with much of Europe—produced epic and romance, courtly song and sacred chant, and volumes and volumes dedicated to the miracles of Our Lady Mary.

Hundreds of churches in France alone were built and dedicated to Mary; liturgies abounded to celebrate her feasts throughout the year. Saturday became "Mary's Day," and people prayed the Angelus (a prayer celebrating the Angel Gabriel's appearance to her) three times a day. Hymns such as "Ave Maris Stella" ("Hail, Star of the Sea"), "Salve Regina" ("Hail, Holy Queen"), and "O Intemerata" ("O Spotless One") were sung daily in monasteries. Artists painted scenes from the *Protogospel* and other extracanonical works. Mary was given titles, such as Gate of Heaven, Morning Star, Health of the Sick, Refuge of Sinners, and Comforter of the Afflicted, that would resonate with the audiences that listened to miracle stories.

No fewer than six important collections of Marian miracle stories appeared under the names of their authors, in addition to large anonymous regional collections. In England, Dominic of Evesham assembled 14 miracle stories between 1120 and 1130; William of Malmesbury finished his 53 Marian miracle tales about 1140; and Nigel of Canterbury (c. 1135–

c. 1200) produced 17 stories, of which 16 also appeared in William's work.[1] In France, shrine collections were gathered at Laon about 1140 by Hériman de Tournai (1095–1147)[2] and in Soissons about 1143 by Hugh Farsit.[3] Both French and English authors wrote in Latin. Bridging the two cultures in about 1165, Adgar wrote his *Gracial*, a collection of 49 Marian miracles, in Anglo-Norman, a form of Old French that was used especially in northwestern France.[4]

Genesis 3 Fulfilled: Mary and the Devil

Above the main doors of the churches that rose in such profusion during the Middle Ages appear scenes of Christ's life, death, and resurrection. At the pinnacle of those scenes, Christ sits in judgment of the human race; below him, Saint Michael weighs their good and bad deeds on a scale, while angels wait to receive the blessed, and devils reach out for the damned. Carved in stone, these images are sharp reminders of the powers of good and evil as well as the ultimate fate of humankind.

In Genesis 3:14–15, after Adam and Eve have sinned, God addresses the serpent: "Because you have done this, cursed are you among all animals and among all wild creatures; upon your belly shall you go, and dust you shall eat all the days of your life. I will put enmity between you and the woman and between your offspring and hers; he will strike your head, and you will strike his heel."

During the first centuries of Christianity, Mary was identified as the "new Eve" or "counter-Eve," the woman whose offspring, Jesus, would overcome the sin and death brought into the world through Eve and the serpent, identified as the Devil. Whether known by the name of Satan or simply called "the Enemy," the Devil embodied the serpent's cunning and shape-shifting; during the Middle Ages, the scripture passage was played out in stories of Mary's striking at Satan to defend and keep her son's followers from the Devil's clutches. Both descriptions and illustrations of the opponents stress the spiritual chasm between them. Mary is beautiful, her face and figure glowing with the glorification of her person in Heaven. She is also supremely intelligent, gifted with supernatural insight as she wields the power granted to her by Jesus. The Devil, by contrast, is physically repellent: He appears as an ape-like figure, his paws clawed, his tail bristling behind him, his head horned, his feet cloven hooves. Although he is clever in his own twisted way, and although he commands legions of lesser devils or demons, he and his gang are no match for the Queen of Heaven and her legions of angels. In these tales, Mary is as mighty as she is beautiful; the Devil and his minions are as feckless as they are ugly. Although

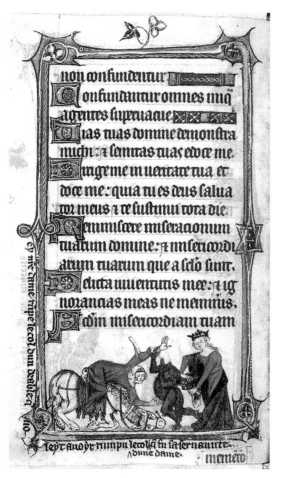

Mary defeats the devil. Miniature illustration of Mary beating a small, dark, grotesque figure easily recognizable as the Evil One. Martyrology of Notre-Dame-des-Près, Valenciennes. BM 838, f. 097v. Arras, France. Institute for Research and History Texts.

evil may appear in many guises—as vicious animals, as alluring sexual partners, as friends or servants or monks—Mary sees through all disguises and deceptions, vanquishing her eternal foe in her ancient role as downfall of demons.

The Feudal World

In the post-Roman West, secular and sacred became intertwined as popes and bishops of the church chose and crowned kings in addition to governing vast properties of their own. (Kings also chose popes and bishops.) Society was divided into three classes: the clergy (those who prayed); the aristocracy, hereditary nobles, and knights (those who governed vast properties and fought for their overlords); and the peasantry (those who worked the land, often in a form of serfdom). Women assumed the status of their spouses. The Christian faith governed the lives of all, baron and peasant alike; dissent was met with excommunication by the church, death, or exile by secular authorities.

The king and members of his aristocracy convened courts—that is, gatherings in the great hall of the palace or manor—for purposes of governance or celebration. Secular courts, assemblies called by an earthly sovereign or lord, were convoked for the great feasts of the church year. It was assumed by some clerics who wrote about Mary that the heavenly court functioned in much the same way.[5] The court of Heaven was taken as a reflection of earthly courts, with God the Father reigning over all, Jesus as savior and judge of humankind, and Mary reigning as Queen Mother.

A thirteenth-century tale, the *Court de Paradis*, presents a cameo of a plenary Court held by God on the occasion of All Saints' Day.[6] At the center of the festivities are Jesus, Mary, and Mary Magdalene. The two Marys begin a court dance, inviting the saints to join them, and Jesus leads a song while dancing with his mother and his friend. Saint Peter has kept out the riff-raff (the souls in Purgatory) during the celebration, but he relents at the request of the Virgin. The fires of Purgatory die down, and the captive souls are released to participate, in a kinder echo of the Marian apocalypse of earlier centuries.

The author, probably associated with an aristocratic household, was well enough acquainted with contemporary court music to insert eighteen refrains into his narrative, all based on songs that were popular in secular courts. The performance would have served as a lively sermon—a poetic interpretation of the feasts of All Saints and All Souls, November 1 and 2. Many other "pious fictions," stories about the lives of Mary and Jesus, were written as alternatives to the secular romances and epics, focused on chivalry and courtly love, that were popular during the Middle Ages.[7]

Mary's Competition: The Noble Lady of "Courtly Love"

Despite his apparent clerical status, Andreas Capellanus, or Andrew the chaplain (late twelfth century), appears to have been an accomplished courtier. He claims to write as a member of the entourage of Marie, Countess of Champagne (1145–1198), who has asked him to instruct a young nobleman on how to conduct himself in courtship. Andreas obliges by writing *De Arte Honeste Amandi* (*The Art of Loving Nobly*) sometime in the late 1180s.[8] Basing his work on Ovid's classical *Art of Love* (and perhaps with the same tongue-in-cheek approach to his subject), Andreas describes the stages and prescribes the techniques of courtship and its consummation in Book I. Book II describes how love may be made to last: by following 31 rules prescribed for lovers. Book III takes it all back, rejecting women and love with misogynistic fervor.

Although it's possible that *The Art of Loving Nobly* was an academic spoof by an enterprising and sophisticated university clerk,[9] nevertheless the popular work codified for the northern French the warmer and more sensual spirit of Occitania to the south. Troubadours there had begun to write love poetry early in the twelfth century. William IX of Aquitaine,

Count of Poitou (1071–1127), had written—in addition to some off-color works—lyrics celebrating the love of a highborn, haughty lady; his close contemporary Jaufre Rudel (c. 1120–c. 1147) sighed after a "far-off" love. In their poetry, the troubadours courted beautiful, noble, unattainable (usually married) women, seeking the "consolation" of their love in embraces and more. Northern French poets followed their example, sighing after noble, often unattainable ladies; courtly romances chronicled the progress of lovers as they sighed, entered tournaments, wrote letters or poetry, begged for signs of affection, and otherwise courted the noble objects of their affection.

The Noblest Lady of Them All: Medieval Marian Lyrics

Of the 145 northern French religious songs in one major collection, 124 contain lyrics focusing on Mary.[10] A significant number use verse forms popularized by Occitan poets, who also wrote lyrics to Mary.[11] These songs and poems address Our Lady in prayer, praise, confession, or a combination of all three. Mary is described as a queen or an empress, the most powerful of women and the most highly valued: Her worth is measured in metaphors of ruby, emerald, diamond, sapphire, jasper, and topaz. She is depicted literally in flowery terms as a rose, a flower of paradise, a lily, or a flourishing vine that bore Christ as its fruit.

One set of images depicts her as the source of living water, recalling Jesus' characterization of himself to the Samaritan woman in John 4:7–13. She is seen as a clear fountain, a current of fresh water in a salt sea, a fount of mercy, pity, and love. Poets emphasize her virginity both before and after Christ's birth, describing the event in terms of sunlight passing through glass, the burning bush of Moses that flamed without being consumed (Exodus 3:2), or the fleece of Gideon dry in the downfall of dew. (This image, found in Judges 6:37–40, is a double one: Gideon also finds the fleece wet on dry ground.)

Many lyrics combine religious and feudal imagery, just as many secular lyrics incorporate religious elements. The feudal code assumes that a vassal serves a lord or lady; in return for such service, the noble protects and rewards the vassal. A winsome combination of the feudal and the spiritual occurs in one anonymous song: The author declares that he has placed his understanding, desires, and habits in Mary's keeping, saying that she is the light that never fails, the sun that never sets, the mother without pain, the land that produces a harvest without seed, chain-mail and shield and lance all in one, and a bright and trenchant sword that defeats all who hold firm in their belief and place their confidence in her. The final stanza addresses her: "Valiant empress, ever-virgin, I offer my soul and my life to you and promise you the allegiance of my body. May it please your power to defend me against the venom of the serpent, so that my body may not come to harm nor my soul to torment."[12]

A poet from the south of France, Daude de Pradas (1214–1282), literally "converts" courtly vocabulary into spiritual veneration. Whoever would wish to sing a truly new song, he says, sings songs of God without a false note. True "courtly love" is love of God and Mary; all other songs turn into tears.

Another troubadour, Peire Cardenal (1180–1278), wrote a lyric that has been called both a hymn and a prayer.[13] "Truly virgin, Mary, true life, true faith," he begins. "True way, true mother, true lover, true love, by your true mercy may your heir inherit (inhere in) me!" He calls Mary a guiding star, the dawn that announces the sun/son; and he portrays her as a queen, dressed lavishly in gray fur and "gold-decked garments." The vision suggests not only the psalmist's queen "arrayed in gold" but also the gold-embroidered chasuble of a priest. "You sit next to God," Cardenal says. "Make my peace with Him."

Whether secular, religious, or a combination of the two, medieval Marian lyrics echo *Mariale* praise books in their imagery and theological assumptions.[14] Worldly ladies, whatever their physical beauty and personal qualities, are no match for the other-worldly splendor of Mary, enhanced as she is by an array of virtues that have no equal.

The Mary of the Medieval Miracle Stories

In medieval times as in antiquity, Mary's power derives from her status as mother of God; her influence, as one who mediates between the demands of Heaven and the failures of earth, extends even to the depths of Hell.[15] The men who wrote about her constructed a figure familiarly winsome and enormously powerful, quite unconscious, I believe, of a subtext that suggested female divinity. Although technically receiving her power from God, Mary acts autonomously in these works, making her the principal agent in accounts of her miraculous interventions. As she appears in many miracle stories, Mary exhibits attributes of Godhead such as goodness, holiness, intelligence, justice, compassion, mercy, and wisdom. She possesses and exercises the power to reward virtue and punish vice, often by herself, sometimes by calling on her divine son (just as Jesus called upon his heavenly Father). Like Jesus, she invites sinners to repent and saves them—repeatedly—from the powers of evil. Like the Holy Spirit, she hovers over a sinful world, ready and able to make its denizens holy, and serving as an advocate of humanity. If she functions as a mediator, it is as a supremely powerful one: Her requests are always granted because she is intimately related to the grantor as well as to the grantee.

At the same time, Mary exhibits attributes of a medieval and very human woman; she is both maternal (giving drops of her milk to cure diseased clerics in two tales) and seductive (appearing in an undergarment with her hair unbound to rescue a drunken monk). She is mistress of the courtly phrase in speaking to the young men she is wooing back to her service. The personification of queenliness and refined, gentle beauty in some tales, in others she berates an ungrateful follower, male or female. She may defeat any number of devils in legal battles over the souls of those redeemed—either through her son's death or her own often arbitrary choice—but if her arguments seem not to persuade as she expects, she is capable of throwing a royal fit in front of Jesus, reminding him of his filial duty to her.

Vincent of Beauvais, an Author in the Latin Tradition

A Dominican monk, Vincent of Beauvais (c. 1190–1264), produced an encyclopedic *Speculum historiale*, or *Mirror of History*, including 70 Marian miracles in his scholarly project.[16] Like the work of his better-known contemporaries who wrote in the vernacular, his Marian stories enjoyed wide circulation for several centuries.

From the number and variety of his tales, we can deduce that Vincent had access to more than one source: probably a *grant mariale*, a large compendium of miracles that included tales of recovery from various wounds, diseases, birth defects, and demonic attacks, as well as stories from Rome, Jerusalem, and Byzantium. He evidently had access to shrine collections as well, from locations as distant as Soissons in the north and Rocamadour in the southwest of France. His Latin style is accessible, in contrast to that of some monks, like Nigel of Canterbury, who wrote in elaborate neoclassical verse that challenged the understanding of the less educated. Vincent's use of realistic dialogue, along with his selection of tales designed to appeal to lay as well as monastic audiences, ensured his popularity.

Vincent records the story of a monk saved from demons—by his day almost a stereotype—in lively fashion. "The Monk of Chartres Whom Mary Saved from Demonic Attacks"[17] begins one night as a monk of Chartres is meditating in his cell on the things of Heaven. Suddenly a troop of demons appears in the form of a herd of wild pigs. Their jaws gaping wide to show enormously long teeth, they run around his cell as if crazed and excited at the prospect of killing him. They surround the terrified monk, who expects his death at any moment. His fear increases beyond measure when he sees an enormous creature enter his cell and say to the pigs, "What are you doing, you lazy louts? Why haven't you taken him away? Why haven't you torn him to pieces?"

They respond, "We tried with all our might, but we couldn't do it." Brandishing a terrifying iron hook with long curved teeth, the creature says, "I'll do it myself." He adjusts it so as to grab the monk (or to carve him into pieces), scaring the poor man nearly to death. But no sooner has the huge creature done this than Mary, mother of mercy in whom the monk has placed all his hope after God, appears. Holding a slender rod in her hand, she says, "How have you dared to come here? That monk doesn't belong to you, and you will exercise no power over him."

When Mary finishes speaking, the whole herd of pigs vanishes like a puff of smoke. After the demons flee, she stays with the still-trembling man and consoles him, saying, "You have been doing well, and your devotion to God is pleasing to me. Continue in this way and strive to improve. And to give you an example of what is demanded of you, eat the most common of foods, dress in used clothing, and zealously perform the work of your hands." With these words she disappears, leaving the monk comforted.[18]

This story is typical of the "monk delivered" genre, a reassurance to members of a monk's community who confront their own demons in the spiritual life. Vincent sketches many of the tales that later writers will expand into narratives containing dialogue and characters such as the pregnant abbess, the hanged thief, and the child delivered from the Devil.

Seafarers Menaced by a Storm Saved by Mary, Star of the Sea[19]

An abbot and his monks are crossing the channel between France and England, a difficult passage due to the storms that often strike without warning. On this occasion, there arises a tempest of such violence that all on board fear for their lives. One prays to Saint Nicholas to spare his life. Others invoke Saint Andrew, Saint Clare, or another saint; each prays to the one with whom he is most familiar, vowing to make offerings at the altar of the saint, as is the custom of those venturing out to sea.

The abbot notices that they are praying to every saint but Mary, the mother of mercy, star of the sea, more powerful than any of the others. "What are you doing, my brothers?" asks the abbot. "Your invocations will be heard if you pray all together, with one voice, to the Mother of God to have pity on her children." And the abbot, weak from fasting, begins to intone the verse, "Happy are you, holy Virgin Mary, and worthy of all praise," from a Marian mass with the refrain, "Pray for your people."

Scarcely have the monks ended their intonation of the verse when a brilliant light appears at the summit of the mast like the flame atop a candle, banishing the shadows of the night and illuminating the upturned faces of the men below. Suddenly the storm ceases, and on the orders of the Queen of Heaven, the sea is calmed. A short time later, the sun rises, revealing the shores they had been seeking.

This tale is one of scores of rescue stories featuring storms at sea, treacherous river fords, and other threats of death by water; it also reflects the displacement of other saints by Mary as her reputation grew to outshine theirs.

Adgar and the First Vernacular French Marian Miracle Collection

Competition seems to have been a major motive for clerical writers to translate Marian iracles into the language of the people. Authors like Chrétien de Troyes (c. 1130–c.1190+) and Marie de France (fl. 1160–1215) celebrated life and love among the nobility, describing what has been called "courtly love." This complex term includes fealty to the god of love, exploits or "adventures" in honor of or service to a lady, and the hope for a physical consummation of that love as a reward from the deity and the lady. Chrétien's lengthy romances and Marie's shorter *lais*, or narrative poems, described the varieties (often adulterous) and vagaries of courtly love in rhyming couplets, entertaining the courts of the French nobility in France and England.

Well-born monks were familiar with courtly literature, if only by reputation, and it's clear from their commentaries that they translated Mary's miracles as an antidote to the temptations described in secular stories. Featuring the greatest sovereign of all and his mother, more beautiful and noble than any earthly queen, miracle tales told of Mary's marvelous works on behalf of those who served her in feudal good faith. This service often took the form of daily prayers—especially the Little Office of the Blessed Virgin Mary, a shorter version of the longer Liturgy of the Hours performed seven times a day. The reward, of course, was the same for every sinner: reconciliation with God and eternal life.

A monk named Adgar (fl. 1160–1191) was the first to translate Mary's miracle stories into Anglo-Norman, the vernacular of France and England that developed after the Norman Conquest of 1066. (English was not used "for any work of importance" until a century later.)[20] What little we know about Adgar we have to glean from *Le Gracial*, or *The Fullness of Grace*, his translation of 49 miracle stories from the Latin.[21] The dates of his birth and death are unknown; the few facts about him come from his work. Writing from England about 1165, Adgar, also called William, undertook his project "for the forgiveness of [his] sins" at the request of his friend Gregory.[22] Like his contemporaries and successors, he told the stories of Mary's beneficence—her own fullness of grace and the abundance of grace she bestowed on others—that he found in "the collections" or "the books" of St. Paul's in London.[23]

Like other clerical purveyors of Marian tales, Adgar strove to make his material as engaging as the epics and romances that were his competition. The marvels of *Le Gracial* are intended to outshine secular adventures as well as to assure their audience of the ultimate happy ending—for themselves as well as for the author's protagonists.

The story of a cure that appears below is one of three instances of miraculous healing wrought by Mary's milk in Adgar's work. Like Miracle 15 below, Miracle 22 tells of a monk afflicted by a cancer of the mouth. Close to death, the man receives a visit from Mary, who praises his faithfulness to her, taking out her breast to give him her milk. Fully cured, the monk scolds his brothers for making so much noise that Mary has left him: an intrusion of the daily on the holy. Miracle 30 celebrates Mary's healing of Saint Fulbert (c. 960–1028), bishop of Chartres, the driving force behind the reconstruction of Mary's cathedral, founder of the famous cathedral school, and the author of Marian hymns as well as an influential sermon on the importance of celebrating Mary's nativity (September 8).

The miracle below draws on two mainstream traditions: the courtly field or meadow where love is celebrated and the dream sequence in which the sleeper is visited by a supernatural being, with life-changing consequences. The translated paraphrase is mine.

A Cleric Cured by Mary in a Field of Flowers
Adgar, Miracle 15[24]

A cleric described only as "a European" is honored by all of the nobility of his region for his piety. He is beloved of Mary as well, for his devoted and faithful recitation of the Office of the Virgin. Stricken by cancer of the mouth, he lives in pain: His lips are deformed by the disease, and his breath is so foul that all his friends avoid him. Only the bishop who appointed him visits him regularly.

God, however, decides that he should be cured and sends the man a dream in which an angel comes to him, leading him to a marvelous field of flowers that flood the senses with their fragrance. Twenty-two plants bearing vari-colored flowers flourish here, as well as one more beautiful bloom that reaches above the others. The cleric asks his angelic guide the significance of this sight, and the angel tells him that each flower corresponds to a verse of either Psalm 119, *Beati immaculata (Blessed the Immaculate One)*, or *Deus, in nomine tuo (O God, by Your Name)* in the Office of the Virgin Mary. The psalms are plants; the verses are flowers of praise, abundant and exotic.

The angel then directs his charge to a temple of unearthly beauty, where he sees Mary, surrounded by dazzling light. "Mother of mercy, mother of tenderness and sweetness," she invites him to approach her. Curing his mouth with milk from her breasts, she tells him that the lips that have uttered her praises so often should not suffer.

On waking up, the cleric tells his friends and the bishop about his miraculous encounter. After the bishop gives him Communion, the man dies; his soul goes directly to Heaven.

No single writer, says Adgar, can tell of all that Our Lady does for her own.

The following miracle is notable for its protagonist, a *vilain* or peasant, and for its depiction of a priest and his concubine, a rarity in Marian stories. I've paraphrased Adgar's tale below.

Enlarging a Country Church
Adgar, Miracle 39[25]

Adgar begins his tale by stating that God loves all humankind, clerics and knights and commoners, all made by his hand. "I know very well that God despises no one, and I'm writing about a peasant in this tale." The events take place in England, "the land of Saint Edmund," where a country church stands, ancient and showing its age. To this church comes a peasant, who stops to rest his horse and say a prayer. He is astonished to hear a strange noise from inside the church and even more surprised to see a young woman whose garments shine so brightly that they dispel the dusk. She takes him by the hand, saying, "Go to the lady in the church. You can do her a service." Asked who the lady is, she replies, "Notre Dame, she who is the lady of all."

Entering the church, he sees a group of virgins surrounding a great lady seated near the altar. She beckons him closer, saying, "Go to the priest of this place and ask him to renovate and enlarge it without delay. My name is Mary, the mother of God." Then, using a staff, she shows him the dimensions she desires and the kind of stonework and masonry that will be required. Awed and frightened, the peasant tells Our Lady that no one will pay attention to anyone of his rank; she responds by giving him a sign to prove that she herself has commissioned the work.

Encouraged, the peasant leaves the church and asks the young woman holding his horse for her name. "Margaret," she replies, "Mary's chambermaid." At that, the day dawns bright and clear, and the peasant goes to visit the priest, telling him of Mary's command. Disdainful of such a lowborn fellow, the priest rebuffs him until the peasant tells him of Mary's sign and mentions the possibility of punishment if he is refused. Impressed, the priest goes to consult his live-in companion, who berates him for listening to such a lowborn fool. "Do you really think," she says, "that holy Mary would ever talk to such a blockhead, an imbecile like him?"

No sooner has she finished ranting when she takes a misstep, falls, and breaks her hip. Knowing that she has been punished for her folly, she begs Mary's pardon, saying, "Have mercy, Lady! I most certainly believe him now!" Confessing her fault, she repents and withdraws her opposition; the priest hastens to begin work on enlarging the church, hoping for her recovery. Taking some dust from the stones that Mary has placed in the church, he makes a paste and puts it on her breast; she is instantly cured.

The tale ends with the church enlarged, the peasant a middle-class mason, and the miracle acknowledged and praised by everyone.

Wace and an Early Vernacular "Life of Mary"

Wace (c. 1100–1174+) seems to have been the first Western writer to incorporate extracanonical works into a narrative about Mary from her conception to her assumption into Heaven. Known as the *Concepcion Nostre Dame*,[26] this 1808-line poem begins with a Marian miracle story and ends with an account of her death. It includes the story of Anna and Joachim as well as an early vernacular version of Mary's genealogy known as "the three Marys." Written during the 1130s or '40s,[27] the work advances arguments for establishing the feast of the Immaculate Conception in commemoration of Mary's freedom from original sin. (The feast had been suppressed in England after the Conquest.)

The *Concepcion* begins with the aftermath of William the Conqueror's victory and the death of King Harold of England, an ally of the Danish monarch. To fend off possible retaliation by the Danes for Harold's death, King William sends Abbot Helsin of Ramsey to learn of any Danish plans for retribution. Helsin's mission is peaceful and successful; he is sent home with honor. Soon after they put out to sea, however, a horrific storm arises, threatening to destroy the ship and its terrified sailors. All call upon God and Mary for help, and an angel appears, calling for Helsin. The angelic messenger is blunt: "Helsin, if you want to leave the ocean behind and reach your own country safely, promise that you will preach the observation of the day Our Lady was conceived on December 8." The angel then specifies which service to use: that of Mary's nativity, celebrated in September, substituting the word "conception" for "nativity." Thanking God, Helsin consents; the storm abates; the abbot returns and keeps his promise.

The story of Joachim and Anna follows, with elements of the extracanonical *Protogospel of James* and *Pseudo-Matthew* as well as extensive citations from the First Testament regarding barren couples who produced eminent offspring. Wace emphasizes Jesse as the father of David, the ancestor of Jesus, setting the scene for Mary's own genealogy. In this segment of the work, based on an obscure work by a ninth-century theologian, Haymo of Auxerre, he tells us that Anna had a sister named Hismeria or Esmeria, who was the mother of Elizabeth (the mother of John the Baptist) and Eliud. Eliud had a son named Eminen, who was the father of Saint Servatius, a patron saint of the diocese of Liège in France.

Anna herself had three husbands: Joachim, Cleophas, and Salome. Her marriage to Joachim produced Mary, the mother of Jesus. When Joachim died, Anna married his brother Cleophas, following Jewish custom; they had another daughter, also called Mary, who married a man named Alpheus. Mary and Alpheus had four sons: James the Less, Joseph the Just, Simon, and Jude. After the death of Cleophas, Anna married his brother Salome; they too had a daughter named Mary, who married Zebedee and produced two sons, James the Greater and John the Evangelist.

Later known as "the Holy Kinship,"[28] this elaborate tale served to explain Jesus' "brothers," interpreted by Saint Jerome (c. 347–c. 419–20) as "cousins" in light of theologians' insistence on Mary's perpetual virginity. It would be repeated almost verbatim a century later in Jacobus of Voragine's *Golden Legend*.

The final segment of the *Concepcion* describes Mary's death and assumption, consulting extracanonical sources such as the *Pseudo Melito*. Mary prays to join her son; an angel reassures her, giving her a palm branch. Saint John arrives before the other apostles and discusses Mary's burial wishes with her. Jesus appears and addresses her with filial love and doctrinal declarations: "Mary, precious gem, most holy virgin, my spouse, come to eternal life in the angelic company.... I am King of Heaven; you will be crowned Queen."[29]

During Mary's funeral procession, John—chosen because of his virginity—leads the way holding the palm branch, which gives off a great light. A crowd of fifteen thousand follows. Unbelievers are blinded, but can have their sight restored by conversion and a touch of the branch. Although Mary's body is taken to Josaphat, the narrator states that the body has not been seen since; he believes that her soul and body were restored to life: "She lives, [in Heaven], better than she had been born." The narrator then adduces the First Testament examples of Jonah, living after three days in the whale's belly, and the three young men in the fiery furnace who survived the flames.

Wace's work influenced both Jacobus of Voragine (c. 1230–1298), who reproduced Mary's genealogy in his entry for the feast of the nativity of Mary, September 8, and a later "sacred romance" that provided a fanciful account of Mary's parentage. The Marian miracle of Abbot Helsin was retold by many authors, including William of Malmesbury, emphasizing Mary's intervention in the storm.

Best-Selling Author Gautier de Coinci (1177–1236)

One of the most popular authors of the thirteenth century, Gautier de Coinci came from the nobility and served as prior of a Benedictine monastery near Soissons. One hundred and fourteen manuscripts of his work—two books of Marian miracles—attest to the popularity of his 58 narratives and 18 songs in Mary's honor. "Part of [his] project was to provide a literary celebration of the love of Our Lady as a superior alternative to the celebration of the *dompna* (Lady) of secular courtly culture."[30]

Gautier translated his tales from the Latin sources he found in his own abbey as well as those in nearby Laon and Soissons. He had access to other collections throughout northern France, and one of his miracle tales comes from Rocamadour. His work reflects images taken from the liturgy, psalms, and commentaries on Mary as well as the popular culture of his time in the form of secular songs that circulated in the courts of the region. One of his favorite ways of describing Mary was to cast her as a chess queen, the powerful White Queen who always checkmates her satanic opponent on the chessboard of life.[31]

Mary as Chess Queen

During the Middle Ages, chess—invented in India, developed in the Arab world, and imported into Europe by visitors and crusaders—became the premier entertainment of the nobility. Often played for high stakes, and with onlookers encouraged to coach the players,[32] chess was a favorite strategy game for knights and lovers. (Many a manuscript illumination and carved ivory mirror backing show a woman and a man seated across from each other over a chessboard.) The king, knight, rook, and pawn pieces maintained their original roles; the *Wizir* or vizir became the *fierce* or queen, and the *aufin* (elephant) became the bishop. Although the moves of the *fierce* were limited to one square at a time, her role was to guard the king—to prevent his being trapped in a corner (*angle*) of the board and thus checkmated (*mat*) and defeated.

One of Gautier's favorite ways of describing Mary, drawing on the phonetic similarity between *fierce* and *vierge* (virgin), was to cast her as a more powerful queen than her chessboard counterpart. Acting for the benefit of the King, her son, she also protects the pawns (peasants) as well as the bishops of this world. (Marilyn Yalom suggests that the power exercised by Mary and the influential secular queens of the time encouraged the development of the chess queen's gambits: "In the fourteenth century, *reine*, the French word for 'queen,' gradually replaced *fierce* and *fierge* ... and during the fifteenth century, *dame*, the French word for 'lady,' began to appear. Both *reine* and *dame* were and are traditionally attached to the Virgin ... and both are used in French today for the chess queen."[33])

In his Prologue to Book I, Gautier plays with the sounds of *fierge* and *vierge* to emphasize that whoever serves Mary with all his heart gains such an advantage in all games that the Devil, who deceives everyone, cannot deceive her servant by any means; Satan can't understand the strategy of Mary, the *fierce/vierge*. When he thinks he has the game, she checkmates him. "God, what a queen!" exclaims Gautier. "What a chess queen!"[34]

All of his miracle stories glorify her prowess on the game board of the world as she protects and defends her king, scattering his enemies and winning always.

The Miracle of the Abbess Whom Our Lady Delivered from Great Distress
Gautier de Coinci, Miracle 20 of Book I[35]

To understand the abbess in this story, it's helpful to know something about religious life in medieval times. Today we speak of a "call" or vocation to the service of God; women and men answer the call to be a nun (sister), brother, or priest. They make conscious decisions, usually as adults, to enter religious life; after a period spent in prayer and study, they take vows in a religious order or are ordained as priests. This was not always the case during the Middle Ages, when noble families were responsible for maintaining law and order in a hierarchical, feudal society. The lord and lady ruled their large households from fortified castles, staffed with servants. They claimed large tracts of land, forests for hunting and fields for livestock and grain, worked and harvested by serfs. They kept their own bands of knights, who protected their territory and helped them enlarge it when the occasion arose. They tended to have large families; they arranged the marriages of their daughters and sons to strengthen political alliances and extend their lands and influence.

Sometimes the lord and lady had too many sons for the territory to sustain, or too many daughters for whom to find dowry money sufficient to attract suitable spouses. These younger children were destined for the church or the convent, willy-nilly; sometimes they were "offered" to a convent or a monastery as young as five or six and grew up learning the prayers of the church by heart. Sometimes they entered religious life when it was apparent that no other options were open to them. No matter their ages, they obeyed their parents.

Many of the nuns in medieval convents were born into the nobility. The austerity of their lives depended on the individual convent and the abbess in charge. Some were very strict; others permitted the sisters to keep small pets, receive visitors, and leave the convent from time to time for visits to family or friends. Abbesses had to be at least 30, old enough to be mature, but (as will be seen in the following story) young enough to know what preachers called "the temptations of the flesh."

This story is retold in Gautier's voice. As in many other miracles, the characters are not named, the better to suggest an application to everyone in their own circumstances.

* * *

The abbess of a large convent loved the Lady of Paradise passionately, setting her heart and attention to Mary's service. That same passion she directed toward keeping order in her convent, to the extent that her nuns grew resentful and complained about it again and again. She led so blameless a life, however, that they could not see anything that they could use to accuse her.

But the Enemy, who knows humans many times over, was furious and distraught by her holding out against him for so long through her upright behavior. He pursued and pressed her so closely that her heart took fire with desire for her steward. The Enemy made her break the seal of virginity, which she had vowed and promised to the King of Truth. Very shortly, the good lady felt a stirring in her womb that grew and grew until she knew for certain that she was pregnant with a living child. Her face, which used to be so fresh and rosy, grew pale and wan, and her nuns noticed it right away, taking great pleasure in her condition. One said, "She should be burnt, the wretch, the hypocrite." "Now she'll pay," said another. "We can't blow our noses without her taking it as a fault, but—thank God—she's done something that will bring her sorrow and shame, and may God grant her enough of both!" And they sent word to the bishop, asking him to address the situation in their chapter meeting.

Knowing nothing of their intrigue, the abbess had the Mass of Our Lady said in her private chapel. After the service, alone, she prayed fervently to Our Lady, sighing and weeping. Brokenhearted, she felt that she was close to giving birth and wished that she could have the child in hiding without incurring shame in the eyes of everyone around her. She didn't know what to say or do, for there was no one in whom she could confide her situation. Softly she began to call upon the sweet mother of Jesus:

"Lady," she said, "have pity on my misery. Sweet glorious lady, you are so gentle and so compassionate that your pity, like your tenderness, washes over the world. Ah, mother of God, whatever I may have done, I cry mercy for my misdeed. Noble lady, high queen, have pity on this orphan child. My heart has turned black with remorse because I have so offended you. Whatever I may have done, never have I denied you—and I will serve you, my gentle Lady, until my soul and body (which have betrayed me) fail. Lady, I beg you, ask your Son, who is so merciful, to help me, for I am beyond human help. Never is a woman unfortunate who places herself under your protection."

The abbess, kneeling and in tears, fell asleep during her prayers before the altar. And holy Mary came to her, accompanied by two angels. She was so beautiful that twenty writers such as I, Gautier, could not describe her, and the angels shone brighter than the summer sun. "Have no fear, good friend!" said Our Lady. "I am Mary the mother of God, who prays for sinners night and day to my dear Son without ceasing. I have seen your bitter tears and heard your prayers. Because of the service you have rendered me, by my prayer the King of Heaven pardons your sins and sends you His grace."

The gentle Lady directed the two angels to approach and help the abbess deliver her child. She told them to take the baby to her friend, a holy hermit, who lived seven miles away. The good man would keep the child with him for seven years, cherishing him as the apple of his eye. The angels did as Our Lady asked, and after delivering the baby, took him to the saintly hermit.

"Good friend," said Our Lady to the abbess, "I have delivered you with great honor from the shame and infamy which caused you so many tears: the birth of a splendid, handsome son. Now guard against falling into such a perilous state a second time, for that would anger me greatly and offend the noble spouse, the highborn husband, whom you once married. For having betrayed him with another, you will have to drink a bitter cup this morning. The bishop will insult you and treat you badly, but you will easily pass his test: I cannot bear to see shamed or wronged those who serve me with sincerity and love."

The abbess woke up, marveling that she felt so light, and was speechless when she began to realize what had happened. Sliding her hands under her habit, she no longer felt a swollen belly; in her elation she didn't know whether she was still sleeping or awake. "Dear Lady Mary," she said weeping, "how you have helped me! How tender, how compassionate, how kind and generous you have been! High queen, great lady, does anyone exist who can express your goodness and nobility? No one. No one can ever say anything that would be enough!"

While the abbess was praying and weeping for joy, the bishop, informed of her condition by the nuns and eager to punish her, arrived at the abbey. The nuns took counsel with one another; they murmured against the abbess, each striving to show her in the worst light. Then they went in search of her. "I don't find anything," said one. "Maybe she's given birth somewhere," said another. "We can't fail to find her, and we'll catch her in the act." After searching chambers and antechambers, wardrobes and even the little houses on the property, they finally discovered the abbess in her own chapel, on her knees before the image of Her who is always prompt to aid and console Her own. The abbess refused to become upset when she heard that the bishop had called for her and was waiting in the chapter room. Making the sign of the cross, she commended herself to the Mother of God. She sought no other advocate, no other jurist.

At the side of the bishop, in the midst of the full assembly of nuns, she sat down in her usual place. But the bishop, boiling with ill-will and angry enthusiasm, publicly shamed her and made her leave her chair; she could not make herself heard in her own defense, and the nuns rushed her out of the chapter room. She endured this treatment as a penance, with Mary's protection as her comfort.

To be sure of his judgment, the bishop ordered two mature clerics to examine the abbess in private, saying, "Her reputation until now has been spotless; I do not want to sully it before I know the truth." The two approached the abbess, who was humiliated and tormented by having to undress in front of them, but prayed softly to Our Lady. The two clerics tapped her here and there for a long time, but their time was wasted; finding nothing, they returned to the bishop. "This was a fool's task," they said. "She is slimmer and more supple than a girl of ten. Those nuns are such slanderers and liars that no honest man ought to believe them."

Far from rejoicing when he heard these words, the bishop thought that the clerics had been bought off. "Sirs," he said, "I believe your eyes, but I believe mine more. I want to see for myself." He went to the abbess, who had been praying unceasingly to God for help. He insulted and blamed her, demanding that she undress again. She did so, her face wet with tears, so ashamed that she did not know what else to do. When she had taken off all her clothes and the bishop saw her stomach and her sides so slender and supple, he was seized with pity for her and fell at her feet, crying: "Lady, I am horribly mistaken and deceived. In the name of the Lord who does not lie, I pray you to pardon me. My heart was darkened and blinded when on bad counsel I defamed you of whom I was so fond." In tears he implored her pardon. But the abbess knelt down beside him and said, "Arise, my good lord. I forgive you everything. May God of His goodness do the same." They embraced each other.

The bishop wished to chastise the nuns who had caused so much trouble, expelling them from the convent; but the abbess took him aside, not wanting her nuns to go wandering from one abbey to another as poor beggars, and confessed everything, praising Our Lady. The bishop was moved to tears, marveling at the miracle. He sent his two clerics to the hermitage, where they found the child, who was so handsome that one could not stop looking at him. After seven years the bishop sent for the boy and taught him his letters, and as a young man he became a cleric in his turn. At the time of his death, the bishop recommended the young cleric to replace him, and he did. A holy man all of his life, he served, honored, and praised the Virgin, and when God called him at the end of his days, his death was saintly and glorious.

"Praise Mary," Gautier says, "for doing what no one could imagine: childbirth without the slightest trace." But, he says, that is what Mary does: "She undertakes nothing that she cannot bring to accomplishment. She even reconciled the abbess with her dear son. May God give us the grace, no matter what our past, to sin no more against Him. And may his gentle mother make us so that we may see them both in Paradise! Amen!"

The Miracle of the Young Nun
Gautier de Coinci, Miracle 43 of Book I[36]

One of the most popular miracle stories of the Middle Ages, the tale of the little nun who left her convent still enjoys currency today (see the "Sister Beatrice, Perennial Penitent" section in Chapter 8). In medieval times, multiple versions circulated throughout Europe and Scandinavia of the story about the young woman who abandoned her post as sacristan or doorkeeper of her convent and its church.

During the Middle Ages, the sacristan's post was one of great responsibility: She held not only the keys to the door of the convent but also those to the tabernacle (where the host or Body of Christ was kept) and to the convent treasury. Caesarius of Heisterbach, a contemporary of Gautier

Chapter 4. The Long Twelfth Century I

de Coinci, gave the errant nun the name of Beatrice and emphasized her position as doorkeeper by noting that she left her keys behind when she fled with her lover. The story that follows combines elements from three medieval versions, but is based largely on that of Gautier de Coinci, whose retelling is more empathetic than those of Caesarius of Heisterbach and others.

Gautier did not name his "nonain" or "little (young) nun," perhaps to emphasize the danger of temptation to everyone in religious life. Unlike others, he did not specify that Our Lady took her place, merely noting that she was received back by her convent. He also put his own spin on the story by including the motif of the worldly abbess, sharply reproving those abbots and abbesses who devoted their lives to the hunt and other entertainments rather than to the *opus dei* or work of God, prayer and service.

The story is told in Gautier's voice since his is the primary version.

* * *

To the glory of the glorious one, I wish to tell of a marvel inspired by the breath of our Holy Mother of God. There was an abbey established in the name of Our Lady where many sisters lived. One of them, who had dedicated her heart and soul to God, was a maid of high lineage, most intelligent and very lovely. Even in the ranks of the nobility there was no more comely young woman, and she was even more beautiful of heart than she was of face and figure. Sacristan of her abbey, she loved our sweet mother Mary with all her heart; never did she pass the image of Our Lady without paying her homage. She never forgot to honor Mary, no matter what her other obligations might have been.

The abbess of this monastery was a woman of high renown who—like many other abbots and abbesses—was forever entertaining her relatives and others, knights, ladies, and squires, shaming the house and making a mockery of God. (Many like her enrich and support their relatives while the monastics in their keeping are impoverished by serving God, having only water to drink and a hard egg or two to crack.) This abbess had a nephew who was accomplished and valiant, full of life, charming and of noble birth. The young man fell madly in love with the little nun, courting her as if the devil had put him up to it. He so pursued her, flattering and begging, coming and going, that in the end the iron melted and water wore away the stone. Out of love he offered to marry her and take her to his lands as his lady and his wife, even setting a time for their departure.

Thus the little nun ceased thinking of Our Lady and listened to her courtier. (The devil, who takes great pleasure in seeing good people do wrong, rejoiced in this affair and fanned the flames day and night so that she was completely smitten with him.)

When the night came for their meeting, the young woman crept out of the dormitory where she slept with her sisters and passed by Our Lady's chapel. Beating her breast and kneeling before Mary's image as she had in the past, she arose after her humble greetings and went to the door, thinking to leave. But the image of Our Lady left its place, went to the door, and held its arms like a cross in front of her, remaining there so that she could not pass by. The young woman marveled that Our Lady was so displeased at her desire to leave that she had to turn back. When she thought of him whom she loved as the apple of her eye, she was sad and mournful; frustrated, and seeing that she could not do otherwise, she returned to the dormitory.

The young man who awaited her was ready to hang himself when she did not arrive. All night he paced, distraught, not knowing what to do or say, but finally he returned to his rooms. The next day he went to her and said, "Dear sweet beautiful friend, waiting for you last night was nearly my death! I'd rather die than go through such a martyrdom again." The little nun did not want to tell him about what had happened to her or what she had seen, but she apologized and promised to meet him at midnight. That night he came back to wait for her.

And the little nun slept not at all, but left the dormitory and went to go past the chapel (for there was no other way to get to the door). Again she genuflected before the altar, and the image of Our Lady did as it had done the previous night. And again she was astonished and dismayed to see the image, arms extended as if to say "Good friend, you will not pass this way." When she saw her way blocked, she was sad and felt herself lost and angry. Quietly she returned to bed, weeping and sighing. She knew not what to do or say; she could neither rest nor sleep, marveling at how the image of Mary had kept her from her love. "But she has made the effort for nothing," said the nun in her heart, "because I am abandoning her service forever. When I leave the next time, I'll run! No more greetings, no more skinning my knees in genuflections as long as I live! I've been imprisoned here, as has everyone who entered the cloister to their sorrow!" So the Devil—that seducer, that deceiver—tempted and assailed the maiden.

In the meantime her lover waited outside the chapel, thinking that she had lied twice to him and betrayed him, berating himself for being such a fool and lamenting the flightiness and changes of heart that beset all womankind. Thus he waited and looked for her all night, vowing that if she failed to appear again, he would give up his quest.

The day passed, and night came. Toward midnight, the maiden fled past the chapel, not pausing to greet Our Lady and pay her homage, but averting her eyes from the image of Mary as she left the keys to the abbey treasury, the keys to the tabernacle, and her lesser keys on the altar. And

Chapter 4. The Long Twelfth Century I

when she had passed the threshold, she would not have turned back for five hundred pounds.

The books say[37] that the young man took her to his own demesne, where he was knighted and made a baron and married her without delay. Thus the maiden forgot her cloister and Our Lady. In all the land there was not a lady more alluring, more charming, more agreeable. She and her baron loved each other dearly and had fine children.

For more than thirty years she lived in the world, never returning to her abbey, but my lady holy Mary did not want to abandon her. That gentle lady's heart, say the books, will not permit her to forget any service done for her. That gentle lady, of her grace, did not wish to lose her little nun who had served her so often. One night, lying in bed with her good baron, she saw the image of her whom she had served with good heart. Our Lady's face blazed with anger brighter than a coal-fired oven. She did not look at the nun directly, but disdained her, saying, "Get up! Get up! Too long have you lain here! If my homage and my due and my salutations you do not give me once again, I will nail the doors of Heaven shut against you. On your feet! Arise! Take up your veil again. Your lamp goes out, there is no more oil. On your feet! Get up! Do not linger here, for the hour of your end is near!"

The lady was abashed, amazed; even as she slept she trembled and shivered, wept and sighed, so much so that the knight woke up, astonished at his wife who was so sad that even in sleep her tears fell on their bed. He held her to him and cuddled and kissed her. The lady awoke in fright; it was a long time before she could say a single word, dissolving in tears time after time before she could speak.

"Lady," said her husband, "it has been thirty-five years and more that we have been together, and I have never seen you so sad." "Milord," she said, "My tears tell you that the Devil, who never sleeps, has kept me sleeping here too long—Milord, I have slept too much and never thought of death, and that's all there is to it. I had too light a heart when I married, I spent too much of myself with you, I shamed the high Lord who created us and every other thing." She told him weeping and sighing of the vision she saw and the fear she felt, and then she recounted how the image of Mary had twice prevented her from keeping her tryst with him. "Sir," she said, "My heart will never know joy in life again unless I return to my cloister. When I left, I was not a worthy nun. I promised and made my vows to the King of Heaven, which I left unkept until now. So must I without delay serve God and His mother night and day. Fasting and doing penance, my body will atone, dear noble friend, for the sweet solace it has found in your arms."

Her knight wept at these words. "Certainly, my love, my friend, I would never want you to lose your soul on my account! Because it is Our Lady who calls you to her service and you will be no longer in the world, I too will leave it and take the habit of a monk, spending the rest of my life repenting my sins and faults. Because you left an abbey for me, dearest friend, I will enter one for you."

Their children were provided for; each one of them was wise of heart, ready to serve God as their parents did. And so the knight entered a monastery, and the nun returned to her abbey, fearing the worst. Timidly she rang the bell for admittance. When the door opened, she was greeted by the Mother of God herself, in the habit of a nun. "For all these years," said the Virgin, "I have taken care of your duties. Here are your keys; take them up and take your place again. Do penance and serve God from now on. No one knows you have been missing." She handed the nun her habit and helped her put it on. At such a welcome the nun was speechless, weeping hot tears of repentance and gratitude that sprang from the depths of her soul. "Lady," she said kneeling at Mary's feet, "I will serve you for the rest of my days and hope to deserve your love." Our Lady raised her up and left her, and the sacristan took up her keys and her duties, devotedly serving God and Mary from that time on. She became known for her sanctity, and her death was holy and glorious.

"There is no one who pays homage to Our Lady and serves her," says Gautier, "who is not repaid five hundred times redoubled. Those who endure the durance of the convent and the cloister will be blessed by God forever."

* * *

Of the many versions of the "Little Nun" tale, the shortest and most moralistic is that of Cardinal Jacques de Vitry (1160/70–1240), a renowned preacher and reformer. The cardinal's abbreviated version foreshadows a future trend: just enough of the story to make a doctrinal point, with both Mary and the protagonist portrayed as silhouettes rather than as heavenly and earthly persons. After describing the little nun's attempts to leave the cloister and her eventual success, the Cardinal states, "Shaken by terrible temptation, she devised a way to leave the church without passing by or paying reverence to the image [of Mary]. In this way, the Devil gained power over her and made her so audacious that she opened the door and rushed out in headlong pursuit of lust. In all your temptations, therefore, turn to the Blessed Virgin."[38]

Given de Vitry's primary audience of churchmen, this admonitory tone is not surprising—but it is chilling in its judgment of the "headlong pursuit of lust," as well as representing a strain of Marian tales that reinforce doctrinal mores rather than inspire devotion.

The Miracle of the Hanged Thief
Gautier de Coinci, Miracle 30 of Book II[39]

This tale, told in Gautier's voice, is the shortest one in his collection. In only 128 lines, the author portrays Our Lady's ability to transcend both sin and social class to rescue one of her own. In the Middle Ages, criminals brought to justice and condemned to death by hanging were left on the gibbet for the public to see, often until their bodies had disintegrated. The staying power of this tale is such that Patrice Martineau, as "the Troubadour of Our Lady," sang his own rhymed version of it ("La Vierge et le Larron," "The Virgin and the Robber") in the 1980s.[40]

* * *

Here I will tell briefly a very appealing miracle. The tale will be short and sweet, because I have many others to recount.

Some time ago there lived a robber who was truly exceptional. He held the gentle mother of the King of Glory in his heart so fervently that every time he went out thieving he commended himself to her care. And as soon as he had done so, as if he had been given permission, off he went boldly. You can know for certain, however, that if he knew anyone was hard pressed—a man or woman living in poverty—for the love of Our Lady he treated them gently and helped them out.

The thief so diligently practiced his profession, and the Devil so ensnared him, that eventually he was caught in the act, and the consensus was that he should be hanged, for his reputation was widely known. Everyone was impatient to see him on the gibbet. They immediately put a cord around his neck and hauled him up.

The gentle Lady of the name revered, who loves her wayward ones so much, kept him in her heart. She who forgets none of her own came quickly to his aid; placing her white hands beneath his feet, she held and sustained him for two whole days so that he suffered neither hurt nor pain. (Foolish indeed is he who does not strive to serve her with all his might.)

On the second day those who had hanged him came to take a look at him. When they saw him there safe and sound they could not believe their eyes. "We must have drunk too much strong wine," said they, "when we hanged this robber—we did a bad job of it. The cord wasn't fastened right." On the spot they took out their swords, wanting to cut his throat. They struggled until they grew tired, but they could not pierce his body, no more than if it had been made of iron or steel. They could do him no harm, for between them and him the mother of the King of Creation placed her hands.

Eble, the robber, cried out, "Begone! Begone! Your efforts are worthless.

Mary, Queen of Heaven. Master of the St. Lucy legend, artist Netherlandish, (active c. 1480–1510). Samuel H. Kress Collection, National Gallery of Art.

Know, all of you, for certain that my lady holy Mary has come to my aid. The gentle lady has held me up and placed her hand under my throat. The kind and merciful lady will let no harm come to me." Those who heard him were filled with joy, giving thanks and praise to the King of Heaven and his mother for the mighty miracle that they had witnessed. That very day Eble and the others presented themselves to an abbey to become monks, where they served Our Lady for the rest of their days.

"The Mother of God," Gautier assures us, "never rejects thieves or robbers, no matter how they have sinned. She takes care of everyone: No sinner, no robber male or female, calls on her who is not cared for and cured by that care. No greater physician exists in Montpellier or Salerno, the great centers of learning that give us so many doctors. Sweet queen," says Gautier, "you are the one who has medicine for all evils and comforts all the desperate. When you comforted that robber, you gave comfort to all who ally themselves with you."

The Knight of 150 Hail Marys
Gautier de Coinci, Miracle 41 of Book I[41]

A well-born Norman, Gautier was familiar with the knights and ladies of the court as well as with the romances and epics they read and the songs that entertained them. This tale, told in Gautier's voice, uses standard elements of courtly romance—the hard-hearted lady, the desperate lover, the kindly cleric, the deserted chapel—to suggest a more enduring relationship.

* * *

There once was a knight—young, handsome, strong, and proud—of wealth and distinction. He lusted not only after tournaments and jousts and assemblies of the great and near-great at court, but also after a lady who had captured his heart. He made lavish gifts and great efforts to impress her and embellish his reputation, but to no avail. Even though he was respected at home and abroad, he was so beset by thoughts of his unattainable lady—his heart burned so hotly for her—that he couldn't see any other woman to woo or wed. He didn't know how to express his sorrow, for the lady would have nothing to do with him no matter how good-looking and accomplished he was, jousting and tourneying for her everywhere he could. The lady was so well-to-do and well connected that the knight would have taken and sacked the fortress and city of Châlons all by himself if there were nothing else that could please her.

But it did him no good. She was so proud and haughty that nothing—not his pleading, nor his riches, nor his success in tournaments—led to love or even friendship. The more he sought her, the more she resisted; and the more coldly she acted, the more warmly he felt toward her. Love assailed him so from every side that it's a wonder he didn't lose his mind. When he couldn't stand it any longer, he visited a holy abbot and told him all his woes. "Good father," he said, "some ladies have a heart of lead, but this one, I'm afraid, has a heart of iron. She may wish me in Hell, but it doesn't matter: I'll not stop until I attain her love. Father, I love her so much, that truly, I can't eat or drink, rest or sleep."

The good abbot didn't dare to scold him; he was well aware that chastisement and blame often make people even more determined to do what they want. He knew that the only useful advice in this matter would come from God and His mother. "Brother," said the abbot, "if you believe me and don't fail to do what I ask of you, this matter will turn out just the way you desire."

"By my gullet," replied the knight, "I'll do whatever you ask. I'll be your man forever if I can have her. There's nothing in the world so formidable, so insurmountable, that I couldn't overcome it if it meant that I'd succeed in winning her love." The abbot said, "Brother, you'll have no great trouble doing this: Every day for a year, on your knees, you salute the Mother of God 150 times, and then come back and tell me about it." "Really!" said the knight. "By God's heart, two thousand times a day, if you say so! I'm so beset by love of her that I'd do anything." The holy man told him, "Good friend, God's mother has handled a lot of weightier affairs. But with the life you lead, I doubt that you can do it after all. You're so fond of knightly entertainments in woods and waters, hunting and hawking, that I'm afraid you'll fail in our agreement." "Sir," the knight said, "I take that as a challenge. By Saint John, I'll be a vowed and tonsured monk in your cloister in a year if I fail to greet our Lady for even one day." Smiling, he embraced the abbot and took his leave.

The knight was so eager to keep his word that he didn't wander far from home. He didn't tourney, he didn't go to court; he was in his chapel more than anywhere else. (He's begun a game that will turn out better than he can imagine.) He made a great effort to greet Our Lady, calling on her day and night in his chapel, asking her to grant him the joy of his lady who was bright and beautiful as the moon. As the end of the year approached, his heart grew light; he felt like singing day and night.

One day, to relieve the boredom of waiting, the knight went hunting in the forest. There, he lost track of his companions; he didn't know which way they had gone, and as he searched here and there he happened upon an ancient chapel that had fallen into ruin. "Ah, Mother of God," he said, "thank you. Noble lady, noble virgin, here in this old place I'll pay what I owe you." He dismounted from his horse and entered the chapel, kneeling before an old statue of Our Lady to say his 150 Aves. Then he pleaded for her to answer his prayer. "There's nothing in the world I desire more," he said. "She's so beautiful—her body, her arms, her hands, her face—never was such a beautiful being created. My heart is set on her; if I don't have her, I'll die." Before the statue of Our Lady he complained and sighed at length.

The Mother of God, who has relieved so many miserable sinners of their misery through her pity and her courtesy, heard his appeal and prayer to her. She appeared to him, crowned with a crown resplendent with precious stones, so glittering and so glorious that he was nearly blinded by the sight. Her clothing shone like the first ray of sunlight on a summer day. Her face was so beautiful, so bright, that no one who looked upon it could admire it enough. "The one who has made you sigh so much, and led you through such meanderings," said Notre Dame, "sweet friend, is she more beautiful than I?"

Bedazzled by the brilliance that surrounded her, the knight didn't know what to do. He hid his face in his hands, so frightened that he thought he would faint from terror. But she who is all pity said to him, "Friend, don't be afraid. I am the one—and never doubt it—whom you should have as your *amie,* your beloved. Be careful of what you do: You will have the one whom you love best of the two of us to be your love." "Lady," he replied, "I could not wish for more than to have you. Truly, you are worth more than thousands of her."

"If I find that you are a faithful lover, dear friend," said Our Lady, "you will find me your loyal friend above in Paradise. You will have joy, solace, and companionship from me as well as my love—more than you could ever hope for. But know that you will have to do as much for me as for your other friend: no more tournaments, no more courtly entertainments. One hundred and fifty Aves a day, without missing a day, you'll say if you want to be the lord of my love. Then you will have me, be assured, and you'll be in my holding and my keeping without limit and without end." And she parted from him.

After she left, the knight did not delay but went to find the abbot. Weeping, he recounted all that he had seen and heard. The holy man rejoiced on hearing his story, and thanked the mother of the King of Creation.

In short, the knight did become a monk, following the counsel of the abbot, putting aside the world and tonsuring the head that was so blond and handsome. He withdrew his attentions from the haughty lady and gave himself to Our Lady with all his heart and soul, sighing as he remembered her great beauty and her appearance to him.

At the end of a year the Mother of God came seeking him, not wishing to leave him on earth. Like a true lover she led him to everlasting life, where he had the joy and solace of her love for all eternity.

Gautier reminds his audience in his parting remarks that worldly *amours*—fixated on charm, good grooming, and family connections—end in bitterness. Mary's love demands only loyalty in exchange for its reward. "Those who embrace her," he reminds us, "find her love bracing to their souls!"

The Miracle of the Misplaced Engagement Ring
Gautier de Coinci, Miracle 21 of Book II[42]

"Those who make idle promises to God and to the Virgin," warns Gautier de Coinci, "had better listen to this miracle story that I read in one of my books."[43] The voice in this story is his.

* * *

During the refurbishment of an old church, workers removed a statue of Mary and placed it in front of the church doors, where passers-by placed offerings at its feet. The young men of the town used to play pelote and run races there, and one day a large crowd of them—all clerics in training[44]—gathered in the square where the statue stood. One young man, quite handsome, wore a ring on his finger that his love had given him. Love had so overwhelmed him that he couldn't bear the thought of losing or damaging that ring in any way. Looking for a place to put it for safekeeping while he played, he walked toward the church and saw the statue, which was new and quite realistic. The young man was smitten by its beauty, and fell to his knees in front of it, bowing his head in greeting.

"Lady," he said, "from now on I will serve you all my life, for I'll never see a lady or maiden who was so pleasing and beautiful. You are more pleasing and more beautiful by a hundred thousand times than the one who gave me this ring. I had given her all my love and all my heart, but for your love I will abandon her and her love and her jewelry. This ring—and it's a beautiful one—I want to give you out of true love, with a vow that never will I have a fiancée or wife but you, sweet lady." He placed the ring on the outstretched finger of the statue, and suddenly the image bent its finger so that no one could have removed the ring without destroying it. The young man was so startled and afraid that he shouted out loud, and everyone in the square came running. He told them what he had said and done to the statue, and they were all amazed. Everyone said that he shouldn't wait another day but should leave the world and enter a monastery, serving God and Our Lady Mary, whose finger had showed him that he should have no other lover but herself.

But the young man didn't have enough sense to keep his promise. He made an effort to forget about it, and in time he thought about it seldom, if ever. The days came and went, and the young cleric grew and prospered. He was so blinded by love of his lady friend that he saw nothing else. He forgot all about the mother of God, to whom he had given his ring and his promise. His lady-love had so won his heart that he left Our Lady and married her.

The wedding was a grand affair: The young man came from a noble lineage and great wealth. Night fell, and the nuptial bed was made. The young man was intent on making love to his bride, who was so beautiful and dainty; there was only one thing on his mind, to lie next to her. But as soon as he reached the bed, he forgot all about taking his pleasure and fell asleep without being able to do a thing.

The kind and gentle Lady, who is sweeter than honey in the comb, immediately appeared, seeming to lie between him and his wife. She showed him her finger—graceful, tapered—with the ring, which fit her to perfection. "You have not treated me fairly or loyally," she said, "but have insulted me by your actions. Here is your little girl's ring, which you gave me out of true love, saying that I was a hundred times more beautiful and more pleasing than the maid you knew. You would have had a loyal friend in me if you had not abandoned me. But you gave up a rose for a stinging nettle, and a blooming rose-bush for a withered box-elder, a honeycomb and honey for poison and bile. You poor wretch!"

Waking up, the young man was amazed and abashed. He felt around the bed with his hands but found nothing there. It seemed to him as if he had been cheated out of making love to his wife, but he couldn't make up his mind about it and went to sleep again. Immediately the Mother of God reappeared, furious. Her face fairly blazed with anger and scorn, so proud and disdainful that the cleric didn't dare look at her. With a look of hatred on her face, she scolded and shamed him fiercely, calling him a liar and a perjurer. "Devils blinded you and led you astray," she said, "when you renounced and left me for your wretched wife. Now go and wallow in the scuppers of Hell where everything stinks like you and your stinking bride!"

The young man leaped up, miserably aware that he was ruined and doomed for having so offended Our Lady, so shaken by his ruin and doom that he didn't—couldn't—touch his wife. "Help me, Holy Spirit," he prayed, weeping, "for if I stay here I'll be lost forever." So saying, he rushed from his bed without hesitating, and Our Lady so inspired him that he left without awakening anyone. He fled to a hermitage, where he took a monk's habit, serving God and our Lady Holy Mary all his life. He didn't want to have anything else to do with the world, but wished to stay with the one on whose finger he had placed the ring out of true love. "Thus," says Gautier, "he married Mary; and monks and clerics who so marry, marry high above their rank. Those who marry little Marians (earthly women) mis-marry, and for God's sake let us not do that!"

The Miracle of Théophile, or the Devil's Charter
Gautier de Coinci, Miracle 1 of Book I[45]

What story is more gripping than the one that tells of the man who sold his soul to the Devil? This miracle concerns a supposedly historical figure, Theophilus, an archdeacon in Cilicia, present-day Turkey. He died about 538.[46] The legend of his pact with the Evil One began soon after his death and was translated from Greek into Latin during the ninth century. By the eleventh century, the story of Theophilus was included in the liturgy of the French church,[47] and scenes from the legend appeared in manuscript illuminations, sculpture, and stained glass in churches throughout France, including the cathedral of Notre Dame de Paris. Theophilus' story appears in every major collection of Marian miracles in Europe; versions appear in Spanish, Dutch, Italian, and Portuguese as well as Anglo-Saxon, German, Swedish, and Icelandic.[48] The French poet Rutebeuf (fl. 1245–1285) turned the tale of Théophile into a play, notable for its portrayal of Mary as making quick work of the Devil as she demands the charter from Satan and threatens to grind his gut under her heel.[49]

The *Miracle de Théophile* appears at the head of Gautier's collection. His version follows the legend closely, making Théophile a *vidame* (a temporary or acting bishop) under the archbishop's jurisdiction. Although other versions of the legend make Théophile's enabler a simple magician, Gautier chose to depict him as a more menacing necromancer—who better to help conjure up the Devil in person? Like many, if not most, of his contemporaries, Gautier was an ardent anti–Semite; this was the age of the Christian Church Militant. In my retelling, Gautier's words appear in quotation marks.

* * *

A lifelong devotee and servant of Mary, Théophile is elected bishop but fears he will become susceptible to vainglory if he accepts the honor. Despite the pleas of archbishop and people, he humbly declines. The new bishop then relieves Théophile of his duties and appoints his own choice for the post. Almost immediately the Devil, the "enemy who deceives many a soul," sees a recruitment opportunity and begins to torment Théophile with regret and anger, to the point where he calls on the Devil to help him regain his "honor" and high position. He even swears a feudal oath to the one he calls *Maufez* (a name meaning "bad faith"), renouncing the service of God and His mother, Mary, and saying, "If you help me in this need, I'll be your man, your cleric, and serve you forever." The Devil, however, does not appear at his call. He needs help.

Théophile, so befuddled by the idea of the Devil that he has no sense or reason left, visits a Jewish necromancer; falling at his feet, he laments the fact that the new bishop has thrown him out of his post. "If I don't regain my position and my honor with your help," he declares, "I'll die of disgrace." The necromancer nods knowingly. "Ah yes," he says, "good friend, I'm acquainted with your prelates and their business. They give benefices to those with the fattest purses. You don't get anything if you don't buy, flatter, and praise them." Théophile is told to return the next night, when the necromancer will lead him by the hand to meet "my lord and king" the Devil, who will make the cleric "a bishop, an apostle, or an archbishop"—whatever he likes.

The following evening, then, Théophile seeks out the necromancer, who greets him affectionately, promises to instruct him in the ways of the Devil, and leads him to a spot outside the city. "Whatever you do, no matter how afraid you might be," says his new teacher, "don't call on God or Our Lady." Good advice, for as Théophile looks about him, so frightened he can't speak, he sees the countryside take fire; in those flames more than a thousand devils parade around the city with a ground-shaking tumult, leading their master. This devil, tall and fearsome, is the lord and prince of the others. Théophile is struck dumb at the sight.

"Tell me, friend," says the Devil to the necromancer, "who is this man, and why has he come?" "He needs your help," replies the other, "his bishop has so mistreated him that his heart is blackened with grief. Have mercy on him." The Devil states his conditions: Théophile must renounce his baptism and his beliefs, God and Mary, all the saints. The Devil will then give him "many honors. That which he has lost will be restored with great celebration, and if he should ask the bishop anything, it will be granted." He emphasizes once again, however, that Théophile will lose all if he does not renounce God and His Mother, complaining that they harass his demons day and night. The cleric must also sign a legal document called a charter, attesting to the sale of his soul. The Devil explains that many Christians have cheated him: When they have received their honors and promotions, their estates and wealth, they go ahead and repent and confess, depriving him of his reward. Therefore, he insists that all Christians hand over a signed and sealed document attesting to the sale of their souls. "They'll not take me again for a fool," he says.

Théophile kisses the Devil's feet, renouncing all; and then, "to firm up his affirmation, and to damn himself more thoroughly," he gives the demon a charter, signed and sealed with his own ring. The Devil takes it to Hell with him.

That very night, the archbishop begins to feel remorse for the way he has treated Théophile ("so learned, led such a holy life"). The next morning, he summons Théophile and celebrates—to the reprobate's delight—the restoration of his position, at almost double his former income. During a visit that evening, the necromancer reminds him to ignore Mary, because he is now a rich man, entitled to "becoming robes, pretty palfreys and noble war-horses, golden trappings, golden stirrups, saddle and spurs of gold." The man delivers a worldly sermon to instruct the naïve

Théophile: The person who doesn't act noble and proud is considered not only old-fashioned but low-class. "The simple man isn't worth a fig. Abandon your hair shirt and penances, eat and drink as you please. You're a handsome man, well formed; if you act the part of a nobleman, everyone will want to serve you."

Théophile takes the advice. He begins to revel in riches, prestige, and a life of ease, forsaking church, chant, God, and Mary. Gautier remarks, "Théophile is in peril of the sea, Théophile is sinking and drowning, Théophile has a heart of iron, Théophile is heading for Hell by leaps and bounds." No longer does he give alms; whereas before he was humble and gentle, now he is haughty and arrogant. "The Devil has extinguished all light around him; blind, he sees not a thing. He is headed straight for Hell, the steed of his soul lacking bridle or reins, when Mary, who forgets none of her own, cannot bear to see him lost." Longing to bring him back to her service and her love, Mary asks her son to help, and God "gives him back the eyes of his heart."

Théophile repents, resumes his hair shirt and his penances, and bewails his sins incessantly, crying night and day. Finally he decides to take his soul-sickness to Mary, who is "so sweet and agreeable that she rejects no one who is ill." He visits a church of Our Lady and throws himself to the floor, sighing and weeping, in fasting and vigils, for forty days. He implores her mercy: "Lady, in whom all sweetness resides, holy and debonair Virgin, I place my soul and my body in your keeping." Mary hears his prayers, but her desire to win her servant back does not mean that she is an indulgent mother. She appears to Théophile in a midnight vision, looking "as if fire and flame would leap from her bright face," not deigning to look at him, and berating him for his faithlessness: "How is your stinking, dirty, sticky mouth presumptuous enough to call on me or my son? You have your nerve, when you've paid homage to the Devil, if you think that I ought to help you." She continues to scold him, claiming that he has angered her and her son for a trifling worldly honor.

After Mary's tongue-lashing, Théophile pleads his case, using the lyric imagery of her titles (high virgin maid, high queen, bright emerald, door of paradise, lady of Heaven and earth, lady and queen of the archangels). He begs her to consider famous penitents of the past: the people of Nineveh, Rahab, David, Saint Peter. If God were not merciful and they had not been penitent, where would they have gone, what would have become of them? Every day, sinners would fall into the abyss were it not for their repentance and Our Lady, who sustains them by her prayer. He begs her to have pity on him and make his peace with her son. Then "she who illumines the whole world, who is the door and window of heaven, who is more honeyed than new honey in a new hive," tells him gently that because of his heartfelt repentance and faith in her, she will intercede with her son for his pardon, but that she must hear without delay his act of faith.

Mary then leads Théophile through a renewal of his baptismal vows, replicating the ceremony on Holy Saturday during which converts and members of the congregation alike profess their belief in God and in Christ's redemptive passion and death. "I believe," cries Théophile, "heart and soul." His act of faith includes the lyrical confession, "I believe and know, bright star, that God willed to make you his mother, that your will is his, and his will is yours. I believe heart and soul that you are the queen and lady of heaven, the lock and key of Paradise, lady of heaven and earth, my surety and my hope." In turn, Our Lady assures him that his prayers and vigils have persuaded her to reconcile her son to him.

Three nights after the first vision, Mary appears to him again. "By my pleadings," she tells him, "the one who was wrongly crucified for you has seen your hot tears and received your prayers. Your repentance is sufficient; see that from now until the end of your life you serve Him single-heartedly so that your soul is refined like gold in a fire before your death." After thanking her, Théophile asks one favor more: that Mary reclaim his charter for him. Even though she reassures him, he continues to fast and pray; after three more days of vigil he falls asleep, worn out. Our Lady arrives and gently places the charter at his feet. On awakening, Théophile weeps for joy. The Devil has lost his power; as soon as Théophile put himself in Mary's hands, the Evil One was routed.

Our Lady returns the charter on Saturday (the day dedicated to her since the tenth century). On Sunday, Théophile attends the bishop's mass, where a large crowd is in attendance. After the Gospel, the repentant sinner throws himself at the bishop's feet and makes a public confession, at which everyone makes the Sign of the Cross and marvels as he shows them the charter recovered by Our Lady and recounts his visions. The bishop offers a brief prayer of thanks to Jesus and then asks the entire congregation to glorify God and the powerful celestial Lady who delivers sinners— to celebrate how she throws the Devil into a fright, how the Enemy is tricked and deprived of his prey. She who never forgets her friends releases sinners from the nets the Devil has cast over them. She is the devils' bane; they cannot win against her. "Let us praise Mary," the bishop says, "her great mercy, her power, and her strength: She has broken the iron bonds of Hell, which trembles and shakes, laments and sighs as devils are routed, scattered, lost as they have lost the souls they have taken and swallowed up." Recalling the father of the prodigal son, the bishop calls for Théophile to receive a rich stole, shoes for his feet, a costly ring. "Kill the fatted calf," intones the bishop, "for it is right that we eat together today in celebration! God has placed our brother among us through the prayers of his mother."

Three days later, Théophile dies, saying, "Lady, into your hands I commend my spirit."

* * *

The street poet Rutebeuf (1245–1285) turned Gautier's tale into a play[50] that presents Théophile's fall, remorse, repentance, and recovery in rapid succession. Although he renounces God, Théophile cannot renounce Mary, whom he addresses plaintively in a lyric poem. Mary is having none of it, replying, "I don't care about your sorry tale. Go on, get out of my chapel!" Relenting, however, she visits Hell and calls out Satan, who complains that Théophile has handed himself over willingly. Our Lady then threatens him: "I'll grind your gut under my heel!" The very next scene shows Mary proffering the charter to Théophile, commanding that he take it to the bishop to read in front of the congregation so that others may learn from his example. The play ends with the bishop's reading of the charter, concluding with a tribute to Mary and a hymn of thanksgiving.

With its rapid-fire dialogue and feisty Mary, Rutebeuf's dramatization offers a more earthy version of the tale, geared to an urban audience whose members lack the leisure necessary for a hearing of Gautier's interpretation.

The Miracle of the Rich Man and the Widow
Gautier de Coinci, Miracle 19 of Book I[51]

"All of our Lady's miracles are so sweet and full of pity that there's no one who recites them well whose heart doesn't melt with compassion. I want to tell one that ought to inspire everyone to serve the highborn maid…." Here Gautier de Coinci begins his tale of two souls who are about to leave this earth. The following tale is my paraphrase, with quotations from Gautier.

* * *

One of the dying souls is a little old lady living all by herself in a tiny hut no better than a pigsty. Having suffered from hunger and thirst most of her life, she now lies alone, barely covered with torn and dirty rags. She had spent her life as a beggar, but on the rare occasion when someone was generous to her, she would buy a tiny candle and offer it in honor of God and Our Lady. The other dying soul is that of a wealthy usurer, lying back against freshly fluffed pillows in an elegant bed covered with luxurious quilts, surrounded by anxious family members. The priest comes in haste to his bedside, adjusting his pillows, comforting him ("You see a lot of men recover who were in a lot worse shape"), and closing windows so that he does not catch a chill.

The old woman sends an even poorer young girl to fetch the priest for her; the child goes straight to the usurer's house, but the priest puts her off, saying that the old woman won't die soon and that the gentleman he is now attending has his regard and his care at the moment. The priest's assistant, young but a good Christian in the best tradition, is saddened and angered when he hears his superior dismiss the prospect of seeing the old woman. Although he dares not say anything, he believes that it would be "a sin and base neglect if no one goes to her," suggesting as much to the priest. The priest, for his part, implies that his young deacon must have taken leave of his senses to suggest that he leave the bedside of this rich man for the pallet of a beggar.

The deacon goes to the old woman's hut and sees it surrounded by such a dazzling light that he is afraid. Next to the woman's thin straw mat he sees a dozen maidens, beautiful beyond description; at the old woman's side sits Our Lady, wiping away the sweat of her death-struggle from her forehead. Mary beckons him closer, asking him to hear the woman's confession. After the old lady has confessed and received the Body of Christ, one of the maidens tells Our Lady that the woman's soul is struggling to leave her body, and Mary replies that the struggle is necessary to prepare for the time when the angels return to take her to Paradise.

Overjoyed by his encounter with Mary, the deacon returns to the rich man's bedside to call the priest. There, he sees the unfortunate usurer throwing himself this way and that to rid himself of what he calls "these chains," but the deacon realizes what is really happening, for he sees what no one else can—more than five hundred demons surround the usurer's bed, tearing him with their nails and sharp teeth while waiting to carry off his soul. "I'll return to my poor old woman," the deacon tells himself. "Her miserable hut, black with dirt as it is, far outshines this room in this palatial house."

He returns to the old woman to give her the last rites and bury her. There, he again sees Our Lady, who has come to act as a kind of midwife or doula in the woman's death, encouraging her and helping her soul to leave her body. "Fear not, happy soul," Mary says, "come forth in all security, and I will lead you joyously before my Son, the King of Glory. You have always remembered me; and all those who love me with a noble heart will leave this world to share the joy of angels." The old woman then dies peacefully, and Mary receives her soul, which is carried to Heaven by angels to the accompaniment of celestial music.

After the deacon buries the old woman, he returns to the usurer's house to tell the priest of his experience, but he finds the house still turbulent with demons. He hears the usurer screaming on his deathbed, the devils taunting him with gruesome descriptions of the torments of Hell, where his moneybags will be hung about his neck while toads, lizards, and lampreys will suck out his eyes and brain. As a demon pierces his neck, the unhappy usurer dies, while the deacon nearly faints at the sight. Our Lady appears to the deacon to assuage his fear, saying that his time on earth will soon be over and he will be saved. The deacon lives such an exemplary life that he earns Paradise for himself.

"By this miracle," says Gautier, "you can know that many souls burn in Hell for their wealth; on the other hand, poverty can be your salvation. What does it profit anyone to conquer the world and be lost to Heaven?"

The Miracle of the Priest Who Knew Only One Mass
Gautier de Coinci, Miracle 14 of Book II[52]

Gautier seems to have had a soft spot in his heart for people of little learning. He must have met some of them, both clerical and lay, in his own region of northern France. The following story is my paraphrase of Gautier.

There was a priest who loved the Lady of Glory and honored her all his life. But I have to tell you, he couldn't read a word: Popular tales, writing of any kind—all were beyond his ability. One liturgy, and only one, he knew: the Saturday Mass of Our Lady that began, "Salve, Sancta Parens," or "Hail, Holy Parent." In season and out of season, in total ignorance of the rubrics that specified which Mass to say when—on Sundays or on holy days or on ordinary days without a saint to honor, for the living or for the dead—he said only the *Salve, Sancta Parens*. Every day he said it devotedly in honor of his noble Lady.

His lack of attention to the rules came to the notice of the bishop, who said that he was ignorant and unworthy to celebrate Mass! He ought to be chased out of his parish with a good sound beating, the bishop fumed, and if he didn't leave the diocese he'd be stripped of everything he had. After telling him that he was forbidden to say Mass anywhere, his superior had him booted out of the chancery office.

But Our Lady took pity on her chaplain in his desperate straits. That very night, about midnight, she appeared to the bishop and said in a temper, "Know this for certain, bishop: If you don't take back my chaplain and restore him to his parish and his rights, you'll die before thirty days are out and spend eternity in Hell." She could not have been more clear, and the terrified bishop called for the priest in a hurry. Falling on his knees at the priest's feet, the bishop begged his forgiveness, saying that he would take him back. The good priest pardoned him and served in that diocese for the rest of his life, saying Mary's Mass every day.

The Miracle of the Peasant Who Could Learn Only Half of the Hail Mary
Gautier de Coincy, Miracle 20 of Book II[53]

In this story about a peasant, Gautier's style is not as lofty as it is in his tales of courtiers, knights, and monastics. I've used more colloquial expressions to translate his down-to-earth writing.

"This peasant," observes Gautier, was "dumb as a rock, but wily enough to plow a few more furrows than belonged to him." Needless to say, he was not well liked. He didn't keep feast days the way he should, but took off work after noon on Saturdays and on Sundays went to Mass, where he stood as silent and stiff as a footstool. When he passed in front of the statue of Our Lady, though, he genuflected. He didn't know a word of the Our Father, but after a long struggle his wife finally got him to learn half of the Hail Mary. That was it, he said, the best he could do, but he didn't stop there: Whenever and wherever he passed an image of Mary, he genuflected and greeted her. And when some poor soul begged him, for the love of Our Lady, for a bit of bread, he always said, "God's heart! You'll have it!" and gave freely.

When the peasant died, a great troop of devils came for his soul but were confronted by a band of angels. "He's not yours!" screamed the demons. "Yes, he is," said the angels, "and despite you we'll have him." "You're a bunch of robbers," said the devils, and started a tirade. "Tell us why, when knights and ladies, priests and clerks, go to Hell in droves, a stupid blockhead—who never said a seemly word or did anybody any good, who didn't have the brains of a beast, took what didn't belong to him, couldn't praise God, did nothing but bellow and destroy bushes and hedges and curse every two words—tell us why he should have a home in Heaven!"

The angels prevailed, however, saying that no one who loved the Mother of God with all his heart could be lost. He loved her with as much sense as he had, they said, and that was enough. The devils flew off, grumbling that Mary was taking the peasant to Heaven by force, and if it weren't for her, their domain would be full to bursting.

This is one of the tales that historian Henry Adams found so compelling, translating a segment of the devils' complaint:

> All the great dames and ladies fair
> Who costly robes and ermine wear,

Kings, queens, and countesses and lords
Come down to hell in endless hordes;
While up to heaven go the lamed,
The dwarfs, the humpbacks, and the maimed;
To heaven goes the whole riff-raff;
We get the grain and God the chaff.[54]

The Miracle of the Candle That Came Down to the Jongleur
Gautier de Coinci, Miracle 21 of Book II[55]

This story comes from Rocamadour, the town and shrine in the cliffs overlooking the Alzou river in southwestern France, about 100 miles north of Toulouse. According to legend, during the ninth century a Saint Amadour lived there as a hermit, and it was he who carved the Black Madonna that has been revered for centuries in the chapel of Our Lady. The buildings around the shrine, cut into the solid rock of the cliff, date back to the eleventh and twelfth centuries, when Benedictine monks assumed charge of the chapel and added a church and fortifications to the site as it became a famous place of pilgrimage. People from all classes and walks of life frequented the shrine during the Middle Ages, and today more than a million and a half visitors visit it every year. The "book of miracles" mentioned by Gautier was written about 1172.[56]

I've retold the tale in Gautier's voice.

* * *

The gentle mother of the Creator has done so many miracles at her church in Rocamadour that they have been recorded in a very large book. I've read it several times and found in it a most courtly miracle that I wish to recount.

In the area around Rocamadour there was a *jongleur*, an accomplished performer, who most willingly sang of the Savior's mother when he visited her churches. He was a minstrel of great renown, a *vielle* or fiddle player, by the name of Pierre de Siglars, and he went to Rocamadour on pilgrimage. There he found many other pilgrims, who came from far-off countries and were celebrating their arrival. When he had said his prayers, he took out his vielle and began to play; the bow resounded on the strings so beautifully that soon he was surrounded by folk both clerical and lay.

When Pierre saw them gather and listen, he played so well that he thought his vielle wanted to speak. After he had sweetly greeted and long praised the Mother of God with his whole heart and bowed before her image, he cried aloud, "Ah, Mother of the King who created all, Lady of all courtesy, if something I say pleases you, I ask that you send me as reward one of those candles that surround you as a gift. Lady without parallel or peer, send me a candle to celebrate my supper." Our Lady Holy Mary, who is the source and channel of all gentility and courtesy, heard the voice of the minstrel, for right away, without further ado, she sent down a most beautiful and well-made candle in the sight of everyone there.

A nasty and mean-spirited monk by the name of Gerard, who was in charge of the church at the time, saw these things through the eyes of melancholy. He judged the miracle to be folly and madness. Accusing Pierre of being an enchanter, a charlatan, and a deceiver, Gerard seized the candle and returned it to its high place. The minstrel saw the enraged and ignorant monk, but didn't quarrel with him, for he perceived and understood that Our Lady had heard his request. His heart was so filled with joy that it brought tears to his eyes, and he wept, revering Our Lady and thanking her from his heart for her great courtesy to him.

He took up his vielle once again and bowed to the image of Mary. He sang and played so well that you would have preferred his songs to the most elegantly performed liturgy. And the candle, large and lovely, descended once again to his vielle. This miracle was seen by five hundred people!

But the frenzied monk, his head full of relics, when he saw the candle come down again, lunged through the crowd more quickly than a goat or deer, so tormented, so enraged that he could scarcely say a word. His anger and frenzy shook the cape from his shoulders, and he told the minstrel as if Pierre were a half-wit that he would never have his candle. (The sheer wonder and marvel of the moving candle simply cemented the monk's belief that never in his life had he seen such a sorcerer as Pierre.) He continued to exclaim that Pierre was a wizard, and then, in a fury and overwhelmed by ire, the monk seized the candle once again, peevishly climbed back up, set the candle firmly in place, and attached it by tying it down. To the minstrel he said that even Simon Magus the magician could not make it descend again.

Pierre the minstrel, who had seen both fools and wise men in his travels, was not at all provoked, putting up with the headlong irascibility of the monk in patience. He took to heart none of the fellow's mutterings but began his song and accompaniment once more. Well he knew that Our Lady would bring matters to a successful end if his songs pleased her. In playing the vielle he sighed and wept, his mouth singing and his heart praying.

Our Lady proved that she was still listening and once again would return to make the miracle even plainer. Twice the ignorant and idiotic monk had taken away the candle in his madness, and twice a great crowd had observed the miracle of its return in astonishment and awe. Now all marveled, all crossed themselves as the candle—twice snatched away—descended once again. Pierre, absorbed, was unaware that his fingers did not even touch the vielle, but sang and played so beautifully for Our Lady that many in the crowd were moved to tears. His pure heart, clear voice, and sweet stringed accompaniment soared in song right up to Heaven, all the way to God and His mother.

And now the candle had risen for a third time. Three times the Lady had given him the candle, to the confusion of the foolish monk, who was stupefied and overcome by the cheering of the crowd. "Ring the bells!" the people cried. "Ring the church bells! Never was there such a miracle, never will we see the like again!" Throughout the church there was such a celebration by clerics and lay, all and sundry, with such ringing of bells, that you could not have heard God's thunder. Everyone there saw the minstrel offer his candle before the altar, thanking God and Our Lady. It would have been a hard heart that was not moved by such a gesture!

And so the minstrel Pierre, courteous, worthy and wise, came each year to Rocamadour carrying and offering a most gorgeous candle. Serving God throughout his life, he never entered a church without playing a song or singing a *lai* for Our Lady. And when it pleased God that his life should come to an end, his soul entered into the glory of Heaven through the prayer of Mary, of whom he had sung so willingly and who received the tribute of a candle each year at Rocamadour, her shrine.

* * *

At the end of his story, Gautier remarks that too often the voices and instruments that seek to praise God are discordant because those who use them are "dis-tempered," literally unattuned to spiritual things. A clear voice, pleasing and harmonious, the sound of harp and vielle, psalter and organ—for none of these does God give a fig, says Gautier, if one's heart is not devoted or attuned to the divine.

A Narrative Theology of Subversion: Mercy, Not Judgment, Prevails

The Catholic church of the Middle Ages was a strict enforcer of orthodoxy. Outside the church there was no salvation, a precept first pronounced by Cyprian of Carthage (200–258) and not revoked until the twentieth century. Persons who died in a state of serious (mortal) sin—after being tempted by the ever-present Devil—would spend eternity in the torments of Hell. Jesus, the "just judge," demanded obedience to God and

Mary, Mother of Mercy. Virgen de la Misericordia, Bonanat Zortiga the Elder (fl. 1403–1440). Plandiura Collection, Museu Nacional d'Art de Catalunya.

church; his enemy, Satan, always lurked, seen or unseen, waiting to seduce and trap the faithful in a moment of weakness, ensuring their damnation.

In her miracle stories, Mary's intervention is a countersign, orthodox (repent and sin no more) and subversive (Jesus' mother will convince her son of your sincerity/repentance/change of life).[57] Her mercy is more abundant than the sins of her unfortunate petitioners; she protects them, rebukes them, converts them until they muster up the strength to change their ways and deserve the grace she bestows so abundantly on behalf of God.

Another Thirteenth-Century Miracle? The Holy House of Loreto

Soon after Mary's death, the house in Nazareth—where she was born, where Gabriel appeared to her, and where she and Joseph lived with Jesus—began to draw visitors and devotees. After the fall of Jerusalem to the Muslims in 1291, the house was perceived to be in danger, and—according to legend—angels transported it to safety. First, it went to Croatia; then, in 1294, the same angelic forces moved it to Loreto, a small town in east Italy. "The dimensions of the House of Loreto are identical to those of the House of the Holy Family that is missing from its enshrinement place at [the] Nazareth basilica."[58] Over the next few centuries, ever greater churches were built to accommodate the house, and Loreto became one of the most visited shrines in Italy. The Litany of Loreto, associated with the shrine, addresses Mary by ancient titles and attributes ascribed to her: Seat of Wisdom, Cause of Our Joy, Refuge of Sinners, Gate of Heaven, Morning Star.

The true story behind the "flight" of the Holy House may be more prosaic. A family named deAngeli is said to have saved the bricks of the house from the Muslim invasion in 1291, bringing them to Italy in December 1294—by sea. Nonetheless, Pope Benedict XV proclaimed Mary the patron saint of pilots and flight attendants in 1920, and the legend (without the possible spoiler) appears regularly in Advent reflections to this day.

CHAPTER 5

The Long Twelfth Century II
Marian Tales from the Continent and England

The universal church ensured that pious and engaging stories about Mary and the wonders of her patronage spread rapidly. Benedictines and Cistercians were joined by a new order of monastics in spreading Mary's miracle stories. Founded by Dominic de Guzmán (1170–1221), the Dominican Order of Preachers set out to foil the advances of new religious movements that had begun to spread in the south of France. Devotion to Mary permeated Dominican preaching; a bishop of that order, the Italian Jacobus of Voragine, included elements of her life story as well as her miracles in his *Golden Legend*.[1] The thirteenth century produced ever more vernacular works about Mary, influenced by the Fourth Lateran Council of the Church (1215), which aimed to educate and reform the clergy so that they could minister more effectively to the faithful. During this century, a king joined the ranks of the "troubadours of Our Lady" as Alfonso X of Spain, called "El Sabio," or "The Wise," wrote and commissioned more than 400 songs in Mary's honor. Collections of miracle tales spread throughout the known world, tributes to her power and honor.

About Gondrée and How Our Lady Came to Be Called Notre Dame de Chartres
Jean le Marchant, Miracle 1[2]

Little is known of this author except that he seems to have been a canon, or member of a group of priests charged with administering church affairs, in Péronne in the northern French region of Picardy. Jean states that he finished his collection of 32 Marian miracles in about 1262. His selections include accounts of cures, some taken from the shrine stories of Laon and Soissons as well as those attributed to Our Lady of Chartres.

Jean writes of dead children restored to life; workers and provisioners of the cathedral protected from accidents and weather disasters; deliverance from prison; and many cures of bodily ills.

Several miracles involve cures of the "*feu des ardents*," an epidemic of ergotism that ravaged the country in 1128. This disease, caused by eating bread made with grains (rye or wheat) contaminated with a fungus, produced painful and frightening symptoms, including convulsions and festering skin eruptions. When it damaged the cardiovascular system, gangrene set in, causing an agonizing death by "sacred fire" or rupturing wounds.

As can be imagined, accounts of the epidemic spread rapidly, appearing in the works of Gautier de Coinci and Vincent of Beauvais as well as in shrine collections and Spanish and Portuguese tales. Le Marchant's story seems to have been based on a Latin version that attributes a miracle performed by Mary at her Soissons shrine to the Virgin of Chartres.[3] (There was indeed competition among shrines.) I recount the miracle below in le Marchant's voice.

* * *

At the beginning of my story, I wish first to tell you where and how it happened that Our Lady became the patroness of Chartres. Some time ago there was a woman named Gondrée who lived near Soissons. Her husband, Theodorus, was distressed and angry when she was stricken by a vicious disease, one that ravaged her face, beginning with her nose and lips and spreading to her teeth and gums, eating her flesh to the bone.

Despite her infirmity she went to the shrine at Soissons, where she called upon Mary and prayed that out of pity Our Lady might visit her and relieve her pain, considering the miserable soul who no longer wished to live but preferred death to her condition.

The Lady of high degree, she who comforts the wayward, the lady of mercy who reconciles sinners to God, the worthy virgin, heard the prayers of the one who had come to her in misery. She put out the fires of the disease, but its traces remained on Gondrée's face: She had lost her nose and most of her lips; she could not hide her condition, which was hideous to see. People avoided her, not wishing to confront such a deplorable sight nor to smell the sickening odor of decay that came from her body. Her relatives counseled her to cover her face with a veil but did nothing to help her.

She then put all her faith in God and his mother, telling Mary about her long devotion and promising to go to the shrine at Soissons and offer a candle in her honor. The next night, wanting to replace her veil, she put her hand under it. To her amazement she felt new skin, supple and tender, and her nose and lips restored, only a little shinier. Calling on Mary, she gave thanks in profusion and asked what she should tell people about her recovery. "Tell them," Mary replied, "that Our Lady of Chartres has cured you. Chartres is my home on earth, my royal palace, my own church, where I hold all of Chartres and its people in my hand."

Mary disappeared, and Gondrée returned to her bed, rejoicing in her cure. The next day, when she went out, her neighbors marveled at the sight of Gondrée's face restored and thanked God and Mary for the miracle. Gondrée herself went straight to Soissons, where she offered a candle before the image of Mary, fulfilling her vow and thanking Mary for graces received and health recovered. When she returned, all those who had previously avoided her now recognized and greeted her once again.

And the cure performed at Soissons appeared in the collection of Our Lady of Chartres.

The Miracle of the Knight Saved from Death by the Undergarments He Wore That Had Touched the Chemise of Chartres
Jean le Marchant, Miracle 21[4]

To the honor and enhancement of the one who illumines the earth by her light, Our Lady of Justice of Chartres, superior to all other loves, whom I wish with all my heart to serve! A knight of Aquitaine had many enemies who hated him and wanted to kill him. He undertook a pilgrimage to Chartres in order to evade those who sought his life and to seek the protection of the Virgin. He reached the church, said his prayers, and made an offering, then visited the Holy Reliquary that held the undergarment that she had worn when she gave birth to Jesus. He touched the holy chemise with several undergarments he had brought with him and, having said his prayers, returned to his estate.

He had such faith in the power of these garments that he wore one of them when he went out, not bothering with any other means of defense, neither sword nor hauberk. One day he was ambushed by those who sought him; they were fully equipped with sharpened steel and iron, ready to run him through. They could not pierce his defense, however, no matter how many blows they struck, and they became furious. The knight, however, mocked them, smiling. "You're wasting your time," said he, explaining that he wore an undershirt that had touched the Holy Reliquary: Their weapons were useless against the fabric inside.

Understanding that they could not harm him, his enemies threw down their weapons and apologized for their hatred and assault. And peace was made among them by the Lady of mercy: She who reconciles enemies brought them together. And the knight believed that she had done two miracles in keeping him from death and making friends of his enemies.

Mary's Royal Troubadour, King Alfonso X of Spain

An extraordinary monarch in many ways, Alfonso X (1221–1284) not only practiced the usual statecraft and led the requisite military campaigns but also maintained courts of exceptional learning and creativity. He brought together Jews, Christians, and Muslims to translate ancient texts into Castilian and maintained centers of learning to support scholarly efforts that transcended religious and regional bias. He patronized a number of poets, including troubadours from the south of France, some of whom wrote Marian songs at his behest. In addition to writing books of law and treatises on astronomy and astrology, he oversaw, supervised, and contributed to 420 songs dedicated to Our Lady, the *Cantigas de Santa Maria*.[5] With each song set to music notated in the text, this monumental work features 362 songs of miracles and 58 songs of praise, illustrated in color miniatures as well as with black-and-white sketches.

Alfonso and his fellow troubadours had access to Continental collections in Latin and the vernacular from England, France, Germany, and Italy as well as shrine collections from Chartres, Soissons, and Rocamadour. At least 55 of the songs are adapted from those sources, along with two adapted from Gregory's *Glory of the Martyrs*. Stories from various Galician localities supplement the more renowned tales. As expected, in addition to cures of every kind of affliction—rabies, paralysis, deaf-mutism, blindness, and ergotism—Mary rescues countless souls in peril at sea. She resuscitates people who have plunged to their death from cliffs or towers; she restores the dead to life, human and animal alike.

Three miracles involve bees, creatures associated with Mary because they were thought to produce honey from their bodies miraculously, as Mary did Jesus, and the wax from their hives was pure. Song 128 concerns a peasant who wanted to raise bees. A fortune-teller told him to obtain a Communion host and place it in the hive, being careful not to damage it in any way. He followed her directions, and when he thought the time was right, he opened the hive. To his amazement, he saw Mary with Jesus on her lap. Taking the hive to church, the peasant joined the priest and congregation in celebrating Mother and Son

Chapter 5. The Long Twelfth Century II

in the hive, which was placed on the altar. The following day, when the hive was opened, they saw only the original host that the peasant had placed there.

A similar miracle occurs in Song 208, where a heretic from Toledo does the same thing with a Communion host. When he opens the hive, however, he beholds a miniature chapel with Mary holding Jesus on the altar, surrounded by fragrance. The heretic converts on the spot and goes to confess to the bishop, who assembles a procession to bring the chapel to the cathedral.

Song 211 tells of a huge wax Easter candle that burned down only one side, distressing everyone. As the churchgoers discussed ways of mending it, they saw a swarm of dazzling white bees enter the church through a hole in the wall. The bees busily began to restore the candle to its original purity; when they had finished, they nested there and produced a great deal of honey.

This song could be interpreted as an example of Mary's ability to purify the things of the church, symbolized by the white bees and their restoration of the candle. Bees are often symbolic of Mary: As she produced Jesus without losing her virginity, they produce pure wax out of their bodies without effort.

King Alonzo himself was the recipient of four miracles. In Song 209 he is relieved of terrible pain when a book of the *Cantigas* is placed on his body instead of the prescribed hot cloths. Song 235 is recounted in the voice of a courtier poet, who describes the king as near death twice at the hands of enemies and three times at the mercy of severe illness. He attributes the king's cures—one of them on Easter—to Mary, who comes herself to lay hands on the king. In Song 279, he prays for deliverance from fever and nausea; he is heard, and in thanksgiving he repeats the prayer he had said. Song 367, again in another's voice, tells of Alfonso's cure at the shrine of St. Mary of the Port in Alcante.

In Song 178, Mary revives a little boy's dead mule, a gift from his father. Although his mother has already begun to skin his pet, the boy measures it and offers a candle of its size to the Virgin. When he returns from church, he sees his mule alive and hurries to feed it.

Song 294 is a fine example of what may happen to people who insult God's mother. A woman is throwing dice with gamblers in front of a church where two angels stand in front of a statue of Mary, all carved from stone. When the woman loses, she becomes furious, picks up a stone, and launches it at Mary. One of the angels, however, reaches out a hand and stops the stone. Bystanders, furious at the insult to Our Lady, seize the woman and throw her into a fire. And ever after, the song says, one of the stone angels has an outstretched hand.

Gonazalo de Berceo, a People's Poet
Miracles, Praises, and Lamentations of Our Lady[6]

Gonzalo de Berceo (c. 1197–c. 1262) was a secular priest (that is, a priest associated with a parish rather than a religious order). His *Milagros de Nuestra Señora* were written in a verse form and a dialect that parish people could understand despite their lack of learning. Educated in a monastery and perhaps a university as well, he fashioned his stories in sets of four-line stanzas that would encourage church attendance and support. The Fourth Lateran Council of 1215, which fostered education of the laity, may have influenced his accessible and appealing style, and his monastery, San Millán de la Cogolla, was a stop on the way to the shrine of Santiago de Compostela. Pilgrims would have welcomed tales of the Virgin at a site where signs of devotion to her abounded.[7]

Gonzalo had access to many of the sources used by Alfonso el Sabio: 19 of his 24 or 25 miracle stories also appear in the king's work—as well as in many other collections. The introduction to his set of miracles recalls both the courtly and the religious tradition as he describes stopping in a verdant meadow while on pilgrimage. In this little paradise, filled with every kind of tree and fragrant flower, echoing with birdsong and refreshed by clear streams, he rests and is restored. In contrast to worldly gardens, however, where courtship and seduction are regularly conducted, this place is dedicated to Marian devotion. Mary is the meadow, ever green; the streams are the four Gospels. (In an evocation of extracanonical works, Gonzalo claims that what the Gospel writers "wrote, she emended. /... It seems that she was the source from which all waters flowed / while without her nothing received guidance."[8])

Some trees are prayers; others, her miracles. Birdsong comes from those who have sung her praises, and the flowers are the many names ascribed to her. Gonzalo completes his extended metaphor by saying, "I want to climb up into those trees for a little while / and write about some of her miracles.... I will take it as a miracle wrought by the Glorious One, / if she should deign to guide me in the task."[9]

Gonzalo's work includes two miracles that Mary worked at Mont-Saint-Michel, an island off the northwest coast of France that is separated from the mainland twice a day by roaring tides. These tides can speedily overwhelm and drown anyone unfortunate enough to be caught walking either to the Mount or to the mainland. Since the eighth century, the abbey there has been called "Mont-Saint-Michel in Peril of the Sea." Miracle 14, "The Image Miraculously Spared by the Flames," describes a statue of Our Lady of Wisdom, Mary enthroned with Jesus on her lap. Richly crowned and garbed, the image wore a cloth wimple that was the pride of the nearby town. A lightning strike ignited a fierce blaze that consumed everything in the chapel, right down to the altar vessels and candlesticks. Only the Virgin and Child were spared, their costly garments intact.

Another miracle of Mont-Saint-Michel was famous by the time it reached Gonzalo, whose version I have paraphrased below.

The Pregnant Woman Saved by the Virgin
Miracle 19 of Gonzalo de Berceo[10]

Both on sea and on land, Gonzalo says, Mary is powerful everywhere. On an island there was a chapel devoted to Saint Michael, but it was difficult to reach because of the tides, which rushed in so rapidly that no one could escape the flood. On the feast day of Michael (September 29), a pregnant woman was among the pilgrims who visited the Mount. When the time came to return to the mainland, the other pilgrims moved rapidly, and the woman, realizing that she couldn't keep up with them, regretted her decision to visit the place. Stranded, she saw the waves coming toward her and realized that her companions were far ahead of her; they also saw her and, recognizing that she was in mortal danger, called on Mary to help. The pregnant woman was obscured by the tidal rush, and when the waters receded, the others looked back to where she had been. They saw a woman with a child in her arms walking across the sand and were amazed. They quickly realized that Christ and his Mother had answered their prayers, and begged the woman to tell them what had happened.

"Listen," says the woman, and she tells how she prayed to Jesus and Mary, "for I knew of no other help for me." Mary arrived and covered her with the sleeve of her cloak; "I felt no more danger than when I slept; if I were lying in a bath I would not be happier!" Mary assisted with the painless birth of her son; "Never did a woman have such an honored midwife!"[11]

Gonzalo ends with praise for Jesus and Mary along with a request that his audience sing a hymn of thanksgiving for this and all the other miracles performed.

Gonzalo's "Praises" recount salvation history, from the creation to the early church, in a series of 122 verses that mention Mary in passing. More interesting is "The Lamentations of the Virgin,"[12] in which Mary tells the story of the Passion to Bernard of Clairvaux, the earlier "troubadour of Our Lady." This work of 197 four-line stanzas presents Mary, returning to earth in answer to Bernard's request that he learn about Jesus' death from her. As she does in the lamentations of Romanos, Mary says repeatedly that she would have preferred death herself to watching her son die, telling Bernard about her son's birth and childhood, his ministry and miracles. She then addresses Jesus, reminding him of their close bond and begging him to take her with him. He responds that he must atone for sins and descend into Hell to rescue those who loved God and to open the gates of Heaven for them. Comforted, Mary understands that he suffers for all, and Jesus promises her that in three days she will be the first to see him.

After Jesus' death, Mary helps to take the body from the cross and goes to John's home. Gonzalo describes the resurrection as two suns rising: "Christ and the Virgin Mary came back to life: / All the bitterness was turned into joy."[13] Like all of Gonzalo's Marian works, the *Lamentations* end with an appeal for Mary's favor.

The Miracle of the Artisan Monk and the Ugly Devil
Jehan Miélot[14]

This story is retold in the voice of Miélot (active 1449–1478), a cleric and translator who adapted more than 100 Marian miracle stories in French and Latin verse between 1448 and 1467. Lavishly illustrated, his manuscripts represent one of the last great Marian collections of the Middle Ages.

In this story, the monk is painting statues above the portal of a church. Portals or entryways often extended upward for several levels; a standard feature of the level directly above the door was the Last Judgment, with Christ as judge in the center, often accompanied by His mother. On one side, demons waited with pitchforks and fire for sinners, while on the other side angels received the elect into Heaven. Different levels of the portal held statues of Mary—sometimes with the Christ Child—and other saints.

* * *

Long ago there was an abbey of Our Lady where there were many good and devoted religious (monks or brothers) who willingly served God and his glorious Mother. They took care to observe the rules of their order and maintained their cloister well. Their church was embellished with paintings and statues; its portal overlooked the street, and passers-by were so struck by the workmanship that they stopped to admire it.

A monk of that order had been an artist; he strove to render the images in the portal as perfectly as possible. An accomplished sculptor and painter, he had already worked a long time and had made a statue of Notre Dame in majesty holding her infant in her arms. He took pleasure in making the likeness of the blessed one and held her always in his heart. He made her as beautiful as he could and seated her in the middle of the portal, for the church was founded in her name. Higher up he had depicted Jesus Christ as He sits in judgment on the souls who have just left their bodies. To the right of Jesus, the monk carved paradise and God surrounded by all His angels, who filled that part of the portal.

To the left of Jesus the monk then depicted Hell, and had begun to work on a devil holding an iron hook and looking hideous, horrible, frightful; I don't believe that the Evil One was ever seen to be so ugly, either in sculpture or in painting. You could see from looking at him that he was doomed by his very nature. The image was so lifelike that it offended the Devil himself, who took human shape and came to the monk who was working on the images. The Evil One said to him: "Hey! What do you think you're doing? Nobody's ever seen anything as ugly as what you're trying to do here."

The monk began to smile, and said to him, "Kind gentle brother, as God helps me, in Hell there is never any beautiful image. You're not accustomed to seeing the Devil; if you were, you wouldn't consider this one so bad. And know for a fact that if I could make him even uglier and disfigured, I would, for he is even more rough and scaly than I know how to make him."

The Devil could not restrain himself. "You do me great shame," said he. "How is it up to you to portray the Devil? I come from Hell, and I consider you a fool and an imbecile to portray me so ineptly. You'll make me lose my followers, people who have served me their entire lives! When they see such a disgusting image, they'll never be able to love someone that repulsive and ugly. So they'll love that woman, whom you've made down there on the next level, for her great beauty. How have I gored your ox? I don't do you any harm, and here with this image you can't make me look any worse than you do. Mend your ways, you're acting like an idiot. I'm asking—not commanding, mind you—that you wipe out this work, while I'm not doing you any harm, and show me as a handsome young man. I don't like to play games with monks. If you don't do what I ask, you'll regret it. I'm leaving now, and you'd be crazy to forget what I said." Then the Devil disappeared without harming the monk. But he left behind such a stink that the poor monk was completely disoriented, and the place where the devil had stood was polluted with the venom and filth that he left there.

The monk, however, never stopped working all day long. And when the Mass of Our Lady was sung the next day and after he had attended it, he said to himself, "Ah, God, what will I do? The Devil has threatened me. He knows so many tricks and deceptions that he could give me a blow that would damage me for the rest of my days. Certainly I'd be a good friend to him if I changed the ugly to the beautiful and embellished it besides."

The monk began to struggle with his conscience. "Alas, poor coward, what have I said? I've begun my own martyrdom. Why should I serve the Devil? Do I not serve God and Our Lady? Those are secure who love God and serve Mary wholeheartedly. And I know that no one can serve two masters; for if he pleases the one he will displease the other. I know for certain that I'd be a fool to leave God for the enemy in Hell; but if I make the Devil's image foul and hideous, I will do him spite and shame."

Thinking harder, the monk argued to himself, "I know well that he defiles the service of God when he can. For that offense I hate him and wish him ill, and I will shame him and cause him grief, if I can." And he declared, "By nightfall I will have made the most monstrous devil that ever was."

Then the monk climbed up to his lofty workplace to begin his labors to make the Devil terrible to behold. But when the Devil saw himself being portrayed as repulsive and fearsome, he appeared on the scaffolding in his true diabolical shape. The despairing monk would not have been there on that scaffolding, facing the Devil, for all the world.

"Monk," said the Devil, "you have done your work maliciously. I commanded you yesterday not to make me look so ugly. Now it's only reasonable that you pay for your mistake. We're going to fly down from here, both of us, and if you fly better than I do, good for you." At that the Devil struck the platform from the scaffolding, breaking it into pieces, and flew down like a bolt of lightning. After him went the monk, in anguish and torment, tumbling head over heels. But he cried aloud as he fell, "Help me, holy Mary, help me or I'll die!" And as he dropped toward the place where he had painted the image of Our Lady, she assisted him without hesitation, reaching out her right hand and bringing the monk to her side, holding him so gently that he suffered no hurt, while the image of the Infant Jesus sustained him on the other side. Between them they held him high above the ground, while a great crowd gathered and marveled that the monk stayed where he was, uninjured.

All the religious ran from the abbey, and lay people from the town. They raised a ladder to help him down, but he did not want to leave, so great was the joy and happiness he felt in the company of Our Lady and her son. He had forgotten completely the terror of his experience with the Evil One. But the monk turned toward the ladder, and the statue let him go, her arm returning to its original position.

Escaping from his mortal peril, the monk went straight to the altar of the Virgin who had saved his soul and body, thanking her with prayers and tears. And he served her willingly for the rest of his life. Certainly it is good to serve such a lord and such a lady, who keep the body from pain and torment and lead the soul to everlasting glory!

The Miracle of Our Lady's Tumbler
Anonymous[15]

Entertainment during the Middle Ages took place in village squares as well as in the great manor houses of the nobility. Animal trainers, instrumentalists, dancers, jesters, and acrobats or tumblers performed in both venues, travelling from court to court and town to town, frequenting fairs and holiday gatherings as they offered their skills to the public. Like other performers, tumblers were looked down upon by the Church; in particular, they were often condemned as threats to morality because some of their poses and gyrations (so said the preachers) bordered on the obscene.

This version of "Our Lady's Tumbler" opens windows into two worlds, that of the entertainer and that of the monastery to which he is drawn. The voice is the author's.

* * *

In beginning his tale, the author claims to have found it in a book of saints' lives and believes it worth telling to a wider audience. The tumbler (whom he does not name) wandered from one place to another, he says, until the day he entered a religious order.

The world had treated this entertainer well: He didn't have to count his pennies, and he had horses, clothes, and silver to donate, good evidence of his success, as he abandoned secular life. He chose the monastery of Clairvaux, which followed a strict version of the rule of Saint Benedict.[16] Almost immediately, the tumbler noticed that, although the monks were well educated and knew their Latin, they refrained from speaking, using instead a system of sign language to attend to the needs of everyday life. With exceptions for necessity and recreation, their voices were heard only in prayer or song as they celebrated the Liturgy of the Hours.[17] The unlettered tumbler, a *conversus* or adult lay brother, was in awe of the literate monks, some of whom had been affiliated with the monastery since childhood, and who used their learning to praise God.[18]

When that young man, so elegant, so handsome and charming, who made so fine a figure, changed his way of life, he had no idea of how to do anything that was useful to the community. He had really done nothing in his life except acrobatics, leaps, and dance steps; he was adept at that and nothing else. He didn't know a single liturgical text, not an Our Father, not a Hail Mary or a Creed or a hymn, nothing that could contribute a jot or a tittle to his salvation.

He saw tonsured monks who spoke in sign language to each other, not uttering a word, and he thought that he himself ought to keep silence. He would have gone for days without saying a word if someone hadn't ordered him to speak, and his timidity caused some laughter in the community, especially since he was only a lay brother and not a choir monk.

He observed priests saying Mass, deacons reading the Scriptures, subdeacons leading the night offices in the Liturgy of the Hours, acolytes standing ready with the psalters.[19] Lay brothers could say the "Have mercy, Lord" of Psalm 50, and even the more ignorant among them could say their chaplets of Our Fathers and Hail Marys. In the different buildings of the monastery, everywhere he saw them, he heard the one lament, the other weep, another sigh. "Holy Mary," said he to himself, "what's the matter with these people that they seem to be so afflicted? They must be truly unhappy for all of them to give vent to such sorrow." But thinking more about it, he realized that they were asking for God's mercy. "And what am I doing here?" he asked himself. "Nothing. Everyone else, even the lowliest, does his best to serve God by doing his duty, but I don't have any duties, and I'm no use to anyone—I don't do anything, and I can't say anything. All I do here is wander around wasting time and stuffing my face for nothing. If they notice that I'm worthless, it'll be the ruin of me, they'll throw me out in the fields with the peasants." Desolate, he called upon Mary.

"Holy Mary, mother! Plead for me with your heavenly father to tell me what to do so that I can serve you both and deserve the food I receive, for I do wrong to eat without doing anything in return." After saying his prayer, he wandered through the monastery, coming upon a little corner niche. He hunkered down inside it, hoping to hide himself. In the niche there was an altar with a statue of Our Lady. "It was no aimless erring," remarks the author, "that brought him here, but God who knows best how to guide His own."

At the sound of the bell for Mass, the tumbler sprang up, dismayed. "Ah," he sighed, "I am undone! Everyone goes to do his part and here I stand like a bull at the end of a tether. But will I stay that way, saying nothing, doing nothing? No! I'll do what I have learned, and serve God and our Lady in her monastery. The others serve by singing, and I will serve by tumbling."

He took off the small cape that covered his shoulders, and his tunic, and placed his clothes before the altar. So that he did not perform naked, he kept on a fine, light undertunic that he fastened with a belt, arranging all with care. Full of humility, he turned to face the statue of Mary. "Lady," he said, "under your protection I place my body and my soul.[20] Gentle queen, compassionate lady, do not disdain what I know how to do, for I want to try to serve you in good faith, God help me, without any move that might offend you. I don't know how to read or to sing for you, but I will show you all of my best feats. Let me be to you like the young kid that cavorts and leaps in front of its mother! Lady, you who are not harsh with those who honor you in a more usual way, know that unworthy as I am, I do this for you."

So saying, he began his leaps and somersaults, bounding high and bending low, turning one way and another.[21] He knelt, bowing to the ground, and said, "Gentle queen, in your mercy and goodness do not despise my service." Then he performed a headstand in the manner of Metz (a city in northeastern France), bowing in veneration before the statue, following with vaults popular in France, in Champagne, in Spain, in Brittany, and in Lorraine: Every move he knew, he strove to make. He performed the Roman vault; he placed his hand in front of his forehead and danced gracefully.[22] After addressing Our Lady again, he danced with his feet in the air, walking on his hands, his eyes weeping with adoration and the joy of serving Mary. "Lady," he said, "I adore you with my heart, my body, my feet, and my hands, for that is all I know how to do. From now on I will be your servant—when the others gather in the church to sing, I will come here to perform just for you."[23]

And so he did. He beat his breast and danced to atone for his sins; he performed a prayer, the only kind he knew how to say. Attempting an elaborate vault, he declared, "Lady, as God is my witness, I've never done this before. It's not a turn for an amateur; I made it up on the spur of the moment just for you." All the while the Mass was being said, he never stopped dancing, leaping, vaulting, so strenuously that—no longer able to stay on his feet—he dropped to the ground, completely exhausted, his body dripping with sweat from his feet to his head. After he had recovered somewhat, he put on his garments again, bowed, and took leave of Mary.

"Lady, I can do no more for the moment," he said, "but I'll be back, believe me, to serve you during each office of the day. How sorry I am that I don't know the Psalms! I'd be so happy to say them for the love of you! And now I commend myself, body and soul, to you."

He kept his word. For a long time, at each office, he paid homage to the Virgin; for him it was a marvelous privilege, even though each performance wore him out. He would not have wished for all the gold in the world for anyone except God alone to know what he was doing, for he was convinced that if the monks found out they would chase him from the monastery back into the world.

The good tumbler lived his life in service to his Lady for a long time—many years, until one day he was discovered by a monk who noticed that he never came to Matins. Determined to find out what this lay brother was up to, the monk followed him and discovered what he was doing. "By my faith," the monk said to himself, "here's a pretty picture: We sing for him and he dances for us, as fervently as if he'd gotten a hundred silver pieces. Look at the poor fool; he's killing himself. Maybe God will take it as a sign of contrition, for he carries on in good faith, and it appears that he doesn't want to look lazy." He could not keep himself from both laughter and tears at the sight, and hastened to tell the abbot about it.

"Don't tell a soul," the abbot told him, "let's keep it to ourselves until both of us can take a look at him. We will pray to God for his sweet mother to let us know if this occupation is legitimate." The two went silently to the altar, where they hid themselves in the shadows. The abbot observed the tumbler's performance of his office, leaping and dancing, prostrating himself before the statue, bounding and tapping the floor with his feet until he was near fainting. Despite his weariness, he continued until he fell, the sweat pouring from his body in huge drops onto the floor of the crypt.

But immediately, his gentle Lady (whom he served with such an honest heart) arrived to help him: She knew when he had need of her to come to his aid. Looking on, the abbot was dumbfounded: From the height of the vaulted ceiling descended a lady so resplendent and so sumptuously adorned that no one had ever seen the like. Never was there anyone so beautiful in the world. Gold and precious stones enhanced the costliness of her garments, and angels and archangels accompanied her to surround the tumbler and sustain him. When they gathered around him, his heart revived and he wanted to resume his service. The noble Lady took a white linen towel and gently fanned her performer to refresh him, neck, body, and face. The man was unaware, for he neither saw nor knew that he enjoyed such celestial company. They did not remain with him long; the Lady blessed him in the name of God and returned whence she had come, in the company of angels who waited for the time when his soul would be free to join them in Heaven.

The abbot and his monk observed this scene four times; each time, the mother of God appeared to comfort and support her servant. The abbot was delighted because God had clearly shown him what he wanted to know: that the tumbler's service was acceptable. The monk, for his part, was ashamed of his lack of charity, saying, "Milord abbot, have pity on me! The man I saw there is a saint."

The abbot kept his counsel for a time, but eventually he sent for the tumbler. Certain that he would be banished from the monastery, the tumbler prayed to Mary for help in pleading his cause: "Lady Mary, come to enlighten me! Dear Lord God, come to my assistance and bring your mother with you—please don't come without her! For I am helpless to defend myself alone." He went in tears to the abbot, who asked what service he had done to earn his bread in the time that he'd been in the monastery. In anguish, the tumbler promised to leave, saying that he hadn't done even half of a good action. The abbot demanded that he respond more fully, citing the monastic vow of obedience. So the tumbler fell on his knees, weeping, and told the abbot of his entire life from one end to the other, without omitting a single thing. At the end of his confession, the abbot raised him to his feet. "Brother," he said to the tumbler, "I promise you that you are one of our company. May God grant that we merit belonging to yours! Dear brother, pray for me, and I will pray for you in return, and now I order you, dear friend, in all sincerity, to continue your service freely. And for a penance, do not torment yourself so with doubts."

Faint with joy, the tumbler had to be seated. He felt a surge of happiness, but it presaged the illness from which he would die soon after. Despite his weakness, he faithfully performed his service, morning and evening, without neglecting even one hour of an office, until the day he became so ill that he could not move from his bed. His greatest affliction was not being able to perform for Our Lady, and he suffered despite the daily presence of the abbot and his fellow monks, who came to sing at the foot of his bed. He confessed his sins, repentant but still fearful as death approached. In the presence of the dying man, abbot and monks alike observed the miraculous appearance of the Mother of God. In the company of angels and archangels she confronted the demons who wanted to carry off her tumbler's soul, and the devils were defeated. Mary herself received the soul of the tumbler as it left this world.

The community buried him with great ceremony; then the abbot told the story of the tumbler's life and what kind of recompense he had received for his faithful service, a reward unequalled on earth.

* * *

The tumbler, called a *conversus* because he changed (converted) his way of life, is converted into a saint through his devotion and faithful service to the Mother of God. When the abbot witnesses the miracle of Mary's appearance and support of her servant, he and the monk with him are converted, and the abbot converts the *conversus* into a monk. The spiritual life and outlook of an entire community are transformed by the example of one who has made his despised profession holy by offering it to God and Mary.

The Miracle of Our Lady at the Tournament
Anonymous[24]

Knights like the one in this story maintained order on a noble's lands, lived at his court, and fought in his name during wars, crusades, and incursions into rivals' territory. Knighthood was an expensive profession; if the liege lord did not provide for all his followers, the knight had to buy a war horse and riding horses for himself and his squire as well as pack animals. He also provided his own armor for warfare and for ceremony, and he outfitted his squire. When he was not fighting on behalf of his liege, he could maintain his skills by traveling to tournaments, where he competed for prizes and took mock prisoners who had to pay real ransoms to regain their freedom.

It was a fortunate knight who could offset the cost of participating in a tournament by "capturing" one or more of his fellows. In one of the most famous Mary stories about knights, below, the protagonist is fortunate in an otherworldly way. I retell this story with quotations from the anonymous author.

* * *

Gentle Jesus, how well he wages war, and how nobly he tourneys who turns of his own will to the monastery, where he prepares to do sacred service and celebrates the holy mystery of the noble son of the virgin mother! For this reason, I wish to tell you the exemplary story of a courteous and wise knight, bold and of great prowess in battle, who loved the Virgin Mary devotedly. To practice his knightly skills and keep fit, he set out for a tournament, armed to his satisfaction. It so pleased God that when the day of the tourney arrived he was hurrying along the road, for he wished to be first on the field, when he heard the bells from a nearby church sounding the call to Mass. Without hesitation the knight went straight to the church to hear the divine service. There, a priest was singing the Mass of the Virgin loudly and with great devotion, and when he had finished one service, he began another. The knight listened well, praying to Our Lady with all his heart. When the second Mass had finished, a third began. "Sir, by the holy body of God," said his squire to him, "the time is passing for the tournament to begin, and you remain here? Come on, I beg you! Do you want to become a hermit or a hypocrite, an imitation priest? Let's get on with our job here!"

"Friend," said the knight to him, "the one who hears the divine service is the one who will tourney most nobly and well, and when the Masses are entirely finished, we'll take to the road again and go tourney as vigorously as God wills." With that, he spoke no longer, but turned his face toward the altar and stayed until the last chant died away. Only then did they mount their horses and ride toward the place where the tourneys were being held.

On the way, they encountered knights returning from the tournament, which had ended some time ago. His fellow knights greeted him, congratulated him, and said that never before had any knight displayed such feats of arms as he had done that day; he would be forever honored for his prowess. Many of them surrendered to him, saying, "We are your prisoners; never could we deny that you have defeated us." It appeared that the knight who had stayed to hear the Masses had taken all the prisoners, all the honors.

Astounded, he began to realize that the one for whom he had stayed in chapel had taken his place in combat. He called his household to him and said, "Now hear me, of your goodness! For I will tell you a marvel the like of which you have never heard." Then he told them word by word how he had heard the Masses and never fought in the tourney, never lifted lance or shield; but the maiden to whom he had prayed in the chapel had done the jousting for him. "How wonderful is this tournament where she fought for me, and how she would have done it in vain if I do not now fight for her! I would be foolish if I returned to worldly vanity. I promise in truth never to tourney again except before the true Judge, who knows the good knight and knows how to judge him and his feats."

Then piously he took his leave of them; many wept tenderly. He parted from them, and from then on he served the Virgin Mary. And we believe that the road he took led him to a fine destination.

The German Novice Master's Masterwork

A chapter in the *Dialogus Miraculorum* (*Dialogue on Miracles*) by Caesarius of Heisterbach (c. 1170–c. 1240) may have been the source of the miracle tale above.

Sir Walter of Birbeck, the Tardy Knight and Saintly Monk
Caesarius of Heisterbach, Dialogue on Miracles, Chapter 37[25]

In this chapter, Caesarius describes the life of an actual knight, Walter of Birbeck. Walter was a nobleman, wealthy and powerful, who spent his youth in "secular warfare" (tournaments) but was nevertheless devoted to Mary. On the way to a tournament in the company of other knights, Walter stopped to hear Mass while the others continued on. Mary, Caesarius says, "filled his place during his absence with marvelous might." We don't know if Caesarius was the source of the anonymous French author's verses recounting the same tale, but certainly the story had currency in the thirteenth century.

In the dialogue with a novice that is the context of Caesarius' story, the novice asks his mentor how Walter's prayers could please the Virgin when the knight was on his way to a tournament—because participation in tournaments was a mortal sin. In reply, the older monk offers evidence of Walter's devotion that offsets his tourneying: The knight's love of Mary was such that he offered himself as a slave to a poor church that was dedicated to the Virgin, paying a ransom for his life every year. He fasted on bread and water on the eve of all of Mary's feast days as well as on Fridays. One day Walter's servant brought him a pitcher of what he thought was water, but when he drank it he found that Mary had turned it into wine. On another day, the priest saw a golden cross at his feet after he had raised the chalice for the consecration. Attached to the cross was a parchment on which was written, "Give this cross from me, Mary, the Mother of Christ, to my friend Walter of Birbeck." When Walter made his profession as a monk, he gave the cross to the abbey of Hemmenrode, where he spent the rest of his life.

Marked by his devotion to Mary, Walter's life produced a number of miracles. He held a book of Marian prayer to the forehead of a man possessed by the devil; the evil spirit flew out, howling and raging. The holy knight was on a ship carrying the monastery's wine when a terrible storm arose and pirates attacked the ship; two huge casks of wine rolled out of the ship and into that of the pirates, sinking them. Producing an image of Mary from his belongings, Walter joined his prayers to those of his abbot back at the monastery, and the storm subsided. Walter's death and reception into Heaven by Mary were revealed to a companion in a vision; his relics cured the paralysis of a local nobleman.

The elder monk assures the novice that Walter's life shows how Mary often gives worldly as well as celestial honor to those who honor her. The sinfulness of the tournament is long forgiven, subsumed in devotion and its reward.

Caesarius includes 64 Marian stories in his work, a collection of 746 tales told in the form of a conversation between an older monk and a novice (probationary monk) in the monastery. Written between 1219 and 1222, the *Dialogue* is based on his own experience as a novice master, or instructor, in the abbey at Heisterbach; the context ensures that the content is highly moralistic. Even so, some tales reflect Caesarius' compassion for the sinner alongside his disapproval of whatever sin is in question. In his account of a nun who was tempted to leave her convent, Mary detains the woman by slapping her so hard that she doesn't recover until her sisters find her the next morning. Needless to say, she does not try again. In the very next chapter, however, the novice master softens the ending of a miracle story about another errant nun, named Beatrice. His treatment of this miracle, which features in nearly every medieval collection, is harsh but ends on a note of compassion. Even though he roundly condemns the "miserable wretch" who "ruined [Beatrice] and abandoned her" and the fifteen years of prostitution that followed (a far cry from the long and honorable marriage she has in Gautier's version), he still portrays Mary as the Mother of Mercy, taking the place of Beatrice at the door and restoring her to her former position, an unexpected happy ending to a sensationalized tale. Caesarius' name for the nun, Beatrice, would follow her through centuries of storytelling and dramatization.

* * *

The sixty-fourth and final tale in Caesarius' collection recounts the vision of a monk who saw Mary in Heaven, opening her cloak to cover all members of the Cistercian order—abbots, monks, novices, lay brothers and sisters—a celestial seal of approval for the order and the author who served her. The image caught the attention of artists, and the Madonna of Mercy—Mary sheltering all classes of people under a voluminous mantle—became a favored subject for painters and sculptors of the fourteenth century and early Renaissance.

Jacobus of Voragine: Mary's Life, Mary's Stories in the Calendar of the Church

Another best-seller of the Middle Ages was the *Legenda Aurea* (*Golden Legend*), written by the Dominican bishop Jacobus of Voragine, Italy (c. 1230–1298). More than a thousand manuscripts and countless editions attest to its popularity since its completion about 1260.[26] Arranged according to the liturgical calendar of the Church year, the work is a collection of (often fanciful) saints' biographies that includes details of the lives of Jesus and Mary compiled from many different sources and accompanied by pious commentary. Because one of the purposes of his compilation was to provide preachers with interesting material for sermons,[27] Jacobus retold many popular miracle stories, including some 20 Marian miracles. His Mary stories tend to be brief and illustrative, anecdotes for a kind of "preacher's digest" suitable for enhancing sermons—a technique that would become a trend.

According to Jacobus, Mary was virtually the co-author of Luke's Gospel.[28] His reason? The episode in Luke 2:49–51, after Jesus had been lost for three days and then found in the Temple. In response to Mary's rebuke, Jesus asked, "Why were you searching for me? Did you not know that I must be in my Father's house?" Neither Mary nor Joseph understood his statement, but Mary "treasured all these things in her heart." Jacobus interprets this passage to mean that Mary remembered all of her son's words and actions, so much so that all of the evangelists turned to her for answers to their questions about Christ's life. Luke, especially, according to Jacobus, relied on her for details about the Nativity.

Jacobus begins his collection with Advent and "The Birth of Our Lord Jesus Christ According to the Flesh."[29] Using Luke's Gospel as his base, he also cites a "Brother Bartholomew" who has read the "Book of the Infancy of the Savior,"[30] and he claims to follow that monk's notes in his telling of Christ's birth, adding some details: Because there was no room at the inn, Joseph and Mary found space in a passageway between two houses, where Joseph set up a manger for his ox and his ass. It was there that Christ was born. Jacobus gives the names of Zebel and Salome to the two midwives present, and when Salome doubts Mary's virginity and tries to test it, her hand withers. An angel tells her to touch the baby Jesus; she does, and is made whole again—details from the *Protogospel*. For the feast of the Epiphany, Jacobus gives the Magi the names Caspar, Balthasar, and Melchior, still familiar to us today.[31]

The Feast of Mary's Nativity and Marian Genealogies

The feast of Mary's own nativity is now observed without fanfare—and without much mention of Mary herself. Jacobus, however, celebrates this feast in style. In addition to recounting Marian miracles, he provides a history of the feast, giving details of Mary's heritage taken from the second-century *Protogospel* (which he attributes to Saint Jerome!), the seventh-century *Pseudo-Matthew*, and the ninth-century *Gospel of the Birth of Mary*. Jacobus uses earlier genealogies in his description of Mary's family of origin and Jesus' relatives, now called the Holy Kinship.[32] His medieval backstory to Mary's life embellishes the *Protogospel* tale of Mary's parents, Joachim and Anna, and explains Jesus' biblical "brothers." His account[33] includes the genealogy and life of Mary used a century earlier by Wace, as well as the story of her mother Anne's three marriages. It was Jacobus' version of the "Life of Mary" that became famous, encouraging the cult of Saint Anne and promoting images of the Holy Kinship (Anna and Joachim; Mary, Joseph, and Jesus with the rest of their relatives). This three-generational family grouping was depicted in many works of art that became popular in succeeding centuries.[34] Mary's birth is now celebrated on September 8, as assigned in the day of Jacobus. The feast itself dates from the seventh century.[35]

A Son Restored to His Mother
Feast of the Birth of the Virgin, September 8[36]

The protagonist of this story is a mother whose maternal strength and assertiveness are a match for Mary's. It is retold here in Jacobus' voice.

* * *

A widow's son was all she had left from her marriage after the death of her husband. She loved her boy dearly, but he had enemies who did not; they captured him, threw him into prison, and left him in chains. When the widow heard of her son's plight, she wept continuously, praying night and day to the Blessed Mother for her son's release. After months of perpetual and unanswered prayer, she went to her parish church, where she waited until she was alone with a statue of Mary holding the baby Jesus.

Standing in front of the statue, the distraught mother addressed the Mother of God: "O virgin most blessed, I have asked and asked you to set my son free, and I haven't heard a word from you in return. So, just as I've been deprived of my son, you'll be deprived of yours. I'm taking your boy and holding him hostage." She stepped up to the altar, snatched the statue of the baby Jesus from Mary's lap, took him home, wrapped him in pristine linen, and locked him in a cupboard.

The next night, Mary appeared to the widow's son and threw open the door to his prison cell. She invited him to leave, saying, "Son, please tell your mother to return my child as I have returned hers!" The young man walked out, free as a bird, and went back to his mother, whom he told about Mary's midnight rescue. The widow promptly unlocked the door to her cupboard and took the statue of Jesus to the church. "Thank you, my lady," she said, "for giving me back my only son. I can now return yours to you—with my gratitude." And she placed the child gently on his mother's lap.

The Monk Who Could Learn Only Two Words of the "Ave Maria"

Feast of the Annunciation, March 25[37]

Some stories are told of those whose quality of soul rather than quantity of knowledge counts for all in the economy of salvation. One of Jacobus' briefer tales, probably based on Gautier, recounts the story of a knight, wealthy and well-born, who gave up the world of tournaments and fighting to enter a Cistercian monastery known for its devotion and austerity. Although noble, this knight was completely illiterate; and because the monks were reluctant to place him with the lower-born lay brothers in the fields, they found a tutor to teach him what he needed to know to be a member of the choir. He spent long, tedious hours with his teacher, but try as he might he could learn no more than the first two words of the "Ave Maria." He clung to those two words, repeating them wherever he went and whatever he did. When his days on earth were finished, he died and was buried in the cemetery of the monastery. There, his brother monks saw a magnificent lily growing over his tomb, each of its leaves adorned with the words *Ave Maria* written in gold. When they dug down into the earth to find the source of this miraculous plant, they saw that the root of the lily sprang from the monk's mouth. They understood then that their brother had said those two words with such devotion that God was moved to honor the one who had honored God's mother.

Mary's Hand on the Scale

Feast of the Assumption, August 15[38]

The motif of weighing souls' good and bad deeds at the end of life was ubiquitous in the Middle Ages. The Four Last Things—death, judgment, Heaven, and Hell, with Christ as judge over all—were carved in stone above countless church entrances. Illustrations of Mary's hand on the scale, not-so-subtle evidence of her role as Mother of Mercy, appeared in "wall paintings, sculpture, manuscript illuminations and woodcarvings throughout France and the rest of Europe."[39] Jacobus tells a cautionary tale in this regard; I retell it in his voice.

* * *

There was a man whose soul was bent under the baggage of all his sins. One night he had a vision of being called before the judgment seat, where the Devil claimed him, body and soul: "This man belongs to me; I have a warrant for him based on the fact that he is descended from those who ate what had been forbidden. Besides, he served me as a slave for 30 years; I have owner's rights to him." Satan further claimed that the man's bad deeds far outweighed the good he had done. God suspended judgment for a week so that the man could gather evidence to refute the Devil's claim. As he left God's court, convinced that he would never be able to beat the Devil, he came upon a kind person who asked why he looked so sad. Told of his situation, this person said that he was called Truth and promised to help. They met another person who also promised assistance; his name was Justice.

Once back in court, Truth said that the man's body had to die, but he did not have to give up his soul because Christ had redeemed humankind. Justice countered the Devil's second claim, that he had owned the man for years, with the observation that although the man was indeed a slave, he had always regretted having to serve so harsh a master. To decide the Devil's third claim, God called for a scale to weigh the man's good and bad deeds. Truth and Justice whispered to him, "Look at who's seated next to the Lord. It's his mother, the Mother of Mercy. Ask her with your whole heart to help you, and she will." So he did, and Mary came to his assistance. On the side of the scale that held his paltry good deeds, she placed her gentle hand, while the Devil tried to pile up the bad deeds on the other side. Mary prevailed, and the sinner went free.

Waking up, the man was convinced by his vision that he should mend his ways.

The Knight Who Sold His Wife to the Devil
Feast of the Assumption, August 15[40]

Jacobus tells of a wealthy knight who had a wife devoted to the Virgin. This knight had distributed his riches with such generous abandon—he was the very embodiment of courtliness—that he was close to poverty. And when a feast day drew near and he was expected to show his largesse, he hadn't a thing left to give. Overcome by shame, he went off by himself to hide until the feast had passed.

On his way to a remote corner of his estate, he met with a giant black war-horse bearing a knight armored all in black. The black knight noticed his drawn face and woebegone look and asked the cause of his sadness. When the poor fellow had told his tale of woe, the armored one said, "If you will be so kind as to grant me one small favor, you will have riches and a reputation beyond anything you have ever dreamed of!" The knight answered the dark one that he would do whatever was necessary, and Satan (yes, it was he) said, "Go home and look in one of your storage chests. You'll find there all the gold and silver and gems you'll ever need. And in return, here's what you can do for me: Bring me your wife on the day I'll assign for you."

The knight agreed and returned to his home, where he found all that Satan had promised. Joyfully he gave gifts, redeemed his holdings from pawn, planned to buy castles. And on the appointed day, he called his wife and ordered her to prepare for a long journey. Trembling and quaking but not daring to deny his will, she said her prayers to the Blessed Mother and took her place on a cushion behind her husband. When the two had ridden for some time, they came to a church. The knight's wife dismounted and went into the church to pray. Exhausted by the ride, and not knowing their destination, she fell asleep during her prayer. As she slept, the Virgin stepped down from the altar, took on the woman's clothes and appearance, and joined the knight outside.

The knight and (now) Our Lady resumed their journey; when they came to the appointed place, the Prince of Darkness came on with a great rush to meet them. When he saw who was there, he reined in his horse and shrank back in fear, exclaiming, "Faithless knight, why have you deceived me and repaid my splendid gifts in this way? I told you to bring me your wife, and instead you have brought the mother of the Lord! I wanted your spouse, and here you are with Mary! Your wife has done me great wrong with her prayers and carryings-on, and I thought I would have my revenge, but now I face the one who will torture me and send me back to Hell!"

The knight was speechless with astonishment and fear, but Mary spoke up at once: "By what audacity, evil spirit, have you tried to harm my servant? You *will* be punished, and this is my sentence: Return to Hell, and never again presume to plot ill against anyone who invokes me!"

The Devil took himself off, fiercely lamenting the loss of his prey. The knight dismounted and threw himself at Mary's feet. She scolded him soundly, commanding him to go back to his wife, who still slept in the church, and to throw out all the Devil's gifts. Returning to the church, he awakened his spouse and told her all that had happened. They went back to their home, rid themselves of their demonic treasure, and praised the Virgin for her goodness. And in time Mary saw to it that their wealth was restored.

Mary at the Apex of Paradise in Dante's *Divine Comedy*

For Dante Alighieri (1265–1321), Mary is associated—almost identified—with the love of his life, Beatrice. Corresponding to Mary, the ultimate highly placed Lady of the highest court, Beatrice appears as the unattainable earthly lady of the poet's courtly desire. Beatrice acts as an *altera Maria*, an "Other Mary" who sets Dante on the way through Hell and Purgatory to Paradise in *The Divine Comedy*.

In the final three cantos, or sections, of the *Paradiso*, we see the "courts of Heaven" with their gemstones and flowers gleaming in an ineffable light. Indeed, Heaven is filled with a supernatural light that is commensurate with—and emanates from—supernatural love. In Canto XXXI, Beatrice conducts Dante to the borders of Heaven; she is replaced by Bernard of Clairvaux, who leads him through a celestial garden. There he glimpses Mary, whose radiance surpasses that of all others in paradise except for God, and who stands at the center of a magnificent white rose.

In Canto XXXII, the saints appear as petals of the rose, and Dante sees Mary fully as "the face which most resembles Christ." Just below Mary is Eve, the "mother of all the living," and saints of both the First and Second Covenants. Canto XXXIII is the culmination of Dante's quest as he experiences the "love that moves the sun and the other stars." God's love encompasses all: the poet, Beatrice, Mary. Paradise indeed.

Mary Tales and Poems in Middle English

Marian devotion developed much earlier in England than did lyrics and stories about her. Thanks to monastic connections with the East as well as the Continent, extracanonical works about Mary's life were available in England. Between the seventh and the ninth centuries, "Anglo-Saxons eagerly read Marian texts, had begun to celebrate her feasts, prayed to her and depicted her in their art; an intense and lively interest in Mary developed in the tenth and in the eleventh centuries."[41] Versions of extracanonical stories in Anglo-Saxon (a Germanic language that came with invading settlers from the Continent) circulated from the eighth century on.[42] Those texts, of course, were available only to those who were literate, an audience composed mainly of monks. Latin texts had an even more limited readership.

The development of Old English from Anglo-Saxon occurred over the course of three centuries. Then, after the Norman Conquest of 1066, sociocultural and linguistic forces combined to produce Anglo-Norman. Marian literature is said to have promoted the development of Anglo-Norman, given a kind of "mirror effect" of Old English and Old French versions of her miracle tales retold by clerics fluent in both languages as well as Latin.[43] In England, Anglo-Norman was the language of the law, the aristocracy, and the literate; (Middle) English served as the vernacular of the middle and lower classes. Only two early collections of Mary stories exist in Middle English; some of her miracles are embedded in saints' lives or sermon collections.[44]

Most manuscripts of the Middle English Mary stories date from the fifteenth century—relatively late in the tradition—and may reflect a slight diminution in the public enthusiasm for Marian tales. (Appreciation of devotional poetry was undiminished, perhaps indicating a preference for more personal expressions of religious experience.) With few exceptions, the authors of Middle English works are anonymous; the tales themselves are scattered among different manuscripts such as *The South English Legendary* (seven tales, ca. 1280), *The North English Homily Collection* (four tales, ca. 1300), and other sources, notably the Vernon manuscript (41 miracle tales, of which 9 remain; ca. 1390).[45]

All of these sources feature tales written in rhyming couplets. *The South English Legendary* pieces include the story of Theophilus as well as Jacobus' tale of the knight who pledged his wife to the devil. *The North*

English Homily Collection, as the name implies, contains four miracle stories designated as sermon anecdotes, including "The Pregnant Abbess" and a version of "The Widow's Candle" translated below. The Vernon manuscript features the saving of Chartres by the Virgin's tunic and the miraculous restoration by Mary of a man's foot as well as the tale of a fornicating priest and "The Harlot's Prayer." Another source, John Mirk's *Festial* (also ca. 1390), like *The North English Homily Collection*, embeds miracle tales as "narrations" in sermons for various feast days. The following story centers on the February 2 feast of Candlemas (also known as the Purification of the Virgin or the Presentation of Jesus in the Temple, described in Luke 2:22–40). On this, one of the oldest feasts in the Christian calendar, members of the congregation brought candles to church to be blessed. (Blessed candles were used for protection against dangerous weather events; they were also lighted at a person's deathbed as part of the last rites.) I have translated the story from Middle English.

The Widow's Candle for the Feast
John Mirk, Sermon for Candlemas in Festial[46]

There was a woman who was so devoted to Our Lady that she gave away all of her clothes out of love for Mary, except for the shabbiest garment, which she was used to wearing. It so happened that on Candlemas Day, when she should have gone to church, she dared not go for the shame she felt that she no longer had the clothing that she used to wear to church. Distraught that she couldn't attend Mass on that holy feast, she went to a little chapel near her home and stayed there in prayer.

While she prayed, she fell asleep and dreamed that she was in a magnificent church, where she saw a great company of maidens coming through the portal. They were led by a maiden who was exceedingly more beautiful than any of them and wore a crown of shining gold. The fairest one sat down with the others. When they were seated, she saw a man enter the church bearing a great bundle of candles; he presented the first candle to the maiden with a crown (Mary, of course), then distributed candles to everyone else.

And so he came to the widow, presenting her with a candle, which made her very happy. She saw a priest and two deacons vested for Mass, accompanied by two candle-bearers, proceeding to the altar. Then she saw Christ as the priest, two angels as the deacons, and two saints as the candle-bearers. Mass began, and at the Gospel, Mary, queen of the maidens, was the first to offer her candle to the priest; after her, the rest of the worshippers offered theirs in single file. When all of them had offered a candle, the priest waited for the widow woman to offer hers; but she held on to it tightly, and Mary had to send a servant to persuade her to part with it. When the servant delivered the message, the woman said that she wanted to keep it for her private devotions. Mary sent another servant to say that it was discourteous of her to delay the service, and if she didn't offer it with a good will, the queen would send someone to take it from her.

The widow refused again: She would not part with her candle. The servant tried to take it from her by force, and the two struggled so mightily that the candle broke, leaving each with half. In the midst of the struggle, the widow woke up, finding half of a candle in her hand. And she thanked Our Lady sincerely that she had not missed Mass that day and had such a relic to keep for the rest of her life.

Geoffrey Chaucer: Mixed Messages About Mary

Toward the beginning of his career, Chaucer (1340–1400) was commissioned to write a poem of praise to Mary. His "Marian ABC," heavily dependent on a French original, is made up of 26 stanzas beginning with successive letters of the alphabet.[47] Starting with "Almighty and merciful Queen, / to whom all in this world flee for help," it ends with a stanza beginning "Zacharias calls you the open well / That washes sinful souls of their guilt." The poem contains almost every title that has accrued to Mary over the centuries; Chaucer invokes Moses and Isaac ("Ysaac") of the First Testament as well as Jesus and Mary. "It's true," he says, "that God shows no pity [to sinners] without you.... He has made you vicar and mistress of this world [as well as] governess of heaven; he forbears to do justice if you ask for mercy, and he has confirmed it by crowning you [Queen of Heaven]."

Mary appears in the prologue to "The Prioress's Tale" in Chaucer's *Canterbury Tales*, written toward the end of the author's life. The Prioress' prologue to her story is a recitation of commonplaces, citing Mary's abundance of graces and bounty, humility, generosity, and guidance of souls to her son. In the (anti–Semitic) story itself, however, the Prioress (the most important person in an abbey after the head, or abbess) shows herself to be both worldly and immature, the kind of religious who would parrot condemnations of any beliefs not firmly held by Christians. Her story reflects the biases of both church and state.

An exception to the anonymity of many English miracle tales—although their collectors and translators may be famous—is Thomas Hoccleve (1368/69–1426), a student of Chaucer. Hoccleve wrote a charming poem, "The Monk and Our Lady's Sleeves," which advocates saying a series of prayers known as "Our Lady's Psalter" (or psalm-book). The "psalter" consisted of five sets of ten Hail Marys (equal to the number of psalms), recited while reflecting on the events of Mary's and Christ's lives. The practice originated in monasteries, where lay brothers—who were often illiterate—were still required to participate in the Divine Office. "The custom of giving them 'Pater Nosters' ['Our Fathers'] and 'Ave Marias' ['Hail Marys'] to say instead spread outside the monasteries and became a common form of [devotion] eventually standardized in its present form."[48]

This Marian tale appears to be unique.

The Monk and Our Lady's Sleeves
Thomas Hoccleve[49]

"Whoever desires to gain the bliss of heaven," the poem begins, "should look to Mary, the mediatrix between God and humans, who obtains mercy for us. She is our shield against the malice of the fiend, who would carry our souls off to that horrible place of eternal pain and torment." The speaker then offers an example of Marian devotion.

A wealthy and worthy man who said 50 Hail Marys each day offered his son to the Church, bidding him follow his father's example. The young man was faithful in his monastic duties; in addition, he duly said his 50 daily Aves, as his father did. Coming home at his father's request, the young monk entered the family chapel to pay his respects to Mary.

When he had ended his prayer, Our Lady appeared to him, wearing a sleeveless garment. Startled, the monk asked her, "Lady, by your leave, what garment are you wearing that has no sleeve?" Mary replied, "You have woven this garment for me by saying 50 Aves every day. From now on, say three times that many, and to every ten 'Aves' add a 'Pater Noster.'" Mary then instructed him to think about a specific event in her life for every set of ten Aves, or decade—such as the Annunciation, the birth of Jesus, her assumption, her coronation as Queen of Heaven.

Returning to the monastery, the monk followed Mary's advice. After the next holiday, when he was again in his father's chapel, Our Lady appeared to him "well arrayed," in a robe well made. "See now what new apparel you have woven for me! My clothing lacks sleeves no more. I thank you." She then told him that he would be rewarded both in this life and the next: When he returned to the abbey, he would be elected abbot. For seven years, he would teach monks and laypeople alike how to say Our Lady's Psalter "according to her teaching and instruction," and many souls would gain eternal life because of their devotion to her.

When Mary ended her prophecy, she ascended into Heaven, and the abbot fulfilled her wishes for the next seven years. At the end of that time, "his soul was brought to God; he received his reward." Hoccleve assures us that whoever serves Our Lady will be "similarly requited." All that is needful is to say Our Lady's Psalter.

Anonymous Marian Lyrics in Middle English

Like their miracle tale counterparts, English poems to and about Mary were gathered relatively late—during the fourteenth century—in a large number of manuscripts. Lyrics could be found in "...liturgical manuscripts, hymnals and sermon notebooks.... [in] books of hours ... [and] in portable collections."[50] Like their Continental counterparts, English authors wrote lyrics on conventional themes like the Annunciation and Jesus' nativity. They described Mary at the foot of the cross, Mary assumed into Heaven, Mary crowned queen. Like their counterparts, too, they engaged in courtly banter, imitating secular forms such as the *pastourelle*, in which a knight rides out into the country seeking a rustic young woman to seduce. In a refutation of one such "country poem," the rider/seeker finds Mary, "my day's life, my night's bliss." The poet then describes the joys of Mary's life in a reversal of the conventional joys of worldly love.[51]

The tone of these lyrics is intimate, simultaneously personal and communal. Church unity would endure for another century or so, with Mary as its guiding star. One of the most famous Marian lyrics in Middle English was written about the Annunciation and Jesus' birth.

> I sing of a maiden
> Who is matchless:
> King of all kings
> For her son she chose.
>
> He came so gently
> Where his mother was,
> As dew in April
> That falls on the grass.
>
> He came so gently
> To his mother's bower
> As dew in April
> That falls on the flower.
>
> He came so gently
> To where his mother lay
> As dew in April
> That falls on the branch.
>
> Mother and maiden
> Was there none but she,
> Well may such a lady
> God's mother be.[52]

Mary is indeed "matchless," both in the sense of "one of a kind" and in the sense of "without a match" or mate. The second stanza declares that Mary chose Jesus to be her son, an assertion of her spirited response to the angel's invitation. The paradox (or oxymoron) of "maiden motherhood" emphasizes Mary's uniqueness and divine motherhood.

Other Nativity lyrics include lullabies for Jesus; in one long poem, a narrator recounts an exchange he has "heard" between Mary and Jesus that begins when the son asks his mother to sing a lullaby for him. Mary responds with a song about the Annunciation, ending with an account of the celestial celebration of Christ's birth and the wonderment of the shepherds. Jesus tells her that he will continue the song and foretells all the major events of his life as described in the Gospels, ending with his death and resurrection and the promise of the Holy Spirit. Jesus then promises to take his mother to Heaven: "I shall take thee when it is time / to me at the last / To be with me, Mother in bliss, / All this I foreordain."[53] The poet ends by saying that he heard this double lullaby as he lay awake on Christmas Day.

This lyric is notable not only for its foreshadowing, in a Nativity double lullaby, of the dialogue between Jesus and Mary as she stands at the foot of the cross, but—perhaps more importantly—for its matter-of-fact description of Mary's assumption, the ancient belief that would not be ratified by the church for another six hundred years. Five additional lyrics address Mary's assumption and coronation as Queen of Heaven. One, heavy with alliteration, addresses her—now assumed into Heaven—as

> God-bearer and daughter divine,
> Mother of mercy and maiden mellifluous,
> Devoid of deceit, dubbed in doctrine,
> Throne of the Trinity, entreat thou for us,
> Defend us from the dolorous dungeon [of Hell]
> And bring us to abide in bliss with thee,
> There to love our God most glorious.[54]

In addressing Mary as "Throne of the Trinity," the poet describes—perhaps unknowingly, perhaps deliberately—the depiction of Mary as a shrine-madonna (see "The Shrine-Madonnas" section in Chapter 6), a carved image of Mary that opens to reveal Christ's life, together with God the Father and the Holy Spirit. In any case, the poem dares what doctrine avoids.

A few poems are dual-language poems, using English to carry the message and French or Latin for the refrain. One of the most famous dual-language poems describes a vision of Mary as a courtly lover wooing a sinner. Mary laments the state of humankind, wishing to be its advocate

"Quia amore langueo," "Because I languish for love." She steadfastly seeks out sinners, hoping to bring them to her son, assuring them that she is their mother, Christ their brother. The poem ends with her assuring the sinner:

> My help is your own, creep under my wing;
> Your sister's a queen, your brother's a king,
> Your heritage is assured: Son, come claim it;
> Take me for your wife and learn to sing,
> Because I languish for love.[55]

What is the Narrative/Poetic Theology of These Works?

During the twelfth and thirteenth centuries, story and song continued the tradition of personal devotion to Mary as authorship expanded from the cloister to the secular world. King or commoner, writing under their own names or under an umbrella of anonymity, authors carried on the tradition of exalting Mary's person and promulgating her miraculous powers of healing body and soul. Although the specter of the Devil lurks in the background (except in the artisan monk's story, where he is prominent), his power is not as manifest in Marian tales of this period as it was formerly. (In Dante's work, of course, he is confined to Hell.) Nonetheless, human weakness ensures the need for Mary's ministrations.

Jacobus and his enormously popular legends represent two strands of Marian miracle stories: one focusing on her power and agency, often subverting received dogma; the other exhorting the hearers of her stories to greater faithfulness to the church and its orthodoxies. Often entwined, the two strands hold the promise of a Holy One who involves herself—indeed, invests herself—in the spiritual and material struggles of all sorts of people, leading them to her son.

English Marian lyrics, developing later in the tradition, combine orthodoxy with poignant expressions of personal devotion and courtly fervor. Dante sees Mary in the center of the celestial rose, closest of any human being to God in the person of her son. His image serves as a metaphor for her presence in song and story during the Middle Ages: As the closest to God, she reflects the Love that animates the universe as she advocates for humankind. The salvation story is not confined to chapel and monastery in the country or shrine and cathedral in the city. Mary and Jesus reach every level of human life, ready to redeem and revive.

The enormity of Mary's importance in the Middle Ages was captured by a poet (François Villon, disappeared 1453) who exemplified the reprobates who called on her. A Master of Arts in theology(!), Villon was a convicted felon as well as a consummate poet. In the *ballade* below, he projects onto his own mother (in whose voice the poem is written) the religious fervor of his time and culture, assuming his audience's familiarity with the tales of two reformed sinners. In this poem Mary transcends the limitations endured by women of that era, represented by the poem's narrator; as "High Goddess" Mary rules over and encompasses both the "painted Paradise" and the "Hell where the damned are boiling"—not only on the ceiling of the cathedral but in the infinity of the universe. Villon's story theology—which encapsulates the story theology of the age—finds expression in a stunning image of the relationship between Mary and Jesus and their mutual redemption of the world. In this last great medieval Marian lyric, we have a glimpse of her power, already fading, that will eventually disappear behind images of a placid, sweet madonna or a fainting and distraught mother.

François Villon's *Ballade of Prayer to Notre Dame*[56]

Lady of Heaven, regent of the earth,
Empress even of the swamps of Hell,
Receive me as your humble Christian
So I may be counted with your chosen ones
Although I never have been worthy.
Your gifts of mercy, my lady and my mistress,
Are so much greater than my sins!
Without those gifts no soul deserves
Or enters Heaven—I'm not just blabbing on, here—and
In this faith I wish to live and die.

Say to your Son that I am His,
Through Him let all my sins be blotted out.
May He forgive me as he did the woman of Egypt[57]
Or as he did Theophilus the cleric
Who through you was acquitted and absolved
Although he'd promised his soul to the Devil.
Save me from ever doing that,
Virgin bearing without breakage of her body
The sacrament we celebrate at Mass—
In this faith I wish to live and die.

I'm a poor old woman, little and unlearned,
Who knows nothing and can't read a word.
At the church where I'm a parishioner I see
A painted Paradise with harps and lutes

And Hell where all the damned are boiled;
One makes me fearful, the other joyful and light-hearted.
Make me be joyful, high goddess,
To whom all sinners have recourse,
Filled up with faith, without pretense or laziness,
In this faith I wish to live and die.

Most worthy Virgin, princess, you bore
Jesus reigning without end or cease.
The All-Powerful, taking on our weakness,
Left the heavens and came down to help us,
Offered his priceless youth to death—
Such is our Lord, such I confess Him to be, and
In this faith I wish to live and die.

Chapter 6

From Story to Drama to Anecdote
The Miracle Tales Evolve

The Holy Kinship as Romance

Jacobus' Marian genealogy enlarged her family tree and seems to have influenced, if not inspired, a thirteenth- or fourteenth-century French prequel to the story of Mary's mother Anne, an exotic hybrid of hagiography and romance.[1] Its anonymous author was undoubtedly a cleric, given his opening statement: Unlike a worldly storyteller, who amuses audiences with sinful songs and profane tales, he will pray for those who listen to him. Like Jacobus, he uses familiar figures, but he adds his own fairy-tale details and romantic flourishes, producing a remarkable hybrid.[2] Below is my account of this peculiar tale.

The Romance of Saint Fanuel and Saint Anne

The story begins a thousand years after God ordered the Tree of Paradise to be uprooted following the sin of Adam and Eve. The Tree is not dead, however; God has sent a cutting to Abraham to plant in his garden. Abraham does so, and the cutting produces a new tree, which bears a flower of indescribable beauty. One day God reveals to Abraham that this tree will be the source of the wood for the cross on which Jesus will be crucified, and from the tree's flower will be born a *chevalier* who will be the ancestor of the Son of God.

Abraham has a beautiful young daughter, who loves walking in her father's garden. One day the girl passes by the sacred tree and plucks its flower, which gives off such a powerful perfume that she becomes pregnant simply from its smell. Her mother discovers her condition and assumes that she is guilty of extramarital relations and hence in peril of being

Chapter 6. From Story to Drama to Anecdote   129

stoned to death; the young woman protests her innocence and offers to submit to an ordeal by fire to prove it.[3] Although Abraham and his wife want to hide the scandal in any case, two servants gossip about it, and soon the whole city knows. Accused and then condemned to be burned at the stake, the young woman says a prayer before she enters the fire, citing prophecies of a savior born of a virgin and pleading for God's intervention on her behalf. Her innocence is proved when a miracle transforms the sparks and flames into a flock of singing birds and the burning coals into thousands of multicolored roses and lilies. Those who wanted the child to be burned alive are themselves consumed with flames, and the site planned for her martyrdom becomes a *champ fleuri*, a field of flowers; the author claims that God will hold the Last Judgment there.

Her family wishes her to marry a powerful knight, but she declines in favor of "the Lord who made the flowers" and delivered her from the flames. In time she gives birth to a son, "delivered of the flower which she carried." She names him Fanuel.

Fanuel grows up to be a good and pious man—so good and so gifted that he becomes king—visiting prisoners, giving shelter to the poor, and reviving the ill. In his orchard, a marvelous apple tree bears fruit that heals all sickness, and one day, while Fanuel is peeling such an apple, he wipes his knife on his thigh, cutting himself. His thigh swells terribly, causing him great pain, and eventually produces a child: a girl named Anna. Aghast, he orders that the child be taken into the forest and killed, but the man assigned to the task is stopped by a pure white dove that perches on the child's shoulder. "Friend," says the dove, "wait a little, hold back that blow. From this child will be born a virgin in whom God will take on flesh and blood when He comes to earth." Instead of killing her, the man abandons her in an empty swan's nest but reports to Fanuel that he has disposed of her.

God provides for Anna, sending her nourishment brought by a splendid deer whose antlers are crowned with flowers. Ten years go by, and one day the king goes hunting with his seneschal, Joachim. Joachim spies and pursues the marvelous deer, aiming to kill it. The deer halts beside Anna's nest, and just as Joachim is about to spear the creature, Anne cries, "Vassal, let the beast alone! It is not yours to kill." Joachim asks her if she is the king's daughter, and she tells him her name, asking that her father come to her. Fanuel does so, and she tells him about the kindness of his servant in sparing her as well as the divine provisions that have been made for her. Joachim, enchanted with her beauty and noble bearing, asks to marry her, and Fanuel consents.

From that point on, the story follows the tradition of the *Protogospel*, telling of Anna and Joachim's long-unfulfilled wish for a child, the angel's announcement to Anna, and Mary's extraordinary birth. The author adds his own embellishments to Mary's first appearance in the world: The newborn holds in her right hand three letters of gold. Jewish leaders visit Joachim to see the child and the golden letters; they threaten that if Anna and her child abolish the Law, she must be put to death. Saint Abraham intervenes and explains to them the significance of the letters: The first indicates that she will remain a virgin all her life; the second signifies that she will have only one child, who will be her son and father; the third shows that this child will be king of the entire world. Mary herself "will be powerful, she will be the remedy of all ills and also the door of Paradise, through which she will lead all her friends." The author then adds his account of Saint Anne's three marriages.[4] Following extracanonical sources through the lives of both Jesus and Mary, the tale ends with Mary's death and assumption.

Trees and flowers flourish throughout this romance, beginning with the Tree of Paradise. Its shoot reflects the "root of Jesse" in Isaiah 11:1, and its flower produces a virgin birth in Fanuel (whose name, the author asserts, means "born of a flower"). Both the conception and virgin birth of Saint Fanuel by the daughter of Abraham and that of Saint Anne by Fanuel anticipate the miraculous conception of Mary. Flowers are showered on the daughter of Abraham, who has conceived through a flower; Fanuel's daughter, immaculately conceived through the agency of an apple (a life-giving fruit, as opposed to the apple of Paradise), is nurtured by a flower-bearing deer. With its accounts of extraordinary conceptions for both Mary and her mother, this peculiar text—a mixture of folk and fairy tale, extracanonical story and legend—makes virginal conception a family tradition, establishing Saint Anne as the worthy matriarch of a family that includes the Son of God.[5]

The Shrine-Madonnas[6]

One of the most daring and suggestive images of Mary as the Mother of God appears in a series of medieval sculptures called *vierges ouvrantes*, or "opening Virgins," in French; *virgenes abrideras* in Spanish; and *schreinmadonnas* in German. Fashioned of wood for the most part, and lavishly decorated and gilded inside and out, these images date from the thirteenth through the sixteenth centuries. Like other statues, some depict Mary sitting on a throne, dressed in flowing robes and holding Jesus: These represent her as the *sedes sapientiae*, or Seat of Wisdom. Other shrine-madonnas show her standing with Jesus on one arm. One image shows her pregnant, perhaps as the patroness of mothers-to-be; she is seated on a throne that could, perhaps, double as a birthing-stool.

Chapter 6. From Story to Drama to Anecdote   131

In all of these images, there is a cut in the wood from Our Lady's neck to her feet that allows her body to open into a triptych, revealing, in its center, either a figure of Jesus or—more often—the entire Trinity in her womb, where the Father holds a crucifix with the body of Jesus and the Holy Spirit appears as a dove above his head. On either side of the Trinity are two wings or panels on which are painted—or, in some larger statues, carved—scenes from the lives of Christ and Mary; angels and saints; and congregations of the faithful, both clerical and lay.

Shrine-madonnas seem to have responded to a medieval "[c]ommonplace to call Mary the bride or chamber of the Trinity so as to celebrate the fulness of the Godhead dwelling in her soul. As a fifteenth-century Frenchwoman prayed, '[I]t was for sinners that the Father, Son, and Holy Spirit wished to lodge themselves in you. For this reason, sweet lady, it befits you to be the advocate or poor sinners, and for this you are the chamber of the whole Trinity.'"[7]

Despite (or maybe because of) the popularity of the shrine-madonna, and despite her presence in churches, convents, and homes "[f]rom Portugal to Poland, and as far north as England and Sweden,"[8] the very concept seemed threatening to the hierarchy. In time, the image would be condemned.

Over the course of the thirteenth and fourteenth centuries, Marian stories began to change, as we've seen in Chapter 5. A major factor was the increasing insistence of the church on instructing the faithful on doctrines to believe and church rules to follow. The church now required belief that during the Mass, bread and wine were changed "by divine power" into the body and blood of Christ. (The "divine power" of transubstantiation, as it is called, remains exclusive to priests.) The church also prescribed annual confession and Holy Communion, emphasizing the importance of these sacraments in the hour of death.

The church's emphasis on educating both clergy and laity influenced two religious orders in particular: the Franciscans, founded in 1209 by Saint Francis, and the Dominicans, founded in 1215 by Saint Dominic. This educational emphasis is apparent in Dominican bishop Jacobus of Voragine's *Golden Legend*; reproduced in hundreds of manuscripts, his enormously popular work appealed to people during the "calamitous fourteenth century,"[9] an era not unlike our own with its plagues, wars, bad or divided governments, corruption, religious and secular divisions, insurrections, and active schism in the Catholic church. During this century, Mary's voice diminished as she began to became the more retiring woman of "traditional" story and song and the sorrowful mother of popular devotion.

The fifteenth century, overshadowed by the devastation of the

Hundred Years' War, saw a concerted effort by the French cleric Jean Gerson (1363–1429) to abolish the shrine-madonnas, which were now found throughout Europe. Chancellor of the University of Paris, Gerson delivered a sermon condemning the imagery of the "opening Virgin," saying that the opened statue could lead to error because it looked as if the entire Trinity had taken on human flesh in Mary. Gerson objected to the "... sheer goddess-like grandeur and autonomy of [the 'opening Virgin']—not to mention the female mystics who emulated her and aspired in their turn to become the Trinity's brides."[10] Consequently, he began a campaign to foster devotion to Saint Joseph as the father of the Holy Family and the protector of both Mary and Jesus. He wrote a treatise on Jesus' stepfather and letters encouraging the establishment of a feast day celebrating Mary's and Joseph's marriage. An epic poem and several liturgical compositions for such a feast served to promote "the patriarchal family."[11] Gerson began the process of "domesticating" Mary that would continue and grow throughout the Reformation and beyond. It's significant that at this time statues of Joseph with the child Jesus began to appear: Mary's husband holds Jesus in his left arm, as she did, and his right hand holds a lily, the symbol of perpetual chastity traditionally assigned to Mary. Gerson's "campaign to replace the Marian Trinity with the Holy Family—to bring the Virgin safely back to earth, where she could be tamed and domesticated by her husband"[12]—would be all too successful in the next centuries.

Shrine-Madonna, closed. Shrine of the Virgin, German, c. 1300. Gift of J. Pierpont Morgan, 1917, Metropolitan Museum of Art.

Chapter 6. From Story to Drama to Anecdote

Shrine-Madonna, open. Shrine of the Virgin, German, c. 1300 Gift of J. Pierpont Morgan, 1917, Metropolitan Museum of Art.

Meanwhile, a defining characteristic of the later Middle Ages was the clerical and popular embrace of "affective piety," a dedication to participating emotionally, through prayer, reading, and contemplation, in the events of Jesus' life, particularly his passion and death.[13] The practice encouraged identification with the suffering of both Jesus and Mary, using images and imagination to participate in Christ's final hours and Mary's anguished accompaniment. (This kind of spiritual exercise had long been practiced in Eastern Christianity; remember the *kontakia* of Romanos the Melodist and the Marian *Lives* of the tenth century, especially that of Symeon Metaphrastes.) One way to engage the audience—emotionally as well as spiritually—was through drama.

Affective Piety Dramatized:
The Miracles of Our Lady Performed

During the fourteenth century, a Parisian goldsmiths' guild sponsored a series of 40 plays between 1339 and 1382, in which Mary's primary role is that of Queen of Heaven and partner of God.[14] In 13 of the first 19 plays, God is absent from the stage, while Mary and her attending angels, Gabriel and Raphael, act in the name of Heaven.

In these plays, called *The Miracles of Our Lady Performed*, Mary restores a saint's lost hand and another man's eyesight; brings back a soul from purgatory; and resuscitates a dead priest who had excommunicated a man so that the cleric may lift the ban that condemned her repentant sinner to Hell. Her roles include those of protector, helper, intercessor, and rescuer; she issues her own commands as well as God's. She also restores to life a murdered young woman as well as the baby of a weary mother in the following play.

A Baby Restored to Life
The Miracles of Our Lady Performed[15]

"The Miracle of the Child Restored to Life" portrays a devoted but childless couple.[16] Prayers to the Virgin occur early in this work; the chambermaid says a Hail Mary, the barren woman's husband pleads for a child to the "Treasure of Consolation, Sovereign Lady of the heavens," and his wife asks the same favor from the "most sweet and honored Virgin who bore the Fruit of Life itself." God and Our Lady enter at the end of her prayer.

God's speech gives the audience a premonition of the mixed blessing that a favorable answer to prayer can bring: "The woman has conceived a child, and whether it will bring her happiness or harm I shall not tell you. But it will be for the salvation of them both." The couple forget about God's words after their beautiful infant son is born, and the father leaves on a pilgrimage of thanksgiving. While he is gone, the weary mother takes a bath with her child and falls asleep in the tub. The baby slips from her grasp and drowns.

Imprisoned and condemned to death by burning for her negligence, the mother realizes the doleful possibilities created by God's favor, saying, "It appears that I didn't know what I asked for, since the answer to my prayer, the one thing that I received, brought me shame and sorrow and death here on earth." Still, she prays to Our Lady, and when her husband arrives home on the eve of her execution, he adds his prayers to hers, saying that the child has cost him too dearly. Mary appears and reassures him, saying that the baby's death is only a trial and that God will give him such joy that it will make up doubly for what he has suffered.

As Mary has promised, the prayers of husband and wife are heard. At the very hour when she is to meet her death (recalling the last phrase of the "Hail Mary," a plea for the Virgin to be present "at the hour of our death"), the woman asks to see her dead child once more, and after a prayer to Mary, she kisses her son good-bye. At her kiss, he begins to cry, and she calls upon the crowd assembled for her execution to "consider the favor that God and the Virgin Mary have shown here today. My child lives—just listen to him howl!"

After the baby revives, it's obvious to the townspeople and the court, as well as the count presiding at the failed execution, that Mary has worked the miracle: The count responds to the child's cry with an address to Mary. "Sweet and merciful Virgin," he says, "We must serve and praise you with all our hearts." From her seat in Heaven, Mary gives credit to God; but the audience knows (and probably God knows) that it was she who gave back life and hope to three of her children.

* * *

The miracle play summarized below features many of the dramatic elements that a medieval audience would appreciate: a demonic promise, a family torn asunder, a trio of pious hermits, and a legal disputation between Mary and a devilish duo. In this play and others, the Devil and his minions appear as *diablotins*, a diminutive name indicating their powerlessness against the might of the Virgin. "The Miracle of the Child Promised to the Devil" is also a parable of the power of the Eucharist, the communion wafer transformed into the body and blood of Christ.[17]

The Miracle of the Child Promised to the Devil
The Miracles of Our Lady Performed[18]

In the first scene, a married noblewoman, Sybille, and her spouse Guy[19] make a vow of chastity to Our Lady. Lurking in the background, two devils vow with equal fervor to make them break their promise. For a time they remain chaste, but eventually, tempted beyond his strength, Guy declares that he wants to make love despite their vow. Sybille is appalled. "You're crazy," she says. "If we do, and if I conceive," she swears in a fury, "I'll give the child to the Devil." Because of his physical strength, the husband prevails. Both of them beg Mary's pardon, but the deed is done, and the devils rejoice: Man and wife have been ensnared. They are doomed.

Nine months later, the disconsolate pair pray to Mary for help as their neighbor Erembourc delivers the child, a handsome son. At the moment when the boy is to be baptized, however, a devil appears: "You speak too soon," he says. "This child is mine; he'll never be a Christian." The distraught mother begs the devil to let her have him for seven years, and he consents. Sadly she and her husband leave the boy—unbaptized and therefore unnamed—with their neighbor, and Sybille tells Mary that she will die of sorrow if her heavenly mother doesn't come to their aid. Indeed, Mary does: She descends from Heaven with Gabriel and Michael singing her praises. "My sister," says Mary, "You have had such great faith in me that I can't fail you." She assures Sybille of her help with a prayer to Jesus that their son will grow stronger and wiser than his peers. She then returns to Paradise, leaving the couple grateful and amazed.

Seven years later, the two devils come for the child; again, Sybille asks for more time. Now, however, the devils demand a written agreement, signed and sealed, that she will hand over her son—still unbaptized—after eight years. "Get out of my sight," she tells them, "but never fear, I'll do what I have to do." Once again they leave, this time clutching the document with her signature.

When at last Sybille and her husband visit their son, they find that he has the stature and the learning of someone far beyond his years. They can only hope that he may find a way of escaping the evil that awaits him. Understandably, their son does not recognize either of them when Sybille greets him tearfully, saying that she has not known a day of joy since his birth. In turn, he tells his parents that he has been treated badly—like an unbeliever, he says—and he vows not to eat again until he knows the reason for his mother's sorrow. Guy tells the sad tale of the vow of chastity; of his desire to break it, and Sybille's fateful oath to the Enemy; of the child's birth and their wish to baptize him. "The devils said that if you were baptized, they would strangle both you and your mother; they came again when you were seven, but the Virgin, source of all grace and mercy, forced Satan to give you eight more years."

"May the gracious Virgin be praised," says the son. "And what is the last year of my respite?" "It has been 14 years," replies his mother. "Next year I must deliver you up to Satan."

Immediately the boy decides to go to Rome and be baptized there to avoid the Devil, asking his parents for their prayers as he will pray for them. All of them depart: the son for the Holy City, and the parents for a pilgrimage to Mary's shrine in Boulogne,[20] where they will beg Mary and her son for their salvation.

Arriving in Rome, the son tells the story of his parents' transgression and his mother's ill-considered vow. He begs the Pope for help in escaping the devils' power, and the Holy Father sends him to the care of a hermit,

Chapter 6. From Story to Drama to Anecdote 137

the Pope's own confessor, but warns him that he will have much woe and hardship before he reaches his goal. The Holy Father gives him a letter to carry with him; he and his cardinals then send the boy on his way with their prayers, asking Mary and her son to protect him.

The young man's journey, anguished and slow, takes him to not one but three hermits, all of whom are so holy that they receive their food at the hand of the angel Gabriel. To the first hermit the boy confesses that the Enemy is following him, watching and waiting to entrap him. The hermit reassures him that the Devil will never have power over him and shares his heavenly repast with the boy, afterward sending him—with another letter—to a second hermit "better than I" for protection and guidance. "Be assured," the hermit says, "that your difficulty is being taken care of."

The archangel Michael visits the second hermit, giving him celestial food for two, and the holy man welcomes the weary traveler in the name of Mary. "Brother," says the young man, "please read this letter and tell me if I have still farther to go, for I haven't much time left before the Devil claims me." Boy and hermit eat the food that Michael has brought; "Son," declares the hermit, "this food has come from Paradise, and it brings grace to those it feeds." Again the holy man sends the boy onward to another hermit, this one named Honnoré, the wisest of them all, who will see to his salvation. Understandably, the young man is disappointed: "I'd hoped to stay here to finish my penance," he says, "And now I'm sent on again to the ends of the earth." "So it is, friend," replies the hermit, "but the Virgin will wipe all sin from your heart so that Satan loses his right to you." Encouraged, the young man goes on his way, giving thanks to Mary.

Honnoré, too, receives an angelic visit from Gabriel, who provides him with nourishment for himself and the guest who will soon arrive. The young man reaches the hermitage exhausted but greets the hermit graciously and presents his letter. "I know quite well what it contains," says Honnoré calmly. "How much respite have you from the Enemy?" "I'll be taken tomorrow," replies the boy, "unless you and the Virgin help me." "Because you have placed soul and body into the care of the Virgin Mary," Honnoré tells him, "she will be your true friend, and I'll pray for you from the bottom of my heart." The boy himself asks Mary to have pity on him, but no sooner does he finish his prayer than a group of devils gathers around them.

"You've led me a merry chase," says one little devil, "but I'll make you pay dearly for all my trouble." Terrified, the young man calls upon Mary for protection, but the demons claim that she can't help him "because she doesn't want to do an injustice"—that is, deprive them of the soul promised by Sybille.

Honnoré calls on the Mother of God to answer his prayer, and Our

Lady appears, chastising the devils for their presumption. "Set your snare somewhere else," she scolds. "Do you think you can take one of my family by your fraud? You'll regret it if you ever lay hands on him." "Look here, Lady," says one of the devils. "Let's take this to your Son for judgment. If he rules against us, we'll leave the boy to you." Mary agrees, drawing the young man to her with a tender acknowledgment of all that he and his parents have suffered, and shooing the devils away from her as they prepare to meet God.

"Welcome, dear Mother," says God. "Where have you been so long?" Mary presents the young man, saying that the devils have taken him for their own. "Grant us justice," say the devils: "He was given to us fifteen years ago, and now Your mother wants to take him from us." The devils then present their case: The child was conceived in sin, his mother asked for and was granted respite twice, and now they claim their gift.

Mary retorts, "Have you found the law to support your claim? I don't think so. Dear Son, listen to me. Even Hell is Yours and mine, and no one can give away something of Yours if it's not in his possession. His mother had no right to give him away." "Hold on," says one of the devils, "I have a document here, with my seal on it. Look at it and believe me." "It's not worth a pear," says Mary. "Give it here, let me look at it." She returns it, calling him foolish and crazy: The document is in tatters, and they have written and sealed it just to deceive her son. Not so, responds the Devil, Mary herself is the one who damaged it, and now it's time to render judgment.

God asks the Devil if the father of the child was present to give his son away. He was present at the promise and didn't contradict it, says the Evil One. At this, Mary begs God to have pity on the boy for love of her, and God gives His verdict: "Satan, I say to you that a wife cannot give what she has without the consent of her husband. This 'gift' is null and void because the father did not give his permission. The child stays with Us; you've wasted your efforts."

The devils snivel that God is always their enemy, that He doesn't dare go against His mother's wishes or He'll be punished, and may God have nothing but grief from their failure, while the delighted young man praises Mary for the grace of his deliverance and begs for baptism. Mary requests that Honnoré baptize the young man, and he consents. God Himself gives the youth a baptismal name, saying to Mary, "Mother, he'll be called Sauveur (Savior) because he has been saved by you."

In a grand finale, Mary and her son become Sauveur's godparents, to the accompaniment of angels' songs, and the boy and Honnoré join the other two hermits in celebrating with Sybille and Guy, all of them praising God and Mary.

* * *

The minions of evil are not always obvious; they can take different forms. In earlier works, they may appear as animals, as hideous hybrid creatures, or even as saints in order to threaten or tempt their prey. Demons, named or anonymous, are primary antagonists in one-fourth of *The Miracles of Our Lady Performed*, and my retelling below of the drama of Saint John the Hermit shows the Devil in disguise while exposing the dangers that can arise in a hermitage. (No fools, those medieval authors.) The sources of this story lie deep in the legends surrounding those solitary souls who retired from the world to avoid temptation but found—like Saint Anthony—that temptation followed them.

Like the *Romance of Saint Fanuel*, this tale shows the influence of folklore.

The Devil in Disguise: The Miracle of Saint John the Hermit
The Miracles of Our Lady Performed[21]

In contrast to the early appearance of God and Mary in "The Baby Brought Back to Life," the first otherworldly being to appear in "The Miracle of Saint John the Hermit" is the Devil, who arrives in the first scene complaining that John is too holy. Disguised as a helpful servant, Huet by name, "the Enemy" is accepted by the hermit and even becomes a kind of confidant. Huet's dark malevolence looms over much of the play, making the hermit's forest dwelling seem godless rather than godly. When the king's daughter becomes lost near the hermitage, she prays to Mary for comfort and solace. There is no indication that her prayers have been heard, for the first person she meets is the diabolical Huet, and neither she nor John can resist the Devil's power. Tempted by the presence of the young woman, John prays to Mary also: "Ah, Queen of Heaven, in these woods I thought to attain salvation, but instead I have incurred my everlasting damnation unless you come to my aid, good Virgin in whose grace I hope." Heaven and its queen are silent; urged on by the devil, John rapes and then kills the young woman, throwing her body into a well.

Despairing, John realizes that God may damn him; only through Mary, he believes, can he find salvation. He resolves to live like an animal in the hollow of a tree.

After seven years, God hears John's prayers and sends Mary to say that he will be pardoned. The tree in which he has enclosed himself—as one "dead to the world" of human beings—becomes a tree of life as Our Lady, again described as she "who bore the sweet fruit of Life," approaches it with her archangels. John is suspicious of the vision, but Mary reassures him, promising him "such great benefits as will move you to marvel." He emerges from the womb-like hollow of the tree at the call of a child, also named John.[22] Answering the child, John is ready to confess his sin and join the human race once more. At his confession, the king forgives him; John then asks Mary in her mercy to let them see the young woman he has murdered. God tells him to call to her in the well; he does, and she replies. Her father's first response is, "Ah, sweet Lady, glorious Virgin, my heart leaps for joy!" The young woman reveals that she has been with Mary all this time, and the king promises John a bishopric, thanking Mary.

The Virgin's role in this play is to balance with mercy and favor what has been lost through sin and its punishment. She has transformed the tree-hollow into a place where life is regained: John emerges reborn, attesting to Mary's ability to renew life, both natural and supernatural.

* * *

By 1382, when the last of the plays was presented, Mary's presence had all but faded from the scene. Her powerful roles of restorer, protector, intercessor, and helper diminished to mere cameo appearances: In the last play, her lines amount to only five percent of the play's total verses,[23] while the elaborate poems that accompanied those dramas—written for a competition—served to reinforce conventional doctrinal images of Mary as Virgin and Mother.

A Prescient Trend

Writing about a century after Gautier de Coinci finished his tale and several years before the first of the miracle plays, in about 1321, a clerical lawyer of Bayeux wrote the most extensive—and arguably the most dramatic—account of Mary's defense of humankind against the claims of the Devil in a long narrative poem called "L'Advocacie Nostre Dame," or "Our Lady's Advocacy."[24] The title recalls a Marian prayer, the "Salve Regina," or "Hail, Holy Queen," which calls on the mother of Jesus, "our life, our sweetness, and our hope," and asks her as "our most gracious advocate" to "turn [her] eyes of mercy towards us."[25] The work dramatizes that prayer: Reverberations of cosmic time echo throughout this tale, situated in an eternal present that reaches back to the era of Genesis and deals with the salvation of souls long after the time of the Crucifixion. Satan's claim to the souls of humankind begins with the story of Adam and Eve's fall. According to the extracanonical fourth-century *Gospel of Nicodemus,* the Devil held captive in Hell all those who had died since the Fall. After his death and before his resurrection, however, Christ descended into Hell and delivered the souls held in captivity, thus depriving Satan of what the Devil considered to be his.[26] Combining law and theology, the author depicts Mary as both brilliant and manipulative. The Virgin in this work is a figure of power; her advocacy is conflated with that of the Holy Spirit, the advocate or counselor promised by Christ in John 14:26. However, she is also portrayed as a dramatically emotional mother, all too similar to her frail earthly sisters; and she is seen as succumbing to an all-too-human propensity to manipulate males (in this case, God the Father and Jesus) to accomplish her will. This view of Mary and of women in general would become increasingly influential over time. My synopsis appears below.

Our Lady's Day in Court, or Why She Is Called Our Advocate
Anonymous

"Our Lady's Advocacy" describes a trial in which Jesus is judge; Satan appears on behalf of the plaintiffs, denizens of Hell; and Mary acts as advocate for the defense. Satan seeks justice from the court for having been deprived of the right to his share of souls, won by Hell and lost to God, as he claims, through the sin of Adam and Eve. After Jesus rebuffs his attempt to bring a criminal suit against the human race, Satan presents a power of attorney from Hell authorizing him to proceed in a civil suit; Jesus accepts it and sets the court date for Good Friday.

Mary as Queen of Heaven hears from her court about Satan's lawsuit and the lack of a defense attorney. She reassures the saints and angels that they need "have no fear. You will see me quite prepared to be an advocate, and I will do whatever it takes to defeat the Devil." She is described as one "who is so wise and learned that she is afraid of nothing, not the Devil nor his followers." When Satan arrives in court, he claims not to see a defendant; Mary declares herself and demands his credentials. She refutes Satan's claim that she should not be admitted as advocate because she is a woman and the Judge's mother, saying that she "can defend all three orders which make up the entire Human Race [virgins, the married, and the celibate]" and therefore should be allowed to do so. In a council of Heaven parallel to the council of Hell that had given Satan his credentials as a prosecutor, Mary accepts the role of advocate for humankind.

To Satan's demands that he be put back in "peaceful possession" of the souls, Mary responds with invective, calling him "dishonest, a son of iniquity, evil one, stinking of smoke, this villainous, filthy lawyer." She reminds Satan that he could not "in good faith own something belonging to another," to which Satan retorts that "if anyone wanted to believe this lady, no one would ever enter Hell." Pulling a sulphurous Bible out of his belly-pouch and quoting Genesis, he points out Adam and Eve's mortal sin of disobedience and challenges Jesus: "Are you not justice and truth? Stand by your words, then, and condemn Adam and his descendants." But Mary observes that Satan deceived the pair and says that he cannot profit from his fraud.

The Virgin asks God to deny the Devil's claim, and although Satan is expert in canon and civil law, Mary proves to be an effective defense counsel. To prove her case during her verbal battle with Satan, Mary cites customary law and Roman law as well as canon law and papal decretals. For more than half the proceedings, Mary conducts herself as a highly capable advocate, poised, learned, and skillful. A little more than halfway through the process, however, the author's voice declares in a clerical bass that

Everyone knows that by her nature,
Woman is a frail creature
and that she is easily frightened and made afraid....
When she saw Satan standing firm
She began weeping with anguish;
... wringing her hands, trembling,
shuddering and sobbing, becoming heated, breaking out in drops of perspiration![27]

When her adversary persists, she moans and tears her robe, showing her son the breasts that nourished him, and throws herself on her knees, appealing to him as his mother. She closes her emotional arguments (made, as the author notes, "like a mother teaching her child"), with the passionate threat: "If you listen to the Devil / rather than your mother or her party, / then take me out of the Book of Life!"[28]

Mary's emotional extravaganza tends to subvert the author's previous depiction of her as rational and erudite; although the arguments she makes afterward are persuasive, they lack the vigor and power of her previous statements. With the encouragement of her divine son, however, she resumes her previous mode of refuting Satan's arguments, stating that Christ's death on the cross outweighed the world's sin, and that when humans repent, God shows mercy.

As they go back and forth, Satan quotes John 13:30 and insists that as "Prince of this world" he should at least have the souls of sinners as his share; Mary responds that shares of good and evil were assigned on Good Friday, when Christ's sacrifice outweighed the world's sin; Satan did not appeal that verdict, and now it should be considered as already judged. The Devil is not finished. If he and his rebel angels were condemned for their disobedience, why not the Human Race? Mary replies that angels sinned against their nature and acted out of malice, envy, and desire. In contrast, it was the human body, continually warring with the soul, that proved to be Adam's fatal weakness. "Man," she states, "was wounded by fragility, but when the Devil sinned, it was out of pure evil, acting against his nature."

Satan tries a final ploy. Adam sinned beyond measure against God and should be condemned eternally for coveting Godhead. Mary responds that Christ's suffering "countered the offense," and Jesus elaborates: "If the fault was infinite and no man can give satisfaction forever, because he must die, then I, who am man and God together, and without end, can provide satisfaction." Mary concludes, "And if any poor sinner makes amends, as soon as he repents, God forgets the sin." Jesus then announces his verdict: "All those of the Human Race who have repented and confessed in devotion, and died in contrition, will remain with Us forever." The Devil is defeated; the court rejoices, saying, "Ah, our gentle lady advocate, you cannot ever be checkmated, but indeed you checkmate all the devils!" Angels and saints then intone the *Salve Regina*, "Hail, Holy Queen."

A Dramatic "Life of Mary" in the Middle English N-Town Plays

Written in the last half of the fifteenth century for performance by guilds (like the earlier Parisian plays), a series of "N-Town" dramas and pageants interpreted the Bible and Christian doctrine to the faithful of England's East Anglia.[29] (The title "N-Town" comes from the generic proclamation that preceded each play: As the performers traveled from place to place, they could insert the name [*Nomen*] of a particular town to make the announcement specific.) Beginning with the creation of Heaven and the fall of the rebel angels in Play 1, the series ends with the Last Judgment in Play 42. Thirteen, or nearly one-third, of the plays feature Mary as a principal character, from Play 7 ("The Root of Jesse and Prophecies of the Savior" and the story of Joachim and Anna [Play 8] to Mary's Assumption [Play 41]).

The compiler was evidently a cleric who drew freely from *The Golden Legend* for a significant number of plot elements as well as dialogue. Stage directions and biblical quotations are written in Latin; celestial figures often speak Latin, as does Mary when she recites the Magnificat in *The Mary Play* (described below). In addition to conventional characters, real and fictitious, the plays feature allegorical figures, or personifications of virtues and ideas. Both canonical and extracanonical sources inform the dialogues in these plays: the *Protogospel* and *Pseudo-Matthew* as well as the biblical accounts of Luke and Matthew. In Play 15, "The Nativity," the palm tree from *Pseudo-Matthew* that had bent down to give Mary its fruit becomes a cherry tree: "Look how the cherries grow on the tree yonder," says Mary. "I would gladly have some if it would please you to labor so much for me." Joseph replies that he will certainly try, but the tree is high and not easily climbed. "Therefore," says Joseph grumpily, "let the one who got you with child pick cherries for you." Mary asks the tree to bend down to her, and it does; Joseph, chastened, acknowledges God as the father of the child in her womb.[30] This play, too, features the unbelieving midwife (here called Zelomy, a variant of Salome) who is then harshly convinced of Mary's virginity—but cured, in this case, after Mary instructs her to touch the baby Jesus' swaddling clothes.

The Mary Play is a microcosm of the world dramatized in the N-Town plays, with its characters biblical, extracanonical, and allegorical, all of them interpreters of both story and belief. In *The Mary Play*, a stand-alone composite of several episodes in the N-town series,[31] the figure of Contemplation introduces the subject and summarizes the actions to follow. The action proceeds from Mary's conception, through her time in the Temple and marriage to Joseph, to the Annunciation, concluding with her visit to Elizabeth.

Preceding the Annunciation, an entirely new set of characters appears in what is called the Parliament of Heaven. Originating in a sermon on the Annunciation by Bernard of Clairvaux (1092–1153), the episode encapsulates the medieval belief that original sin was so great that humanity required an equally great redeemer (as depicted in the *Advocacie Nostre Dame* above). To illustrate this belief, Bernard developed a parable based on Psalm 85:10: "Mercy and truth have met; justice and peace have kissed." Bernard used this "prayer for the restoration of God's favor"[32] as the basis for his story about the Redemption: Humans were created with four virtues, personified as sisters—Mercy, to guide the humans; Truth, to teach them; Justice, to govern them; and Peace, to cherish them. Adam was deprived of all four when he sinned, and the human race was in danger of extinction by Death. Much as they wished to redeem humanity from Death, the sisters could not agree on how to accomplish the task, which required a person without sin. Despite a diligent search, none of the sisters could find someone sinless. God then intervened, sending Gabriel to visit Mary, who would bear God's own son. God ordered Truth and Mercy to go before Christ; asked Justice to prepare a throne for him; and told Peace to go with him. At this resolution of their difficulties, Mercy and Truth were reconciled, and "Peace and Justice kissed."[33]

The Mary Play dramatizes this parable, beginning with Contemplation's introduction of the Parliament of Heaven, set 4,604 years after the onset of humanity's captivity to the Devil. The entire Trinity participates in the process; after the sisters fail to agree on what can be done to redeem humankind, it is the Son who proposes the solution: "You must know that the one who will die must be sinless himself, so that Hell cannot hold him ... and his death shall be man's redemption." When none of the sisters can find such a person, the Son convenes the rest of the Trinity, saying, "Father, he that [redeems] the human race must be both God and man; let me see if I can take on that likeness: I am ready to do it." The Holy Spirit assumes the task of the Son's embodiment, declaring that as Love he will lead the Son to his "lover," the one of whom he will be born. Mercy declares, "Now is the loveday made of us four, finally now may we live in peace as we were wont to do."[34]

During the scene of the Annunciation itself, Gabriel greets Mary with "Eva turned Ave" and flowery celebrations of her grace. Mary is more impressed with his message than his presence, saying that she is used to seeing angels, but none looking like a regular human being. Unfazed, Gabriel tells her that her son will rescue all the souls in Hell who are waiting for release—and he will wait for her answer. Mary agrees; Gabriel, overjoyed, addresses her as "God's mother dear, God's sister and God's playfellow, God's chamber and God's bower!" Mary thanks him for his "travel here" and asks him to visit more often "for [her] consolation," revealing her deep understanding of the responsibility she bears. In departing, Gabriel addresses her by her "new" titles: Throne of the Trinity, Queen of Heaven, and Empress of Hell.[35] The angel then departs.

The remainder of the play shows Mary and Joseph deciding to visit Elizabeth and Zachary. As Mary pronounces the words of the Magnificat in Latin, Elizabeth repeats them in English, with Mary explaining Gabriel's message and describing Jesus as "perfect God and perfect man." Continuing her catechetical role, Mary prescribes the recitation or singing of the Magnificat every evening; Elizabeth acknowledges her as the "throne of the Trinity," and Joseph asks about Zachary, who remains silent.

Contemplation ends the play by describing it as an enactment of how the "Hail Mary" was composed between Gabriel and Elizabeth, with additions by the church: "With *Ave* we began, with *Ave* we conclude," says Contemplation, inviting the audience to join in singing "Hail, Queen of Heaven."

The persona of Mary in the N-town interpretation of Christ's passion and death (Plays 28–32) exhibits strength and fortitude as well as grief and sorrow—qualities missing from her role in the French religious dramas of the period. In Play 28, she mourns for the suffering of her son and suffers her own pain, asking God the Father, "Where are all the promises You made when You made me a mother? Why should Your own son suffer all this?" Ever thoughtful, she concludes that all of this is happening for the salvation of humankind, and says that it will soothe her woe to know that people "are saved by my child and brought to a good end."[36] At the Crucifixion, her expression of sorrow is brief and touching: She asks why her son is dying so shamefully and why her heart cannot leave her body, asking for death before she faints. We see her briefly with John and Mary Magdalene, and John leads her away to pray in the temple before her son dies.[37]

After the harrowing of Hell in Play 35, Jesus appears first to Mary, addressing her with "Salve, sancta parens," her familiar liturgical greeting. Her assumption is dramatized in Play 41. Play 42, the last in the series, is "Judgment Day," a brief showing of God, Gabriel, Michael, demons, and souls awaiting judgment. At a mere 139 lines, this play seems like an anticlimax after the solemnity of Mary's arrival in Heaven.

In contrast to earlier dramatic works such as Rutebeuf's *Théophile* and even most of the Parisian guild plays, the N-Town plays present Mary as a vibrant and even earthy woman, however extraordinary. "There is an undercurrent of affirmative sexuality in [scenes of pregnancy and childbirth] that challenges the dominant view of the Virgin as totally 'other'—impossibly immaculate, impossibly ideal—and of women as [deficient by contrast]."[38] The N-town Mary is confident of herself and her calling, an enthusiastic partner in the work of salvation.

A Marian Lament/Lament for Mary

One of the most famous medieval Marian lyrics is the Latin "Stabat Mater" ("Stood the Mother") attributed to Jacopone da Todi (c. 1230–1306), a lay Franciscan.[39] Still sung in Catholic churches during Passiontide, his song describes Mary standing and weeping at the foot of her son's cross. Successor to Euthymios and Symeon Metaphrastes, Jacopone asks, "Who is the one who would not weep, seeing the Mother of Christ in such torment?" The singer implores, "Holy Mother, fount of love, make me feel the force of sorrow, so that I may grieve with you.... Make me feel the wounds of the Crucified, your Son, who suffered for me, so that I may share his pain.... Let me be wounded with his wounds, inebriated by the Cross and the blood of your Son." The author asks that for his devotion, he be "defended in the day of judgment, guarded by the Cross, strengthened by the death of Christ, favored by grace" so that his soul, at death, may "be given to the glory of Paradise."

Echoing ancient hymns, this invitation to join Mary and her son reflects the practice of affective piety, reaching out to the lay people who responded to the drama of the miracle plays and who gathered in droves to watch Passion plays, enactments of Christ's death and Mary's own suffering.

Mary in the Passion Plays of France

In the N-Town plays, we see Mary as a whole person at various stages in her life, from conception to assumption. In Passion plays, whose *raison d'être* is to depict the circumstances of Christ's passion and death, Mary's role is most often limited to mourning, her persona distinguished by submission to the will of God, humility, patient suffering, and obedience in the face of death. Here, Mary embodies the conventional Ave countering Eva, that disobedient, proud woman so impatient to be like God that she was responsible for the original sin that brought death into the world and placed humankind in bondage to the Devil, waiting for millennia to be released by Christ. In patristic and medieval clerical parlance, women are daughters of Eve, constantly reminded of Augustine's pronouncement that Adam, not Eve, was made in the image of God, and that women therefore are to be silent and obedient to their husbands and their church.

During the fourteenth century, the pervasive misogyny of ecclesiastical writings and sermons spilled over into broadsides that vividly described women's many shortcomings, among them gossiping, extravagance, pride, and jealousy. Women were volatile, spiteful, idle, selfish, deceitful, irrational, lustful, greedy, and a danger to men's bodies and souls.[40] Farces and *fabliaux* (short, ribald tales of philandering and adultery) in the marketplace as well as sermons in the sanctuaries emphasized women's spiritual weakness and emotional fragility.

The Mary of the Passion plays provided a different paradigm of womanhood. Devoted mother, acquiescent to the will of the Father, the Son, and the apostle John, in these dramas Mary models an ideal of faith in her heart-pierced compassion and her lyrical expressions of theological and doctrinal truths. In these enormously popular productions of the fourteenth and fifteenth centuries, Mary's previously diverse and powerful roles are reduced to one: the suffering woman at the foot of the cross. The words she speaks may harken back to Romanos—but they do so without the strength and fervor of that early Marian voice and the recognition of her importance in the economy of salvation. In the set speech of the Passion plays known as Mary's lament,[41] the former *mulier fortis*, the valiant woman of the twelfth and thirteenth centuries, becomes the *mater dolorosa*, the sorrowing and sorrowful mother of the waning Middle Ages. The dramatization of Mary's suffering, which invites the spectator to identify and suffer with her, has the effect—intended or not—of emphasizing the frailty, emotional extravagance, and helplessness of the woman—and women—embodied in her.

In the early fourteenth-century *Passion of Palatinus*,[42] Mary grieves for her son but wonders what will become of her: "In you was all my delight

... in you my faith and hope.... Sweet son, think of me. After [your] death, what will I do?" Her next speech regrets the loss of her "dear son and father," condemns the Jews and Judas, and expresses her wish to join Jesus in death. She feels her heart pierced by a sword, as Simeon had predicted (Luke 1:35); the sharpest swords are those of Jesus' wounds that caused his death, which she felt as he died. Despite the comfort offered by Saint John, she continues to lament: "John, what will become of [this] worn and weary woman whom death will not take? I have no will to live longer. God, who will comfort the comfortless? In truth, never was one more sorrowful born of a mother."[43] Chided by John for her excessive grief, she tells him that she will abide by his wishes and says farewell to Jesus. Obedient to male authority, Mary displays none of the strength that is her standard in other genres, other times.

A more lyrical portrayal of Mary's own passion occurs in the late fifteenth-century *Passion d'Auvergne*. In this drama, Mary speaks to her son on the cross in the form of a poem, giving her lament a stylized but nonetheless poignant tone and infusing it with a dignity lacking in other works: "O cross, that you would bend down! Give me my son, my fleur-de-lys!" After Jesus gives her into the keeping of John, she says: "Must the son become the nephew [and I] leave the master for the disciple? My God, that is a terrible thing for me: The prince changes into a knight, the lord into a squire, the creator is exchanged for a creature, and the artist for a portrait.... You see a pitiful mutation change joy into suffering. My child, is it for the best? Tell me, my son, my glorious God! My son, console your mother!"[44]

At the end of this play, Christ's resurrection is celebrated by none other than Pilate and his wife; a Roman centurion; Gamaliel, a pro–Christian Jew; and Mary, who ends the play with another *ballade*, or long lyric poem. The very model of theological correctness, her speech celebrates the "essential unity" of God, "one in being and substance" in the Trinity (a phrase from the Nicene Creed), and it asks God to preserve the lives of her servants from all perils and danger. Although in this play Mary moves from the foot of the cross to Heaven, her earthly role is still limited to that of a sorrowful mother, a distressed and disconsolate woman deprived of her only child. Her heavenly role is likewise limited to that of a faithful proclaimer of doctrine.

The much longer fifteenth-century "great Passion plays"[45] give Mary a speaking part in the Annunciation, of course, but heavily emphasize her obedience to God and to Joseph. She appears in the public life of Jesus but takes no active role. The virtues she exhibits—humility, patience, long-suffering, submission, and compassion—form her essentially static character. In these plays, too, she expresses the anguished wish to die with her son. The dramatization of her suffering, inviting the spectator to identify and suffer with her, once again has the effect of emphasizing her frailty, emotional extravagance, and helplessness. "The humanity of Mary, then, came to be associated generally with her earthly suffering; the most prominent image of her humility, and her most immediate cooperation with the redemptive act, came to be joined with her motherhood."[46] In the Mary of the Passion plays we fail to find the unassuming but assertive woman of Scripture. We cannot recognize the powerful woman of ancient legend and medieval miracle story whose partnership with God continued the redeeming work of her son. Mary has been reduced to a fainting figure at the foot of the cross.

Our Lady of the Sermon: Marian Devotion as a Guarantee of Heaven

Although the practice of devotion to Mary permeated the miracle stories about her during the "long twelfth century" and beyond, church doctrines other than her perpetual virginity did not figure prominently in miracle stories. (Despite Eadmer and others' advocating for the celebration of her immaculate conception, the concept did not become a required belief in the Catholic church until 1854.) As the teachings of the Fourth Lateran Council spread throughout Christendom, however, pastors were directed to preach about the necessity to confess one's sins and to receive the body and blood of Christ in the Eucharist at least once a year, at Eastertide. The increasing importance of deathbed repentance and confession was reinforced by grisly reminders of the fate that awaited unconfessed sinners in the newly emphasized Purgatory as well as Hell.

By the fifteenth century, these doctrines were widespread, and a German preacher, Johannes Herolt (?1386–1468), compiled a series of 99 miracle anecdotes that invoked Mary in the cause of requirements for salvation. Borrowing heavily from Vincent of Beauvais and Caesarius of Heisterbach[47] and writing in Latin, Johannes condensed the tales into brief episodes suitable for illustrating church teachings about what was necessary for salvation. Edifying but stupefying, the collection illustrates the sort of pious excess that the humanist Erasmus and the Reformers would criticize.

Herolt's Miracle 50 describes the near-death experience of "a man who was religious in name only." As he grows weaker, the man sees devils coming for his soul, and God, knowing all his sins, grants it to them. Mary, however, has been counting up all the "Hail Marys" the man has said during his lifetime and places them on the scale of judgment. The devils counter with entire "books" of his sins. Mary beseeches her son,

"Remember, Beloved, that Thou didst receive of my substance, visible, tangible and sensible substance; give to me one drop of Thy blood shed for sinners in Thy passion." Jesus consents, and "…all those sins of the religious weighed against it as light as ashes."[48]

In this retelling, we see one drop of divine blood as far outweighing Marian tributes; Christ's blood has replaced Mary's hand on the scale, diminishing both her power and the efficacy of prayers to her.

Herolt's stories emphasize fasting on Saturdays, Mary's day; recitation of numerous Aves; and adherence to church practices. In Miracle 28, Mary visits on his deathbed a man who cannot hear or speak, enabling him to call for a priest to administer the last rites. A dead monk revives in order to be anointed and receive Communion; afterward, he expires again in Miracle 29.[49] Miracle 52 features a robber who is caught and beheaded. A priest is summoned but refuses to have anything to do with the robber unless his head is restored to his body, and his executioners comply with the request. After confessing, the thief confides that he had fasted four times a day on Saturdays in honor of Mary, adding, "I never did anything else that was good in my life," and dying immediately afterward.[50] Presumably he then enters Heaven.

Herolt's depiction of Mary's indulgence toward sinners may have reached its apex in Miracle 72. This miracle, he says, concerns a woman who never did a good thing in her life except to say Aves every day and sponsor a Saturday mass in praise of Mary. On her deathbed she says, "Lady Queen and mother, although I have never done anything good, yet I trust in thy mercy and commend my soul to thee." At her passing, the usual scores of devils arrive to harvest her soul but are thwarted by Mary, who snatches it for herself. The devils howl, but Mary prevails, reminding them of the Aves and the masses. In response to the devils' recitation of the woman's "many crimes," Mary replies, "That soul may never be damned that hath served me and hath committed her soul to me." Vanquished, the devils flee, and Mary takes the woman's soul to Heaven.[51]

Stories like Herolt's, and the Marian devotion that they depicted and were designed to inspire, may well have exasperated those pastors who were more concerned with the quality of their flocks' spiritual lives than the quantity of their devotions.

What Is the Narrative Theology of the Waning Middle Ages?

Throughout the fourteenth and fifteenth centuries, Mary's presence and active advocacy declined and faded in both story and drama. *The*

Romance of Saint Fanuel and Saint Anne is paradigmatic of the way in which some Marian stories evolved, resembling fairy or folk tales rather than stories of accompaniment and accomplishment. In the French goldsmith guild's dramas, Mary's role fades to a shadow. The N-town plays' portrayal of the fullness of her life is offset by the Passion plays' emphasis on her helplessness and near-despair. Mary's powerful defense of humankind in the *Advocacie Nostre Dame* barely survives the author's attempt to sabotage her learning and authority by mocking her appeal to Jesus the judge, attempting to diminish her person while celebrating her victory.

As Mary's presence grew fainter in miracle tales, and her speech came to echo human doctrine rather than divine compassion, she assumed the roles of poet, catechist, and mourner. Marian stories like those of Johannes Herolt had the effect of edification rather than conversion, privileging pious practice and doctrinal conformity.

CHAPTER 7

What Happened to the Stories?
That's Another Story

The last great compilation of Mary stories appeared in the mid-fifteenth century, the work of Jehan Miélot, who added pious furbelows to his adaptations of earlier writers. Some tales survived in printed editions of *The Golden Legend*. Others were turned into anecdotes that preachers used to enhance their sermons, following the tradition of Jacques de Vitry, Caesarius of Heisterbach, and Johannes Herolt. In an era preoccupied with sin and punishment, these little episodes still spoke of the possibility of Heaven even for sinners. It would take three hundred years for stories about Mary's miracles to begin circulating again; they disappeared, replaced by doctrine (teachings) and dogma (required beliefs). Mary became an object of study and proclamation, rather than a subject who acted on behalf of sinners. By the beginning of the sixteenth century, that change was beginning to occur.

Between Devotion and Reform: Erasmus of Rotterdam (1469–1517)

As her devotees visited her shrines and said their Aves during the fourteenth and fifteenth centuries, the figure of Mary herself began a metamorphosis caused at least in part by tumult in both church and state. The Hundred Years' War between England and France (1337–1453, with periods of respite) brought chaos to the citizens of both countries. During the Papal Schism (1378–1417), two or even three rival popes simultaneously claimed authority over the church, one in France and one or more in Rome, each with his own supporters. Adding to Christian woes, the Muslim Ottoman Turks conquered Constantinople for Islam in 1453.

Despite chaos both civic and religious, institutions of learning continued to foster scholars, among them the brilliant and quirky Erasmus (1469–1517.) A figure of both the Renaissance and the Reformation,

Chapter 7. What Happened to the Stories?

Erasmus may have had as colleagues some of the Byzantine scholars who fled Constantinople during the Muslim invasion, bringing to Europe their learning in the Greek tradition. Erasmus was one of the first to incorporate Greek into his studies; his edition of the Second Testament paved the way for the study of the Bible in its original languages. His 1511 best-seller, *The Praise of Folly*, reflects the heart of the Renaissance critique of the Middle Ages and the church, skewering traditional university learning, monks, friars, inquisitors, cardinals, popes, secular clergy, theologians, miracles, and shrines. The expansive range of his writings and influence marked Erasmus as a humanist and a scholar trained in classical languages, rhetoric, and literature rather than the typical medieval regime of dialectic and scholastic debate. Like those of other humanists, Erasmus' writings were marked by an inquiring skepticism that irritated both church stalwarts and advocates of reform such as Luther.

In "A Pilgrimage for Religion's Sake," Erasmus criticizes "...those who with much ado have thrown all images out of the church; also those who are crazy about pilgrimages undertaken in the name of religion."[1] The work recounts a dialogue between two neighbors: Menedemus, a skeptic, and Ogygius, an enthusiastic visitor of shrines, who has just returned from a six-month pilgrimage. Laden with shrine-tokens (scallop shells from St. James of Compostela, rosary beads, medallions embossed with images of saints or their shrines), Ogygius has visited shrines in both Europe and England. At the shrine of St. James in Compostela, he fulfilled a vow made by his mother-in-law to go on pilgrimage if her daughter delivered a healthy boy. Menedemus questions the practice: What risk would there be to his friend if he were to fail to keep his relative's vow? Ogygius says the risk is that his future prayers might be ignored.

The conversation continues: Ogygius mentions a letter written "by Mary herself" and presumably delivered by an angel to the very "pulpit from which the recipient speaks."[2] In Mary's purported letter, she complains about the requests she receives: A merchant requests a fortune as well as protection of his mistress as he travels overseas; a nun asks for the preservation of her reputation as she prepares to run away from her convent and live a life of sin; gamblers promise to share their winnings with her but curse her if they lose. A soldier prays for plunder, a prostitute for customers ... the list is endless.

"If I deny anything," Mary says, "straightaway I'm cruel. If I refer to my Son, I hear, 'He wills whatever you will.' So am I alone, a woman and a virgin, to assist those who are sailing, fighting, trading, dicing, marrying, bearing children; to assist governors, kings, and farmers?"[3] Mary continues her plaint: She used to be addressed as Queen of Heaven, dressed in silk and satin, with precious stones galore; now she's lucky to have a mouse-nibbled cloak to her name, and offerings have dwindled until they scarcely pay for one wretched candle.

Erasmus then changes tack to decry how reformers have reacted to the excesses of pilgrimage piety by abolishing images and destroying shrines. Mary's persona says, "And yet, all these hardships I could have borne if you weren't said to be plotting even greater ones. You're trying, they say, to remove from the churches whatever belongs to the saints." She then lists the formidable weaponry of Saint Peter, whose keys can lock shut the gates of Heaven, and of other, more heavily armed saints, including the "sacred fire" of Saint Anthony (the object of so many of her miraculous cures). Finally, she delivers an ultimatum to aspiring reformers: "But me, however defenseless, you shall not eject unless at the same time you eject my Son whom I hold in my arms. From him I will not be parted. Either you expel him along with me, or you leave us both here, unless you prefer to have a church without Christ."[4] A mighty threat indeed—and a brief glimpse of the powerful Queen of Heaven whose threats are not to be ignored.

Erasmus' parody of Marian devotion continues with portraits of shiftless monks, greedy shrine-keepers, thieving pilgrims, fake relics (including the extraordinary abundance of Mary's milk as well as articles of her clothing, saints' bones, and pieces of the True Cross), extravagantly decorated churches, and sumptuous clerical vestments. He describes offerings of gold, silver, and precious stones, given to decorate statues and altars as well as to enrich the keepers and fill the coffers of the shrines. Furthermore, his credulous pilgrim relates, to reach all of these marvels, the faithful face hazardous travel fraught with robbers and cheats on land and sea.

The conversation ends as Ogygius invites himself and his wife to dinner at the house of his friend. (Has he been influenced by the dark side of pilgrimage?) After saying that he would prefer stories he doesn't have to pay for, Menedemus consents and leaves, as he says, to "say his Roman stations," or attend to his household affairs.

Erasmus' critiques found a ready audience in the humanists and reformers of his time: The Renaissance was reawakening Europe to the beauties of the past, and Martin Luther was about to challenge the universal authority of the Catholic Church.

Renaissance and Reform

The writings of Erasmus reflect the beginnings of a renewed interest in the cultures of the past, especially the Greek and Roman ideals of the beauty to be found in both humans and nature. From the often stylized but majestic statues and paintings of Mary as Queen of Heaven or enthroned as Wisdom with her son on her lap, artists moved to softer, more "contemporary" depictions of mother and son, often in roundels that encircled the pair. Mary was depicted in more natural settings and as maternal rather than regal, with Jesus nestled against her breast or standing in front of her, supported by her sheltering hand. Madonna and Child, accompanied by Joseph, appeared in domestic settings as the Holy Family, for example in Nativity scenes and depictions of the flight into Egypt.

Saint Anne and the "Holy Kinship" became a popular artistic theme in the fifteenth and sixteenth centuries,[5] and the cult of Saint Joseph grew. Mary's sphere of influence was shrinking—her dominion over Heaven, earth, and Hell fading as she took her place in domestic scenes of relationship. Although the figures in "Holy Kinship" paintings place women in the forefront, it is the men, particularly Jesus and Joseph, who are emphasized in the pious literature of the time. An increasing number of statues depict a four- or five-year-old Mary standing at the knees of Saint Anne, who is teaching her to read—a literal diminution of her presence.

The Marian spring of tradition, strong in the Middle Ages and running through the Renaissance, was overwhelmed by the flood of religious reform movements that swept through sixteenth-century Europe. Erasmus' lampoon of shrine-keepers and credulous pilgrims, his parodies of Marian miracle stories, and his critiques of the Church resonated with the advocates of reform.

Martin Luther (1483–1546) had a personal devotion to Mary. He affirmed her status as Theotokos, Mother of God, and defended her perpetual virginity, but he abolished the feasts of her conception, birth, and assumption as apocryphal. (He kept the annunciation, the visitation, and the purification.) He translated the Magnificat into German, citing her as an "example of the grace of God." He emphasized her humility and joy in housework while extolling her as an image of the Church. His belief in *sola scriptura*, *sola fide*, *sola gratia* (only Scripture, only faith, only grace) as the necessities for salvation influenced the entire Reformation. Other reformers expanded the list of necessities to five, adding *solus Christus*, only Christ, and *soli Deo gloria*, to the glory of God alone.[6]

Ulrich Zwingli (1484–1531) rejected images of Mary, saying that Christ was the only mediator between God and humankind. Accordingly, her statues were removed from churches in Switzerland. Although Zwingli affirmed Mary's status as "the highest of creatures next to her son," he emphasized her poverty and lowliness.

John Calvin (1509–1564) outlawed veneration of Mary but saw her as a model of faith. An iconoclast, Calvin believed images to be idolatrous, and statue-smashing riots took place in Switzerland, Scotland, the Netherlands, and Belgium, causing enormous destruction.

In England, the "stripping of the altars"[7] under Henry VIII and his henchmen ravaged entire churches, abbeys, and shrines, including the renowned Marian center of devotion at Walsingham. Like other reformers, the English tended to stress Mary's obedience and domesticity, although they retained feast days, hymns, and prayers in her honor.[8] Queen Elizabeth I succeeded, at least for a time, in displacing Mary as a center of devotion through her assumption of the title "Virgin Queen."

Over the course of the Reformation, Mary became "biblical rather than devotional or mystical."[9] She was "[t]he totally human Maid of Nazareth, a peasant girl snatched by the initiative of God from her ordinary life to take her great and historic part in the drama of salvation."[10] Her presence—formerly dynamic and personal—became domestic and didactic, a model of maidenly modesty, motherly devotion, and humble servanthood.

There were no more stories, only religious tracts arguing for different sets of orthodoxies.

Apparitions I: Our Lady of Guadalupe[11]

While reformers were occupied with removing the slightest trace of Mary from churches, and pilgrimage sites were being pillaged, a local event of international import took place in the Americas. In December 1531, at a hill near Tepayac (not far from modern Mexico City), a Nahuatl peasant named Juan Diego Cuauhtlaoatzin saw Mary, who instructed him to ask the local bishop to build a chapel in her honor on the hill. Dismayed by the class difference between himself and the venerable Bishop Zumárraga, Juan put off the visit, and Mary appeared to him a second time, telling him to pick the flowers nearby and take them to the bishop as a sign of the authenticity of her message. Juan gathered the flowers in his cloak and took them to the bishop. An interpreter recorded the meeting, at which the bishop expressed some skepticism about Juan's request. When Juan opened his cloak, a shower of December roses fell at the bishop's feet; and from the rough brown fabric of maguey cloth that covered her messenger shone the image of Mary, an image that spoke to each of them in his own language. The bishop knelt in homage.

The chapel was built, of course, becoming what is now the Basilica of Our Lady of Guadalupe in Mexico City, the most visited Catholic pilgrimage site in the world. The mestiza Madonna would support her followers for centuries, her image becoming an icon of heavenly support for the less privileged of the earth.

Chapter 7. What Happened to the Stories?

The Virgin of Guadalupe with the Four Apparitions. Nicolás Enriquez, Mexican, 1773. Purchase, Louis V. Bell, Harris Brisbane Dick, Fletcher, and Rogers Funds and Joseph Pulitzer Bequest and several members of The Chairman's Council Gifts, 2014, Metropolitan Museum of Art.

The Counter-Reformation: Mary and the Church Militant

Battered by the schism of the late fifteenth century and the rise of the reformers in the sixteenth century, the Catholic church responded by convoking an international council to clarify theological issues. The Council of Trent (1545–1564) affirmed the canonical books of the Bible, including those that had been rejected by Protestants. Trent also promulgated rules, or canons, that forbade the sale of indulgences; established the church as the final authority in interpreting Scripture; affirmed relics, pilgrims, and pilgrimages; and declared the number of sacraments (which Protestants had reduced to two) to be seven. Canons also affirmed the tradition of art and sculpture in churches, encouraged the elimination of heretics through the Inquisition, and banned shrine-madonnas.[12]

It could be said that Trent ushered in its own, Roman form of iconoclasm, forbidding statues and paintings that represented extracanonical or classical interpretations of Scripture. New and refurbished churches featured ceilings festooned with cherubs, walls covered with vast paintings of scriptural subjects in elaborate gilded frames, and monumental marble statues of saints and public figures. The Catholic Baroque was a flamboyant reproach to Protestant simplicity as architecture and art "triumphantly celebrated all the dogmas attacked by the Protestants."[13]

Not threatened only by reformers, the Church faced a growing challenge from Islam in the sixteenth century. Menaced by a growing Turkish Ottoman (Muslim) presence in the Mediterranean, a "Holy League" of Christian nations gathered its fleets at Lepanto off the coast of Crete in October 1571. Pope Pius V invoked Mary, urging the European faithful to pray the Rosary in petition for victory. The Battle of Lepanto ended in a decisive Christian victory; Mary's role as defender of the faithful merged with that of defender of the faith, and the title "Our Lady of Victory" became a symbol of Catholic triumph over opposing religious forces.

Most of Mary's traditional miracle stories remained out of sight and out of hearing, confined to manuscript pages as the church sought exclusive control over depictions of divine and saintly figures. Many religious plays, including those that depicted Mary, were banned. Writers of the counter–Reformation placed Mary on ever-higher doctrinal pedestals, and over the next few centuries she became a passive object of devotion—despite efforts, orthodox or not, to emphasize her importance as a companion to her son, active partner in his work of salvation, carrier of his message for the rest of her life, and prolific miracle-worker after her death.

A Cover-Up and a Revelation: Mary as Bishop—or Pope

The Cover-Up

At some time during the seventeenth century, the Vatican decided to refurbish the Saint Venantius chapel in the baptistery of the papal church, Saint John Lateran. A huge Baroque altarpiece replaced the smaller, less elaborate altar of previous centuries with massive marble columns that held up a towering triangular pediment above an altar draped in cloth edged with gold. At the center of this altarpiece, which reached almost to the ceiling, was placed a diminutive painting of a demure Madonna, head bowed and smiling sweetly, holding the infant Jesus. Above the pediment, the head of Jesus appeared in mosaic against a golden background, flanked by two angels.[14]

The Revelation

Behind the altarpiece, however—and removed from public access by a red velvet rope—is a complete seventh-century mosaic of Jesus blessing Mary, "[t]he Eucharistic leader of sixteen men," among them Peter and Paul and several bishops. "Mary herself wears an Episcopal pallium with a red cross and ... red shoes. Both the pallium and the shoes are

"Demure Mother Mary," Renaissance painting over the altar in the Chapel of Saint Venantius, Rome. Ally Kateusz, "Two Marys, Two Traditions." The demure mother is on the left, the powerful mother on the right in Slide No. 1. https://www.allykateusz.org/art-as-text-powerpoint/two-marys-two-traditions. Courtesy Ally Kateusz.

still insignia of the bishop of Rome, the pope."[15] Mary's arms are raised in blessing, directly below the blessing of her son, in a true "imitation of Christ."

The altarpiece and the mosaic of Mary behind it are indicative of what has been done to obscure the image of Mary as ecclesiastical leader—an image not only depicted vividly in this seventh-century mosaic but also inscribed in a fifth-century stone (see the "Mary as Minister in the Temple of Jerusalem" section in Chapter 1), alluded to by Euthymios, suggested by John the Geometer, implied by medieval writers, and celebrated by François Villon.

Despite such efforts at suppression, a fifteenth-century painting titled "The Priesthood of the Virgin" shows Mary vested for Mass in an elaborate chasuble. Her left hand holds the hand of the child Jesus; her right hand holds the Eucharistic bread. There is no doubt about her power to make her son present in the host, a power clearly equal (or even superior) to that of the miniature figure of the Pope at her feet.[16] The Mariologist Quirino de Salazar (1576–1646) put that image into words: "[T]he salvation and redemption of the human race must be in a way attributed to [Mary], that with Christ she gave and offered the price of our redemption truly and directly.... What clearly brought the Virgin to this glory and made her

Seventh-century mosaic of Mary, wearing red (papal) shoes, flanked by two apostles. She wears a white episcopal or papal pallium with a red cross that has been replaced by a black one. Numbers 16 and 17 on this web site show Mary as a celebrant of liturgy, flanked by saints and prelates: *https://www.allykateusz.org/art-as-test-powerpoint/two-marys-two-traditions.* **Courtesy Ally Kateusz.**

a collaborator and helper with Christ was that … she offered him who was hers to us and for us … in a manner singular and proper to herself she obtained life and salvation for the human race."[17] In France, "Mary was invoked and contemplated as the model of the priest, and honored as 'Virgo Sacerdos,' the Virgin Priest."[18] This motif ran quietly through the seventeenth and eighteenth centuries, to emerge more widely and more vividly later in the nineteenth and twentieth.

Most Marian writers of the seventeenth and eighteenth centuries focused on the refutation of Protestant views and the development of devotion, treating Mary not as a subject active in salvation history but as an object of pious practices, the more numerous the better. The exuberant storytelling of the shrine-madonnas, literally embodying salvation history, gave way to stately, larger-than-life marble statues and massive paintings of Mary assumed into Heaven, surrounded by the angelic host. Post-Reform Catholic writers placed Mary in the verbal equivalents of those massive artworks, creating masterpieces of apologetics that rarely reached people in the pews (who might not have understood them). It was enough for Catholic churchgoers to know that Mary triumphed over pagan and heretic alike, reserving the salvation of her son for those who still believed in her and her church.

Defenders of Mary I

Post-Reform Catholic writers like Peter Canisius (1521–1597) brought a Jesuit balance to some of the more heated responses to Luther and others. Canisius' work, *On the Incomparable Virgin Mary*, drew on both scriptural and extracanonical sources to affirm Mary's vow of virginity, her upbringing in the Temple, and her divine motherhood. Canisius restored some of Mary's autonomy by rejecting Luther's depiction of her as preoccupied with domestic duties. But there were limits; he denied that she could command her son. Still, he defended Marian miracles, finding them perfectly acceptable if they seemed "probable and edifying."[19]

Other Catholic writers, responding to the wholesale rejection of most Marian attributes, doubled down on praising her abilities, among them Francisco Suarez (1548–1617). Suarez defended Mary's sinlessness and extraordinary graces, and—following Pseudo-Albert—declared her to possess both natural and supernatural knowledge as well as theological wisdom, "…for she was the teacher of the Apostles."[20] He taught that she was freed from original sin immediately after her conception, and he affirmed her bodily assumption. He emphasized the difference between veneration due to God alone—*latria*—and veneration due to saints, or *dulia*, assigning Mary a special kind of veneration called *hyperdulia*. Suarez used this distinction, first articulated by Augustine in *The City of God*,[21] to refute the reformers' accusations of Mary-worship. His argument appears not to have had much effect; the concept of different forms of veneration remains virtually unknown today, even among Catholics.

During the seventeenth and eighteenth centuries, confraternities or sodalities—associations of men and women dedicated to promoting special works of piety—achieved prominence in Catholic circles throughout the world. Marian confraternities grew from their roots in the guilds of the Middle Ages into organizations that survive today. Among the most prominent of these organizations were the Confraternity of the Most Holy Rosary (founded in the fifteenth century, greatly expanded in the eighteenth) and the Confraternity of the Immaculate Conception, an eighteenth-century foundation dedicated to the promotion of that doctrine.

Defenders of Mary II: The "French School"

Early refutations of the reformers tended to exaggerate Mary's exceptional gifts of body, soul, and mind. Later apologists emphasized her holiness, her union with her son, and her active role in salvation history. The feasts of the Presentation of Mary and the Presentation of Jesus became important celebrations "in connection with devotion to the *Virgo Sacerdos* ['Virgin Priest']" as exemplars for priests.[22] Writing about Mary's presentation of her son in the Temple, Giovanni Battista Guarini (1538–1612) adds a layer to its meaning by noting that, years later, "the Blessed Virgin was standing near the Cross of her son, as priests customarily stand at the holy altar when, under the species of bread and wine, they sacrifice and offer to God the sacred body and precious blood of his Son."[23]

Quirino de Salazar (1575–1646) quotes the church patriarch Epiphanius (310–403) to the effect that Mary can be called a priest and altar: "she who, holding the table [altar], also gave us the eternal bread for the forgiveness of sins." Salazar comments: "Weigh these words. He calls the Virgin *priest* because, acting in the manner of a priest with her son the Priest, she offers to the eternal Father the host of the redemption."[24]

Jean-Jacques Olier (1608–1659) advanced the idea of Mary's participation in the sacrifice of the cross, commemorated in the sacrifice of the Mass, thereby suggesting her priesthood.[25] Jean Eudes (1601–1680) considered priests to be wedded to Mary, drawing up his own marriage contract with her and wearing a wedding ring.[26] Eudes also fostered devotion to the Immaculate Heart of Mary, a concept related to the promulgation of

Chapter 7. What Happened to the Stories? 163

the Immaculate Conception.[27] Later, Jean Crasset (1618–1692) represented a more nuanced view of Marian intercession in his work, *True Devotion to the Holy Virgin Established and Defended*. He pooh-poohed the ideas that devotion to Mary outweighed a person's sinfulness and that belonging to a Marian confraternity was sufficient for salvation: "On the Day of Judgement [sic] Mary will say, like her son, 'I do not know you' to those who have been only externally devout to her without the practice of good works."[28]

Crasset's less dramatic attitude toward Mary and Marian devotion did not prevail in some later religious works. Marie-Louis Grignion de Monfort (1673–1716), whose *True Devotion to the Blessed Virgin* would inspire millions, advocated an approach to God much like that of the *jongleur* in "Our Lady's Tumbler" when he feared the interview with his abbot: It was essential to have the personal support of Mary. As Hilda Graef notes, "Grignion ... subscribes to the medieval idea that Christ always obeys his mother.... For Christ was subject to her for thirty years, and by this subjection has given more glory to God than if he had converted the whole world by his miracles, and in her womb ... he was 'a captive and a loving slave.'"[29]

Grignion's *The Secret of the Rosary* combines a history of the prayer with instructions for saying the Rosary, illustrated with anecdotes. Describing Mary's tender care as well as her punitive powers, Grignion tells two tales. The first tale describes two young sisters who meet a beautiful lady while they are out walking. The lady leads the younger sister away with her, and the older sister sadly returns home. For three days, their parents search everywhere for the lost child; returning home, they find her, radiantly happy, at their front door. She tells them that the Lady to whom she has been saying the Rosary had taken her to a lovely place, where she ate delicious food and played with a beautiful baby boy. Overjoyed, the parents send for the Jesuit priest who had instructed them in the faith and taught them to say the Rosary. Grignion learned of the story from that very priest.[30]

A second anecdote concerns two medieval priests famed for their eloquence in preaching. Jealous of Dominic's legendary success in promoting the Rosary, they begin to inveigh against joining the Confraternity of the Rosary, and they persuade large numbers of people. One priest is found dead after preaching an anti–Rosary sermon; the other is struck dumb and becomes paralyzed. After admitting his sin, he is cured.[31]

Grignion de Montfort's devotional writing was eclipsed by the monumental work of a Spanish Franciscan abbess, Maria of Agreda (1602–1665). Maria's *Mystical City of God* weighed in at nearly 2,000 pages, divided into four books that describe Mary's life. Book 1, "Conception," covers her first fifteen years. Book 2, "Incarnation," ends at the flight into Egypt. Book 3, "Transfixion," concludes with Jesus' ascension into Heaven, and Book 4, "Coronation," describes Mary's life from Pentecost to her death and crowning as Queen of Heaven. The work was based on a series of revelations by God, the author claims, who also provided her with six angels to guide the work.[32] Based on a series of visions—encounters with God the Father, Christ, and Mary—the *Mystical City* includes both extracanonical and biblical episodes as well as the author's conversations with her heavenly sources.

Both of them truly Baroque authors, Grignion de Montfort and Maria of Agreda continued the post–Tridentine tendency toward effusive piety, a tendency that would increase and influence Marian devotion on both sides of the Atlantic during the succeeding centuries. Stories of this period, such as they were, encouraged an emotional spirituality that was focused on personal salvation.

A Response to the Enlightenment: *The Glories of Mary*

Eighteenth-century rationalism, with its secular focus and disdain for religious observance, governed Europe during a period fraught with civil strife, suppression of religious orders, and determined opposition to the church. The result was the disappearance of "serious Marian literature."[33] One reaction to anticlericalism and secularism was to encourage ever greater and more varied devotion to Mary, epitomized in the work of Alphonsus Liguori (1696–1787). A gifted preacher, Alphonsus aimed his sermons at the common people. His great personal devotion to Mary resulted in *The Glories of Mary*, a comprehensive work designed—like that of Jacobus—to help the preachers of his day inspire the people in the pews.

Part 1 of *The Glories of Mary* explains the "Hail, Holy Queen." The mother of penitent sinners, Mary is the hope of all, protecting those who invoke her against temptations. Mortals need her intercession for their salvation; she is a "peacemaker" between sinners and God, rescuing souls from Hell and Purgatory and conducting them to Paradise. Part 2 is a compendium of Marian feasts and devotions. Alphonsus lists her virtues and describes devotional practices (novenas, meditations, rosaries, prayers for every day of the week).[34] This extravaganza of fervor is marked by suggestions of Mary's near-omnipotence and influence in divine decisions.

Despite its exaggerated piety and dubious teachings, *The Glories of Mary* was both popular and influential. Like the *Mystical City of God*, it is still in print today.

Apparitions II:
Mary and the Miraculous Medal

As if in reaction to the rationalism of Enlightenment philosophers and the destructive secularism of eighteenth-century revolutionaries, the nineteenth century witnessed an exponential increase in the number of Marian appearances, particularly in France. Marian scholar George Tavard notes that "[t]he Mother of God is alleged to have appeared in France alone in at least twenty-one locations between 1803 and 1899."[35] One of the most famous series of appearances occurred in July 1830, when a young nun, Catherine Labouré, heard a voice in the middle of the night urging her to go to the chapel of her Paris convent. Following the voice, she found Mary sitting in the chapel and had a conversation with her. During that session, Mary told Catherine that she had been "chosen for a special mission."

Mary appeared to Catherine again four months later, in November. This vision revealed her in a different guise: She appeared beautifully robed, standing on a globe and holding a smaller globe in her hands. The smaller globe then disappeared, showing Mary's hands covered with rings that flashed rays of light from dozens of precious stones. As Mary explained, the rays represented "graces for those who ask for them." A frame around the Marian figure was inscribed with the words, "Mary, conceived without sin, pray for us who have recourse to thee."

Catherine was instructed to have a medal struck depicting the Mary of her vision; the reverse side was to show a circle of twelve stars surrounding a capital M above the hearts of Jesus and Mary, his surrounded by a crown of thorns, hers pierced with a sword. "All who wear it will receive great graces," Catherine was assured. Following the advice of her confessor, she remained anonymous; her confessor communicated Mary's messages to the local bishop, who eventually gave permission for the production of 1,500 medals in 1832. The reception of the medals was so enthusiastic, and the reports of cures and conversions were so compelling, that thousands more medals were struck. Catherine died in 1876 after a life spent in anonymous service to the poor and elderly.[36] By that time, millions and millions of miraculous medals hung from the necks or occupied the pockets of believers in Mary's saving grace.

The story of the miraculous medal concerns a private revelation that was destined—commanded—to become public. It's a narrative that, by way of the events described next, would reinforce a change in Mary's perceived role from subject in her own story to object of official church teachings.

The Pope and the Dogma: Pius IX and the Immaculate Conception

As we've seen, the idea of Mary's personal *holiness*—her prerogative as the mother of God—was promulgated by early church fathers. The idea of Mary's *sinlessness*, however, took centuries to develop, beginning with Augustine of Hippo (354–430). In addressing the problem of evil in the world, Augustine concluded that the whole human race was damaged—indeed, damned—by the sin of Adam and Eve, to the extent that only God can save us through Christ. "Augustine linked Original Sin with concupiscence (i.e., the human person's spontaneous desire for material or sensual satisfaction). It is an effect of Original Sin and is transmitted through sexual intercourse, that is, by the libido in the parents' love by which a person first comes into existence."[37] Adam and Eve committed the first, original sin of disobedience, with the result that they passed down that sinfulness to every human being on earth—except, according to a growing consensus, Mary.

Only two decades after Mary's appearance to Catherine Labouré and the massive distribution of medals stamped with the words "Mary, conceived without sin," Pope Pius IX (1792–1878; pope 1846–) issued a papal bull, or proclamation, declaring the Immaculate Conception a dogma of the Catholic Church. A dogma is "[a] doctrine that is taught definitively and with the fullest solemnity, i.e., so that its formal rejection is heresy."[38] Under the title of "Ineffabilis Deus," or "Ineffable God," the bull cited a history of belief and devotion dating back to the fifth century. Pius invoked both Scripture and "Tradition" (the church's catch-all term for extracanonical writings) in presenting his reasons for the proclamation. He noted that the Council of Trent, "in declaring that all men [sic] are born infected with original sin," had declared Mary exempt. He emphasized the widespread support of the world's bishops as well as the will of the faithful in support of the teaching. The "Supreme Reason," however, according to Pius, was Mary's "Divine Maternity." As the Mother of God, she had to be exempt from the fatal effects of the Fall.[39]

After centuries of debate and discussion, Mary's immaculate conception had become an article of faith for Roman Catholics. As a symbol of "post–Reformation Catholic Marian devotion," it was "understood as opposition to Protestantism embodied in the Immaculate, i.e., pure and strong woman representative of God's grace among us."[40]

Predictably, Protestants and members of the Orthodox church rejected the idea: Members of the Reform tradition interpreted it to mean that Mary was "unlike the rest of the human race," and Orthodox believers "dissented from the dogma's underlying notion of Original Sin."[41]

Apparitions III: Mary and Lourdes

There was nothing particularly remarkable about the town of Lourdes in the mid–1800s. A small village in the foothills of the Pyrenees in southwestern France, it was home to about 4,000 people. On February 11, 1858, a barely literate 14-year-old peasant named Bernadette Soubirous was told by her mother to look for firewood at the grotto of Massabielle, an unsavory spot locally known as the pigsty because of the refuse regularly dumped there. Prone to sickness, Bernadette nevertheless obeyed. Her sister Toinette and her friend Jeanne went with her. Looking up at the grotto in the rocks above the River Gave, Bernadette was astonished to see a young woman there. Dressed in white, with a blue sash around her waist, the woman was barefoot, with a yellow rose on each foot. She held white rosary beads; when Bernadette saw that the lady appeared to be saying the rosary, she took out her own set of beads and began praying. When the lady beckoned her nearer, however, she hesitated, and the vision disappeared.

Her sister and friend saw nothing, and Bernadette swore them to silence about the encounter. Breaking her promise, Toinette told their mother about Bernadette's experience. Both of them were punished and warned not to go there again. After her daughter consulted their parish priest, however, Madame Soubirous relented, and Bernadette began a series of visits to the grotto. The lady spoke to her in Occitan, the local language of the south of France, rather than French (which Bernadette would not have been able to understand). During her third appearance, the lady asked her to come to the grotto for 15 days, and Bernadette complied. Word of her experiences spread quickly, as word does in small towns, and soon she was accompanied by larger and larger crowds.

Between February 21 and March 4, the lady appeared to Bernadette every day except two, requesting that a chapel be built on the site and that Bernadette and others "pray for sinners." Despite being asked repeatedly who she was, the lady did not reply, and Bernadette referred to her as "Aquero," the Occitan word for "that one."

During her ninth appearance, on February 25, the lady told Bernadette to drink from a fountain nearby. Seeing only a muddy puddle, the young woman scrabbled at it until clearer water appeared and she could drink a little. During February and March, Bernadette was grilled repeatedly by both church and state: Local priests feared imitations and fakes, and government officials denigrated religious demonstrations. Both authorities bullied her and tried to dissuade her from visiting the site, but she was not deterred.

On March 15, the Feast of the Annunciation, Bernadette asked the lady her name yet again. Finally she had her answer: "I am the Immaculate Conception." Not knowing what that meant, Bernadette repeated the words to herself so that she could remember them for her parish priest. Father Peyramale was flabbergasted. The dogma had been proclaimed only four years before; there was no way that Bernadette could have known about it. He and other Church investigators were eventually persuaded that Mary had indeed appeared to Bernadette.

Bernadette saw Mary for the last time on July 18, 1858, from behind a barricade that had been erected by the French government. She later became a Sister of Saint Bernard, living out her short life in service, pain, and prayer. She died in 1879.

Today Lourdes is "the most important place of Catholic pilgrimage in the world after the Holy Land and Rome."[42]

Other Nineteenth-Century Visions of Mary: Priest and Goddess

In addition to the apparitions that attracted notice on both sides of the Atlantic, the 1800s saw the establishment of a new religious order as well as increased attention by international scholars to the history of art and literature surrounding Mary.

The Daughters of the Sacred Heart, founded in 1872, was based on the concept of Mary's priestly participation in salvation through her intercession.[43] Devotion to the Virgin Priest centered on prayers that addressed the sins of the clergy, the corruption of the times, and attacks on the Church in the midst of political and religious turmoil.

Also in 1872, a Belgian priest, Oswald van den Berghe, published *Mary and the Priesthood*, featuring a preface by none other than Pope Pius IX.[44] Harkening back to thirteenth-century ideas of Mary's exemption from the deficiencies of ordinary women and her extraordinary participation in Christ's original sacrifice on Calvary, Pius IX encouraged devotion to the Virgin Priest, alleging that Church Fathers had attributed that title to Mary. Pius commissioned a prayer to her, accompanied by indulgences. Depictions of Mary as Virgin Priest spread throughout the world.

That priestly image of Mary, suggesting her partnership with Jesus in offering the bread and wine of the Mass, did not last beyond the first two decades of the twentieth century. In 1912, the Holy Office [of the Vatican] placed the devotion to the "Virgin Priest" under surveillance, concerned about the title itself, about images of a priestly Mary, and (perhaps above all) about the propensity of women to identify with Mary in her sacerdotal role. There was a fuss about religious sisters who might see themselves as virgin priests in the Marian tradition. On March 29, 1916, Pope Benedict XV (1854–1922; pope 1914–) issued a decree ordering that depictions of Mary as a priest be rejected. The suppression was confirmed under Pius XI (1857–1939; pope 1922–) by the Cardinal Secretary of State, Rafael Merry del Val, who wrote that "...the concept of Mary as Virgin Priest was one which 'less enlightened minds would not be able to fully understand.'"[45]

Feminists, Philologists, and Mary

Victorian scholars of ancient Middle Eastern texts, like pioneering medieval scholars before them, found Mary to be a source of inspiration. The brilliant Agnes Smith Lewis (1843–1926) discovered and translated ancient texts from Arabic, Syriac, and other Middle Eastern Languages. She published her translation of the *Protogospel* and the *Transitus Mariae* (*Passing of Mary*) in 1902.[46] Both remain among the classics in the field of early Marian manuscript studies.

Anna Brownell Jameson (1794–1860) authored a 500-page *Legends of the Madonna*,[47] a collection of sketches depicting Mary in scores of paintings, frescoes, woodcuts, and other visual media, interspersed with Marian stories from extracanonical texts. One tale, found in a ballad from the south of France, tells how, on her arrival in Egypt, Mary encounters a gypsy woman who offers the Holy Family shelter and reads Jesus' palm. She foretells his death on the cross and consoles Mary, who will be honored for the sake of sinners. The gypsy then asks for payment—not in coin, but in true contrition for her sins and life eternal, through Mary's agency.[48]

Jameson's reverence for Marian art was more than matched by her personal appreciation for Mary herself, as expressed in her description of the Sistine Madonna.

> [T]here she stands—the transfigured woman, at once completely human and completely divine, an abstraction of power, purity, and love, poised on the empurpled air, and requiring no other support; looking out, with her melancholy, loving mouth, her slightly dilated, sibylline eyes, quite through the universe, to the end and consummation of all things; sad—as if she beheld afar off the visionary sword that was to reach her heart through HIM, now resting as enthroned on that heart; yet already exalted through the redeemed generations who were to salute her as Blessed.[49]

Jameson's words evoke the idea of Mary as an icon of divinity, an idea and ideal suggested throughout her work.

For her commentaries on the art of different eras, Jameson familiarized herself with Marian history, doctrine, and devotion as well as many extracanonical stories. In her discussion of paintings of the Immaculate Conception, for example, Jameson described events from the Council of Ephesus; medieval pronouncements by Bernard of Clairvaux; preaching by both Dominicans and Franciscans; and papal documents supporting the liturgical celebration of the teaching. Describing artistic depictions of Mary immaculate, she anticipates by two years the declaration of dogma by Pius IX.

Along with Margaret Fuller (1810–1850) and Marian Evans (George Eliot, [1819–1880]), Anna Jameson celebrated what Kimberly VanEsfeld Adams has dubbed "Our Lady of Victorian Feminism." Adams writes that these authors present "Jesus and Mary as the masculine and feminine representations of the divine, signifying the spiritual equality of men and women. They thus bring Mary into the orbit of Godhead … this move is simultaneously orthodox and radical, a high claim for women's status and power."[50]

Feminist as they were, these women defied the popular piety of their time. Throughout the nineteenth century (and well beyond), Mary "[the] Virgin Mother was also assimilated to the ever-pious and obedient True Woman…. Mary's domestication [was] a deliberate attempt to strip her of her traditional supernatural and regal powers: No longer queen of the universe, Mary became a Hebrew housewife who looked after the needs of husband and child."[51] She was, in effect, demoted to the status of "Angel in the House,"[52] the ideal of a self-sacrificing woman submissive to her husband and preoccupied with domestic duties and cares. This ideal, so eagerly celebrated since the Reformation, has shown an unfortunate staying power.

Affective piety—promoted in books like *The Glories of Mary*—was reflected and promoted during the nineteenth century as devotions to Mary proliferated in parishes throughout the world. Replicating devotion to the Sacred Heart of Jesus (depicted with a crown of thorns around the image), the Sacred Heart of Mary—pierced with a sword—appeared on medals and scapulars (cloth images worn around the neck, both front and back). Pilgrimages multiplied; Marian shrines increased in size and number throughout the world. Mary was invoked in daily celebrations of the Mass, weekly stations of the Cross, monthly communions on first Fridays and Saturdays, and feasts great and small throughout the year. Innumerable cities and towns throughout the world claimed a particular Mary as their patron under innumerable titles of "Our Lady." The church continued to treat her as an object of veneration, especially in her presumed capacity as Mother of the Church. Laypeople tended to have more personal relationships with her as advocate in times of trouble and as defender of the faith.

Mary Stories and the Medievalism Phenomenon

The work of Jameson, Fuller, and Evans acted against the "Hebrew Housewife" trend, as did—dramatically, but very differently—the work of Henry Adams (1838–1918), who brought back the medieval ethos and some of the old stories about Mary in his *Mont-Saint-Michel and Chartres*.[53] It's safe to say that Adams absolutely doted on Mary. He recited litanies of her cathedrals, delighting in details of the one at Chartres. He translated some of the stories of Gautier de Coinci and others in the eight-syllable rhythm of the original rhyming couplets, reveling in Mary's dominion over Heaven, earth, and Hell. Although Adams tends to romanticize Mary in the fashion of the nineteenth century, we see evidence of her power in his work, made plain in the towers of her cathedrals as well as in the tales of her miracles. Here is his version of some verses from "Our Lady of the Tournament":

> His friends, returning from the fight,
> On the way there met the knight,
> For the jousts were wholly run,
> And all the prizes had been won
> By the knight who had not stirred
> From the masses he had heard.
> All the knights, as they came by,
> Saluted him and gave him joy,
> And frankly said that never yet
> Had any knight performed such feat,
> Nor ever honor won so great
> As he had done in arms that day;
> While many of them stopped to say
> That they all his prisoners were:
> "In truth, your prisoners we are;
> We cannot but admit it true:
> Taken we were in arms by you!"
> Then the truth dawned on him there,
> And all at once he saw the light,
> That She, by whom he stood in prayer
> —the Virgin—stood by him in fight!
> ....
> "Glorious has the tourney been
> Where for me has fought the Queen,
> But a disgrace for me it were
> If I tourneyed not for her.
> Traitor to her should I be
> Returned to worldly vanity.
> I promise truly, by God's grace,

> Never again the lists to see,
> Except before that Judge's face,
> Who knows the true knight from the base,
> And gives to each his final place."
> Then piteously he takes his leave
> While in tears his barons grieve,
> So he parts, and in an abbey
> Serves henceforth the Virgin Mary.[54]

Adams was not alone in his attraction to the Middle Ages. During the course of the nineteenth century, both Europe and America developed an enthusiasm for the medieval and what was called "the Gothic" in architecture and literature. In the United States, the publication of *Mont-Saint-Michel and Chartres* coincided with the construction of neo-Gothic churches and public buildings, particularly in the East. At once exotic and conservative, medievalism in architecture and literature became a trend. Both in Europe and in the United States, Marian miracle stories were published by both scholars and amateurs of the Middle Ages. The popularity of miracle stories would increase during the twentieth century as Marian apparitions continued to attract the attention of millions, believers and unbelievers alike.

What Are the Narrative Theologies of the Post–Reform Era?

Both the Reformation and the Council of Trent changed narratives about Mary. Like her image in the chapel of Saint Venantius, Mary's leadership and power were obscured as her stories virtually disappeared, replaced by homiletic anecdotes and scholarly appreciations of her relationship to Jesus and her personal privileges and graces. From active subject and powerful agent, Mary devolved into an object of devotion for most Catholics and a virtual nonentity for members of the Reform tradition. Liturgies, hymns, and devotions replaced story collections in the Catholic tradition. Neither in popular nor in scholarly writings did Mary speak for herself; instead, she appeared as a passive object of study and speculation.

Yet hidden behind the altarpiece of popular devotion, a vision of a more active Mary survived and found new life. Harkening back to the intimate association of mother and son described by John the Geometer and Euthymios the Athonite, Marian writers of the seventeenth century "emphasised that the priest's consecration of the elements is a new realisation of the mystery of the Incarnation that was first accomplished

Chapter 7. What Happened to the Stories?   173

in, and by, Mary."[55] Still, this vision remained in the shadows; these new treatises on Mary, emphasizing her active participation in the events of the Redemption, were not directed to average churchgoers as the stories had been, and a papal decree effectively effaced depictions of Mary's priesthood.

During the nineteenth century, Mary's appearances—made public in news media—focused international attention on her and her miracles once again. Shrines were built in the locales of her appearances, and stories of miraculous cures began once again to circulate (although there were no official shrine collections). Scholars on both sides of the Atlantic participated in a "Gothic Revival," leading to a renewal of public interest in the stories of Mary's might.

The most persistent narrative of the post-reform writers is Mary's priestly role in the life of both Jesus and the church, drawn in a through line from the more enlightened church fathers to the apologists of the early modern era.

As the following chapters show, old stories took on new forms, and new stories emerged over time.

Chapter 8

A Tale of Four Stories from Then to Now

Mary's journey from subject of her own story to object of veneration has taken her over continents and centuries. This chapter follows the evolution of four major Marian story traditions as interpreted in turn by medieval, early modern, and contemporary writers.

A Life of Mary from the Byzantine Tradition, Medieval Version

Segments of the *Lives of Mary* produced in antiquity and the early Middle Ages were adapted by Jacobus de Voragine for several entries in his *Golden Legend*. In a commemoration of the Nativity, he cites the *Book of the Infancy of the Savior* as well as numerous saintly commentaries on the virgin birth. Whatever his sources, Jacobus' account of Christ's birth describes all of nature celebrating: the heavens, rivers and streams, animals, and the entire natural kingdom—beginning a tradition of Christmas tales that are quite fictitious yet compelling.

For the Birth of the Blessed Virgin Mary, Jacobus creates the Marian genealogy described in Chapter 3.[1] For the Feast of the Annunciation of the Lord, he echoes the *Protogospel* and *Pseudo-Matthew* to describe Mary's Temple stay and her vow of chastity.[2] For the Feast of the Resurrection of the Lord, Jacobus says that Jesus appeared to his mother "...before all the others, although the evangelists say nothing about it." Paraphrasing Euthymios, he continues, "[I]t may be that in this case the evangelists kept silence because their charge was only to present witnesses to the resurrection, and it would not be proper to have a mother testifying for her son."[3]

For the Feast of the Assumption, Jacobus uses a variety of sources, including both the Palm and the Six Books traditions, although he claims that his account "...is related in a small apocryphal book attributed to John the Evangelist."[4] He disagrees with Epiphanios, who said that Mary

"...lived for twenty-four years after her Son's ascension, ... dying at the age of seventy-two." Jacobus believes that she was sixty. Stating that "[i]t is said that the Virgin's garments were left behind in the tomb for the consolation of the faithful, and that the following miracle was brought about by an article of her clothing," he relates the miracle of her tunic in the defeat of the Norman attack on Chartres. He asserts that Mary was taken up bodily forty days after her death, adding quotations from Saint Jerome regarding the date (August 15) and import of the event and describing six miracles she worked after her death.[5]

Jacobus uses previous Marian *Lives*—augmented by citations from Saints Jerome and Bede, among many others—to authenticate his reverent accounts of her earthly existence. The miracle tales of Mary's prowess accompanying many of his entries offer models to other clerics for teaching and preaching. A thousand manuscripts attest to his success.

A Life of Mary from the Byzantine Tradition, Modern Version

The Eastern Orthodox Church has honored and maintained its liturgical tradition for more than a thousand years. A twentieth-century *Life of the Virgin Mary, the Theotokos*[6] blends Scripture and extracanonical sources, saints' commentaries and iconography, pious legends and liturgical elements, with theological speculations by Byzantine church fathers from Romanos to the present. The result is a vivid portrait of Mary, set in a highly colored landscape.

Mary receives the Angel Gabriel as she is weaving royal purple threads into the Temple veil. Jesus is born in a cave, with the virgin birth heavily emphasized. There is an extensive account of the Holy Family's journey to Egypt—led by eighty-year-old Joseph—and their life there, complete with a map of their travels and miracles. We hear the story of Gestas and Dismas, who would be crucified with Jesus. Instead of the miracle of the palm tree, Jesus causes a spring to flow, "into which the Virgin bathed the child and washed His clothes. This place today is called Al-Mahammah or 'the Bath.' A tremendous number of visitors, both Egyptians and foreigners still frequent [it]."[7] After the destruction of the Egyptian idols (see the "Mary in the Gospel of Pseudo-Matthew" section in Chapter 1), two miracles are performed: one by Mary, who cures a woman possessed by demons; the other by Jesus, who restores the power of speech to a woman who could not talk.

On the return home to Galilee, Mary is described as leading the life of an ordinary Jewish housewife: "She is not swollen with pride nor vaunts herself; she brings no attention to herself as someone special or as the 'Mother of the Messiah,' but remains in the shadows. Her whole existence can only be viewed in relation to her Son."[8]

The story continues with a discussion of Jesus' stepbrothers and the death of Joseph, based on the fourth-century *History of Joseph [the Carpenter]*.[9] Although he is spared the ailments of old age, Joseph reaches "a very advanced age." His last illness is sudden, but Jesus is at his deathbed, and Joseph acknowledges his foster son as God.

Although this Orthodox *Life of Mary* notes that "[r]espectable women did not travel alone nor with their hair unbound or unveiled," Mary "risked the hazards of traveling to catch a glimpse of her son addressing the crowds. She is also among the women who would comfort Him and the disciples by ministering to them.... Understandably, the women disciples who followed Jesus traveled in a group, thereby making it possible for them to appear respectable."[10]

What a contrast this twentieth-century concern for respectability makes with Euthymios' confident, assertive Mary!

Although the Orthodox *Life* contains a lengthy description of the Passion, it omits the Last Supper entirely. Faithful in every other way to Scripture, tradition, and saints' commentaries, the authors simply pass over one of the most significant events of Christ's life and death. (We can only surmise that following the text of Euthymios, with its implication of Mary's concelebration, would prove problematic for Orthodox theologians; although women can serve as deacons in that tradition, they still are not eligible for Holy Orders.)

Mary is, however, the first to see the risen Savior, despite the evangelists' silence on this event. Like Euthymios and others, the authors explain the absence of this detail from the Gospels by suggesting that her testimony as a mother would have been taken for the wishful thinking or outright delusion of a mourning woman. Be that as it may, Mary receives the gifts of the Holy Spirit more abundantly than the apostles at Pentecost. When the apostles cast lots to see where they should go to preach the gospel, Mary asks for a lot also. The lot of Iberia (Spain) falls to her, but as she happily prepares to leave, Gabriel appears to tell her that her lot is not in Iberia but in Macedonia's peninsula, Mount Athos. (This area, in northeastern Greece, is home to some 20 monasteries, at least five of them devoted to Marian feasts.)

The Orthodox text follows Euthymios with its description of the apostles' checking in with Mary when they return to Jerusalem from their missions: "The Apostles loved to see the Mother of God as often as possible to learn from her. They honored her as the prolocutress [*sic*] of their assembly, and would gaze upon her most glorious countenance as that of

Christ himself. Listening to the gracious words of the blessed Virgin filled them with ineffable joy."[11] Mary is a source of wisdom for visitors from afar, a kind of lodestone drawing people to Jerusalem to hear her. Saint Luke paints an icon of Mary with Jesus in her arms, and "[f]or centuries, the Mother of God has mercifully visited us in her wonder-working icons that are resplendent with grace, and have illumined and helped them that approach to venerate them with love."[12]

This text recounts Mary's travels with St. John to avoid persecution by Herod, first to Ephesus, then to other cities. (The "house of Mary" in modern-day Ephesus is a shrine visited by both Christians and Muslims. Built over small first-century rooms, a chapel surrounds the "house.") Returning to Jerusalem, Mary learns that Lazarus (yes, the Lazarus whom Jesus had raised from the dead), now living in Cyprus, longs to meet her. With John and others, she sets sail, only to be washed ashore on Athos in northeastern Greece. After a statue of the Roman god Jupiter shatters at their approach, Mary disembarks to destroy all pagan idols and convert the inhabitants, predicting that monks will occupy Athos and promising them her protection. She then returns to Jerusalem.[13]

Mary's dormition, like other events, is drawn from extracanonical texts, liturgies, and the interpretations of Byzantine elders. Mary receives a palm from Gabriel on the Mount of Olives, foretelling her death. This dormition narrative follows the tradition, with the apostles brought from abroad. Jesus comes to receive her soul; Mary dies on August 15. Her soul visits Hades, and her body is carried to Heaven three days after her death. Thomas arrives late and receives her sash. Later, she appears to the apostles, reassuring them that she will be with them forever.

A marvelous mixture of canonical and extracanonical texts, saints' commentaries, liturgical excerpts, and pious tradition, this *Life of Mary* combines narrative and devotion, both reflected in the many icons that illustrate the encyclopedic text. It seems more than odd, however, that the authors of such a monumental work fail to describe the first celebration of the Eucharist, since the commemoration of the Last Supper is at the heart of both Roman and Orthodox Catholic worship.

A shorter work of "patristic theology," *The Life of the Virgin Mary [Attributed to Maximas the Confessor]*,[14] published in 2022, mingles a description of Jesus' blessing the bread and wine with an account of his washing the apostles' feet. The text mentions that "…during the Last Supper, … He entrusted the care of those women who followed him to His mother, that they might not fall into disarray."[15] The text also affirms Mary's fortitude during Jesus' Passion and his appearance to her first of all.

This version of Mary's life has all the piety but none of the engaging details that distinguish the earlier work.

Theophilus: From the Seventh Century to the Twenty-First

The oldest story of someone's selling his soul to the devil is that of Theophilus, a sixth-century archdeacon living in what is now Turkey. Elected to the bishopric, he refuses the post out of humility, and another man takes up the crosier and miter. The new bishop then deprives Theophilus of his position, rendering him destitute. In despair, Theophilus signs and seals a contract with Satan, only to regret his decision and beg Mary for deliverance. After securing a pardon from Jesus, delivered by Mary, Theophilus worries about his contract. Mary confronts the Devil, takes the contract, and restores it to the repentant sinner, who takes it to the bishop, confessing to him and the entire congregation.

First recorded in Latin translation from the Greek by Paul the Deacon in the seventh century, this tale forms the basis for "25 Latin versions, a half-dozen or so French versions, at least four versions in English, six in German, several in Italian, at least four in Spanish, at least two in Dutch, one in Old English, three in Icelandic, and at least one in Swedish."[16] These numbers reflect only a smattering of the medieval versions; the poet Rutebeuf, a secular contemporary of Gautier de Coinci, dramatized the legend in his *Miracle de Théophile*, first performed in the 1260s. Scenes from the legend appeared in manuscripts (where the most popular illustration seems to have been the Virgin snatching the contract from the Devil), stained glass, and sculpture in churches and cathedrals throughout Europe, most particularly in France.[17]

The legend emerged later, in the wake of fifteenth- and sixteenth-century prosecutions of witchcraft, with Christopher Marlowe's *The Tragical History of Dr. Faustus* (1604). Goethe's nineteenth-century *Faust* (1808, 1830) became an opera by Charles Gounod (1859) that is performed today. In popular culture, the trope known as "deals with the Devil" has taken diabolical shape in a plethora of comic books, novels, short stories, films, musical works, TV shows, stage plays, and games.

In the course of its proliferation, the Theophilus legend lost Mary's redemptive agency; the story came to focus on the conflicted relationship between man and demon—ambition and knowledge versus supernatural intelligence and cunning. Except perhaps for games, in later "deals with the Devil," the Devil usually wins: Mary's absence leaves a hole in the universe, one that is often filled with violence, anguish, despair, and death.

Sister Beatrice, Perennial Penitent

Close in popularity to the story of Theophilus is that of the little nun who left her convent, which appeared in nearly every collection of Marian

Chapter 8. A Tale of Four Stories from Then to Now

miracles in the Middle Ages. Since then, 200 or more prose versions of the story, with Beatrice or Marguerite as the protagonist, have circulated, in English as well as European and Nordic languages.[18]

In the 1820s, French scholars published a prose translation and an Old French version of "La Sacristine."[19] Charles Nodier (1780–1844) brought out a short story, "La Légende de Soeur Béatrix," in 1836.[20] Villiers de l'Isle-Adam (1838–1889) changed the name of the "little nun" in his 1888 story, "Soeur Natalia," imbuing the story with nostalgia for the Middle Ages and the presumed purity of its naïve piety.[21]

In 1901, Maurice Maeterlinck (1862–1949) wrote the libretto for an opera, *Soeur Béatrice* (*Sister Beatrice*), in three acts. The plot, like Nodier's and Villiers' versions of the tale, depicts Beatrice as the guardian of a statue of Mary. After Beatrice elopes with the military officer who has wooed her, Mary's statue comes to life and takes the place of the wayward nun. The sisters of the convent, angry at the disappearance of their statue, accuse Mary/Beatrice of stealing it and threaten to beat her, but they are disarmed by the one who performs miracles of healing and performs the tasks of the convent. Mary/Beatrice continues to placate the sisters, while the all-too-human Beatrice, abandoned by her lover, sinks into poverty and illness. At last Beatrice returns to the convent, where Mary welcomes her and returns the statue to her niche. When Beatrice confesses her flight from the convent, the sisters attribute her guilty admissions to delirium and declare her to be a saint who has miraculously restored their statue.[22] Maeterlinck wrote librettos for at least three other operatic productions of this story in the twentieth century, and the latest performance was recorded with Catherine Hunold singing the title role in 2022.

In 1912, a silent film, "The Miracle," also produced in French and German, brought Sister Beatrice to the world's screens under the name (who knows why?) of Megeldis. Using a special color process and featuring a full symphony orchestra and chorus as well as special-effects crowds and church bells, the film included an intermezzo "Lake of the Fairies" and a scene in which Megeldis is accused of witchcraft. The final episode takes place on Christmas Eve, when Megeldis returns to the convent with her dead child and is received by Mary.[23]

In the early twentieth century, the story was used in the formation, or training, of religious sisters, who carried it into the Catholic schools where they taught. (I first heard about the little nun from my fifth-grade teacher, Sister Sanctina.)

Soeur Béatrice had staying power on the Web as well. In 2005, the story appeared in a blog, "Saints and Sinners," as "The Keeper of the Keys: The Legend of Beatrix the Nun and the Virgin Mary."[24]

Some few Marian stories became folktales[25] and entered folk custom in their passage from one century to the next, one country to another. The Brothers Grimm, for example, published "Mary's Child," a tale of a poor woodcutter's daughter adopted by the Virgin. Given a task and a command by Mary, the young woman fails and lies about it. Mary punishes her with exile from Heaven, and she lives in a hollow tree within a wilderness. A king goes hunting there, discovers her—now unable to speak—and marries her. She has three children, all of whom Mary takes after inviting her to repent and hearing her refusal. Accused of murdering her children, the woman is about to be burned as a witch when she finally repents, regains her voice, and confesses to Mary. Rain falls immediately, extinguishing the fire, and Mary appears with her children, saying, "Whoever repents a sin and confesses it will be forgiven."[26]

The Grain Miracle Legend

An intriguing and enduring example of one legend's evolution is the Grain Miracle.[27] In one of the Six Books manuscripts, Mary promises to bless the fields and crops of those who pray to her.[28] Assuming the role of Ceres, the goddess of the harvest, as she had the roles of Diana in fertility and childbirth, Mary was thought to ensure good harvests as her image was carried in procession around the fields before plowing. The custom of Marian processions in spring—and often at harvest time—became common in agricultural areas in Europe, lasting well into the twentieth century.

According to a thirteenth-century tale, which takes its inspiration from *Pseudo-Matthew* and the *Arabic Infancy Gospel*, the Holy Family had just begun the long and eventful way to Egypt. As they hurried along, fleeing Herod's soldiers, they passed a farmer sowing his wheat. The farmer greeted them, and Mary spoke to him: "Farmer, if any come this way and ask if you have seen a couple with their child pass by, tell them that it was when you were sowing this field." No doubt puzzled by Mary's request for the obvious, the farmer agreed. As they left him, Mary blessed the field, and instantly the wheat sprang up, waving gently in the wind. Soon after, Herod's troops came galloping up. "Ho, farmer!" their captain shouted. "Have you seen a man and a woman pass by with their child?" "Indeed, sir," responded the farmer, gesturing with his scythe. "I saw them while I was planting this wheat." Angry and frustrated at having missed the family by so long a time, Herod's man ordered his soldiers to turn back.

Another version of the story is found in *The Play of the Three Kings*,[29] an anonymous fourteenth-century work set in the context of the Magi's journey to Bethlehem, their encounters with Herod in Jerusalem, and their decision to return to their lands by another way to avoid seeing the murderous king again. In this play, it is Joseph who greets the farmer planting his wheat, asking if he would direct them to the road to Egypt. "If anyone comes after us and asks if by chance you've seen someone pass by, would you tell them that you haven't seen a soul? Friend, you would do so much for us!" The sower, saying he can see that Joseph is a worthy man, reassures him. Later, just as Herod's men ride up, the sower observes that his wheat is ready to cut, and he answers their question with the statement that he hasn't seen anyone—large or small, coming or going—since he sowed his wheat. "And now," he says to Herod's minions, "I need to cut it right away." There is no need to lie; the field speaks for him.

Mary is no longer the center of the action; even though we may assume that she continues to bless the fields where she is honored in procession at the seasons of sowing and harvest, this tale centers on the actions of two men.

From Story to Ballad

In the nineteenth century, Francis James Child found the legend of the sower in several verses of a ballad, "The Carnal (i.e., crow) and the Crane."[30] In this mixture of Christian doctrine, extracanonical story (*Pseudo-Matthew*), and grain miracle tale, the Crow instructs the Crane about Jesus' conception by the Holy Spirit and his nativity in the stable. After Herod's decree, the Holy Family flees to Egypt, where a "lovely lion" and other wild beasts worship Jesus. When they set out again:

> Then Jesus, ah, and Joseph,
>   And Mary, that was unknown,
> They travelled by a husbandman,
>   Just while his seed was sown.

The ballad has Jesus performing the miracle, this time producing corn:

> "God speed thee, man," said Jesus,
>   "Go fetch thy ox and wain, [wagon]
> And carry home thy corn again
>   Which thou this day hast sown."

The husbandman acknowledges Jesus as the redeemer of humankind, and Jesus requests that if anyone inquires after the Holy Family, to "[t]ell them that Jesus passed by / As thou thy seed did sow." Soon after, King Herod himself comes riding with his army and asks if Jesus had come this way. The husbandman replies:

> "Why, the truth it must be spoke,
>   And the truth it must be known;

> For Jesus passed by this way
>   When my seed was sown.
> "But now I have it reapen, [reaped]
>   And some laid on my wain, [wagon]
> Ready to fetch and carry
>   Into my barn again."
> "Turn back," says the captain,
>   "Your labor and mine's in vain;
> It's full three quarters of a year
>   Since his seed has sown."

As Mary's stories have disappeared, so she herself has vanished from this ballad—as a voice and as a worker of miracles in partnership with her son.

From Ballad to Folk Tale

Known also in the poetry of Germany, Belgium, Sweden, and Denmark, the story was collected from the south of France in the twentieth century.[31] The French version, in my translation below, focuses on Mary, adding details from folklore that dramatize the flight.

* * *

Once upon a time, Mary and Saint Joseph had to take to the road with the Infant to flee the wrath of Herod in the form of his ruthless soldiers, a whole brigade of them on their horses, their captain in the lead, who had massacred the innocents with dagger and sword. Blades in hand, spattered with blood, they hunted, they searched throughout the country.

By nightfall the Lady was at the end of her strength, but still Herod's minions came on at a hellish pace, the hoofs of their horses striking sparks from the road. Mary ran and ran and ran as long as she could, holding tightly to her son Jesus, whose throat Herod had promised to cut. Suddenly, spent, she fell breathless beside a sage plant.

"Sage, sage, save Jesus!" said our Lady, and the sage heard her and hurried to grow until it became a spreading bush. When Herod's soldiers arrived on their horses, they looked all about. And the mint plant, that traitor, whispered as loudly as it could, "Under the bush, under the bush." But with all the brandishing of swords and clopping of horses' hooves, the soldiers heard nothing, and left, defeated. "Mint, mint," said Our Lady, "you are a liar, and you will lie forever: You will flower but never bear seed." And to the sage, she said: "Sage, sage, God save you! You will flower and bear seed." Thus we take some sage when we feel sick; and when we're healthy, we do well not to forget it, as it is the hand of God.

But Herod's soldiers continued to scour the plain. They saw Our

Chapter 8. A Tale of Four Stories from Then to Now

Lady from a distance and raised a shout. Spurs flashing, raising clouds of dust, they raced headlong across the fields. Our Lady took refuge under an aspen tree, but the aspen trembled and shook, shedding its leaves and exposing her and her son to the sight of the soldiers. But the brave hazelnut tree was there, too, fluffing its leaves to make them large, hiding Mary and Jesus from Herod's men. And since that time, the aspen, livid and scarred, shakes as if it had a fever, while the hazelnut tree is the healthiest of all trees: At its touch, snakes die, and it has the privilege of flowering several times a year, on the feast-days of Our Lady.

But Egypt was far away, and the road was long. In her flight to escape her ferocious pursuers, those blood-soaked riders, always on the hunt, Mary had constantly to find new places to hide. Mary asked the cuckoo to hide her child in its nest in the stubble of the fields, but the bird betrayed them, calling to their pursuers. By chance, the oriole was nearby; it took the infant and hid him in its nest. Since then, the cuckoo, grey of plumage and bereft of a nest to call its own, lays its eggs in others' nests, while the oriole's feathers glow golden. Our Lady also gave the oriole the gift of signaling the approach of rain with a special cry at sunset.

Still the good Lady fled, followed by Herod's soldiers on their huge horses, galloping, galloping, armored with iron, in dust and lightning, crushing all under their feet, sweeping everything before them; they had sworn that nothing in the fields, nests, hedges, or clumps of trees would escape their eyes.

In the countryside lived a ploughman with his family in their little house, crying with hunger. They had not eaten for a week, and the season was bleak, the very dead of winter. How would they live until the harvest?

A voice said to the ploughman, "Go, go, go out to the valley and sow your wheat!" He obeyed the voice. And while the wheat was being sown, the Virgin passed by. "Good day, good day, fine ploughman! What lovely wheat you are sowing!" "Good day, good day, lovely lady! What a fine child you are carrying!" "Tell me, tell me, ploughman, would you be willing to protect him?" "Oh yes, oh yes, good lady, I'll do all that I can!"

The Virgin asked him to make a deep, deep furrow to hold her and her infant. And he leaned on the plow-handle, digging a furrow so deep that the Lady could hide within it, with the Child on her lap. Over them he threw his cape.

"Tell me, tell me, good ploughman, the wheat has not failed you this year?" "Oh, but it has, good Lady, it has! We haven't eaten for seven days!"

"Well, then, take your scythe and you'll harvest your wheat." "And how would that be possible, when it's not even all sown?"

"You only have to go, take up your scythe; the wheat will be ripe for the harvest." And from the bottom of the furrow the good Lady chanted to the wheat what was necessary for her to chant: "O wheat, O wheat, flower and seed, hurry, hurry to ripeness!" And the wheat sprang from the ground above the Lady and the Child: all at once, green shoots of wheat, then wheat in stalks, then wheat in ears, then wheat ripe for the scythe.

"Go, go, go to the Valley: The wheat is ready for harvest!" The good ploughman obeyed the voice. And while the wheat was being harvested, Herod's troop rode up.

"Good day, good day, good ploughman! What fine wheat you're harvesting!"

"And you, Herod's captain, what a handsome horse you are riding!"

"Tell me, tell me, my man, haven't you seen the Lady pass by? She's carrying that Child we are ordered to kill!"

"I did, I did, captain, she passed by when I was sowing."

"Ah, turn around, brigade! She passed by last year!" They raved, they swore, Herod's captain and soldiers, but they left at a gallop: Spurs jingling and hoofs pounding, they left like dust in the wind that disappears over the fields.

The good Lady rose from the furrow, and the infant blessed the wheat. In an instant the wheat rose up from the earth, as if from the heart of the infant, as if from his very flesh. There was enough for the ploughman, good man, for his wife and his children.

Of that wheat blessed by Jesus, there is some for the bread of humankind, there is some for the bread of God, alleluia!

A Nineteenth-Century Grain Miracle in the Upper Midwest

During the 1870s, a series of grasshopper/locust swarms descended on the prairies and farms of north central Minnesota. According to *The Story of Mary and the Grasshoppers*, a twentieth-century account of the event,

> As many as a hundred would attack one stalk of grain, chew until the stalk was gone, then fall into a bunch on the ground, only to jump up for a new attack. In a short time not even stubble remained.... Grasshoppers, sixty to eighty per square yard, could devour one ton of hay per day for each forty acres they covered.... They ruined clothes.... Altar boys swished them from the altar and brushed them from the priest's vestments at mass. The grasshoppers went everywhere, and in a short time they spelled out a total crop failure for the farmers in central Minnesota.[32]

By the spring of 1877 the situation seemed dire, with grasshopper eggs covering two-thirds of the state. The governor proclaimed a Day of Prayer, and the regional Benedictine pastor, Father Leo Winter, extended the prayer over the next months and persuaded the people to offer a chapel dedicated to Mary in gratitude should she come to their aid. The chapel would be called Mary's Help, and every Saturday a Mass would be said in thanksgiving if "…she would free us from this horrid plague through her mighty intercession."

On April 26, 1877, the day dawned sunny and bright, but by evening it began to rain. The temperature dropped; the rain turned to snow; and the snow turned into a blizzard that howled through the next day. The grasshoppers were wiped out, and grain yields soared up to 200 percent over the previous year.

The chapel was built; the people came as they had promised and offered thanks. When a tornado destroyed the structure, it was rebuilt in solid Minnesota granite. Over the lintel of today's chapel is a bas-relief of Mary in glory, with two penitent grasshoppers lying at her feet.

From Tumbler to Juggler, *Converso* to Child: Our Lady's Minstrel

In *fin-de-siècle* France, the scholar Gaston Paris and others encouraged the study of Old French. In his work on medieval French literature, Paris praised the tale of the tumbler for its "delightful and childlike simplicity,"[33] and Jacques Anatole François Thibault (Anatole France) unwittingly started an entire cottage industry when he published his version of the story called "The Juggler of Notre Dame."[34] After hundreds of years of obscurity, it took less than a decade for the thirteenth-century tale of a lay brother's conversion of his monastery to become the inspiration of a century's worth of adaptations and exploitations.

In Anatole France's version of "Our Lady's Tumbler," the performer is a juggler, reflecting the popularity of juggling as street entertainment during the nineteenth century. The performer's name is Barnaby, and he juggles six copper balls with his hands and six knives with his feet. Although he is poor, he loves Our Lady, never failing when he passed a church to enter and say a prayer before her image.[35] One cold and rainy night on the road, he meets a monk, whose description of monastery life—particularly the praise of God and Mary—inspires him. The performer declares that he would be delighted to sing the hours of the Virgin, to whom he has a special devotion. The monk, who happens to be the prior of his monastery, invites Barnaby to join him, and so he does.

France gives names to the men who use their gifts in service to Mary: Brothers Maurice, Alexander, and Marbode, whose talents impress and depress Barnaby. One day he overhears the monks talking about the religious who could learn nothing more than the Hail Mary: At the man's death, five roses grew from his mouth, one in honor of each of the five letters of the name "Maria." Inspired, Barnaby finds an empty chapel, and while the monks are busy at their work, he performs his juggling act for Mary.

It is the prior himself who observes Barnaby, accompanied by two elders, who are scandalized and declare the performance a sacrilege. The prior, however, believes that the simple Barnaby has lost his mind. As they prepare to remove him bodily from the chapel, they see the Virgin descending from the altar to wipe the sweat from his forehead with the edge of her mantle. Falling to the floor, the prior declares, "Happy are the simple, for they shall see God!" "Amen!" the elders exclaim. The end.

True to Gaston Paris' interpretation, France made the tale and the tumbler/juggler "simple and childlike," and that's what the powerful story of the Middle Ages became as it was popularly interpreted during the course of the twentieth century. In 1902, the juggler appeared in an opera as Jean, performing in the Latin Quarter with Notre Dame and the monastery of Cluny in the background. Barnaby was the boy hero of half a dozen children's books (or more) "based on a French folk tale," and he appeared in gothic-scripted translations for adults. During the Golden Age of radio in the '30s and '40s he offered his performance as a Christmas gift to Our Lady, a forerunner of the Little Drummer Boy. There was an MGM short subject (1942) and an animated cartoon (1958) based on R.O. Blechman's account for children, *The Juggler of Our Lady* (1953). The 1960s saw a British TV adaptation; a dance/movement theater piece filmed and telecast; a student-written musical for which the renowned poet W.H. Auden wrote "The Ballad of Barnaby"; and a turn by Tony Curtis as "The Young Juggler" in a film of that name. Tomie de Paola published *The Clown of God* in 1978; *The Acrobat and the Angel* came out in 1999, and *The Little Jester* in 2002. Disney and the Paulist Fathers collaborated to produce a feature-length 1982 film, "updated and Americanized," in which Barnaby "ekes out a living" after the death of his wife but finds "the meaning of Christmas and giving," in the words of the Ignatius Press videos brochure for *Catholic Family & School*.[36]

All of these interpretations were just a prelude to 2018, when a mammoth exhibition, "Juggling the Middle Ages," opened at Dumbarton Oaks in Washington, D.C., to celebrate a six-volume work, *The Juggler of Notre Dame and the Medievalizing of Modernity* by Jan M. Ziolkowski.[37] The exhibition had been preceded by scholarly presentations on the work at the International Conference on Medieval Studies. The subject of the exhibition was introduced in a 64-page catalogue, illustrated with images of Mary and the "juggler" from medieval stained-glass windows to twentieth-century opera playbills. The exhibition reception featured live juggling performances that preceded lectures by renowned scholars and a film screening. A series of commemorative concerts lasted into 2019.

Where and who is Mary in that monumental tribute to her performer and his story? Silent in her chapel niche, she acts only to wipe the face of her devotee (or to throw him a rose, in one version). An object of religious devotion in the thirteenth century, she becomes an object of scholarly devotion in the twenty-first. Our Lady's tumbler loses his profession, with all its forbidden, racy moves; Mary forfeits her accompanying angels and redemptive power and is left alone on that pedestal of intellectual and artistic attention.

Pseudo-Matthew at Christmastide: The Cherry Tree Carol

In Chapter 20 of the *Gospel of Pseudo-Matthew*, a palm tree bends down to give Mary fruit to relieve her hunger. The story resonated through the centuries in sculpture and painting, and it resurfaced in N-Town Play 15, when Mary wishes for some cherries and "the one who got [her] with child," the Creator, responds to her prayer. The tree "bows down so that she can gather them herself and eat her fill."[38]

Francis James Child assigned no date to "The Cherry-Tree Carol" in his late nineteenth-century description of the ballad based on the drama. He reproduced several versions of the lyrics, one of which appears below.

> Joseph was an old man,
>   and an old man was he,
> When he wedded Mary
>   in the land of Galilee.
>
> Joseph and Mary walked
>   through an orchard good,
> Where was cherries and berries
>   as red as any blood.
>
> Joseph and Mary walked
>   through an orchard green,
> Where was berries and cherries
>   as thick as might be seen.
>
> O then bespoke Mary,
>   so meek and so mild,
> "Pluck me one cherry, Joseph,
>   for I am with child."
>
> O then bespoke Joseph,
>   with words so unkind,
> "Let him pluck thee a cherry
>   that got thee with child."

> O then bespoke the babe,
>> within his mother's womb,
> "Bow down then the tallest tree
>> for my mother to have some."
>
> Then bowed down the highest tree
>> unto his mother's hand;
> Then she cried, "See, Joseph,
>> I have cherries at command."
>
> O then bespake Joseph,
>> "I have done Mary wrong;
> But cheer up, my dearest,
>> and be not cast down."
>
> Then Mary plucked a cherry,
>> as red as the blood,
> Then Mary went home
>> with her heavy load.
>
> Then Mary took her babe,
>> and sat him on her knee,
> Saying, "My dear son, tell me
>> what this world will be."
>
> "O I shall be as dead, mother,
>> as the stones in the wall,
> As the stones in the street, mother,
>> shall mourn for me all.
>
> Upon Easter day, mother,
>> my uprising shall be,
> O the sun and the moon, mother,
>> Shall both rise with me."[39]

With the exception of the last five stanzas—which serve in the original as elements of catechism—the carol is sung today by scores of artists in dozens of settings, choral and solo, vocal and instrumental, its popularity constant for hundreds of years. In it we hear Mary's wish as Jesus' command: The cherry tree bows to her prayer and to his power (which is also hers). Jesus reaffirms the bond between mother and son as he describes his mission, which ends as he rises in triumph over death and darkness. This is an Easter carol as well as a Christmas carol.

Narratives and Theologies Across the Centuries

In the wake of the Reformation, the stream of ancient and medieval stories about Mary seemed to disappear. In reality, that stream simply went underground, to surface in different genres at different times. The stories themselves evolved in different ways. For Jacobus, they become feast-day enhancements. The modern Byzantine *Life of Mary* gives us a missionary Mary whose travels result in monasteries on Mount Athos. In the evolution of the Theophilus story, Mary disappears after the Reformation, and her absence deprives the story of hope. In contrast, the tale of Beatrice survives with Mary as its center: Even as a statue come to life, Mary works miracles for the convent sisters and welcomes the penitent back to grace.

In few of the post–Reform stories does Mary speak: She literally loses her voice. In the thirteenth-century grain miracle, for example, Mary directs the farmer. In the fourteenth century, Joseph is the one who takes charge of the field; and by the time the ballad is collected in the nineteenth century, it is Jesus who is the principal actor and voice. Yet, in the French folktale—where we might least expect it—Mary recovers her medieval power and authority: Although she must ask bushes, birds, and a peasant ploughman for aid, she rewards her helpers and punishes her betrayers, speaking for herself. The folktale ends with Mary presiding over a harvest of wheat that Jesus has blessed, a harvest that feeds the ploughman and his family as well as "all of humankind." Jesus and Mary together produce the bread of life in this folk parable of the Eucharistic liturgy.

A chapel in the Minnesota countryside serves as a reminder of Mary's ancient power as it commemorates a nineteenth-century grain miracle. The stone grasshoppers at Mary's feet will not threaten crops again.

It's the story of the nameless entertainer, "Our Lady's Minstrel," that undergoes the most significant change from the thirteenth to the twenty-first century. Although modern versions lack the nuance and spiritual depth of the original, the story itself contains the power of the Marian presence that can transform lives.

And it is Mary's presence that animates all of the stories through the centuries. Her exercise of power may be brief, but it is always effective; her miracles are always something to marvel at, whether concealing a penitent's sin or rewarding an acrobat with Heaven itself—or a rose. I find the narrative theology of the latest version of the grain miracle to be the most compelling of all these tales: Jesus and Mary concelebrate a liturgy of plenty, transforming a ploughman's grain into the bread of life, continuing their partnership in the work of salvation.

CHAPTER 9

End of Stories, End of Story?
Where Is Mary in Modernity?

Mary as Messenger I

The Mary of the early twentieth century echoes the Counter-Reformation in her appearances at the Cova de Iria near Fatima, Portugal, in 1917: Her voice on these occasions is reproving, warning of dangers both to faith and to world peace. The year before, roiled by political strife and economic challenges, Portugal had entered World War I, with enemy German forces in neighboring France. Like Lourdes, Fatima was an insignificant village, and the seers of Our Lady were children. For Lucia dos Santos and her cousins, Jacinta and Francisco Marto, visions of Mary were preceded by two visits from an angel, who gave them a prayer to say before they met Our Lady.[1] The visions themselves occurred over a period of six months in 1917, beginning in the month of May. Mary asked the children to pray the rosary for world peace; she predicted the early deaths of Jacinta and Francisco. She requested that people pray for "the conversion of sinners" and showed the children a vision of Hell awaiting the unrepentant.

Like Bernadette of Lourdes, the three children were threatened by secular authorities but refused to deny their visions; in August of 1917, Mary asked for a chapel to be built in the Cova de Ira, where she had appeared, and promised a miracle in two months' time. By October, the crowds that had gathered previously were dwarfed by the more than 70,000 people who visited Fatima, waiting in a downpour for the promised miracle. Suddenly, the sun appeared, seeming to leave the sky and plummet toward the earth, a movement repeated three more times. As rapidly as it had started, the phenomenon stopped; the sun returned to the sky, and members of the crowd found their clothes as dry as the ground beneath them.

The chapel was built, then a church, a shrine, a basilica. Francisco and Jacinta died (they now are saints of the Catholic church); Lucia died in 2005 after having received additional visions.

The Fatima phenomenon reflects Mary's status in the Catholic Church during much of the twentieth century as she took on the role of "Cold War Mary."[2] Popes became cold warriors, inveighing against the evils of atheistic communism and national socialism. Mary was chosen to lead the first line of defense, recalling her early roles as downfall of demons and intercessor for her followers. Her biblical authority—from crushing the head of the serpent in Genesis to evading the dragon in Revelation—was vital, and the rosary her chosen weapon. The Legion of Mary, founded in 1921, followed the teachings of Grignion de Monfort, emphasizing prayer and devotion to Mary. In 1947, the Blue Army of Our Lady symbolized the Church Militant as it championed prayers for the conversion of Russia and devotion to the Immaculate Heart of Mary. Now known as the World Apostolate of Fatima, USA, the organization advocates conversion and reparation as its members pray for world peace.[3]

Our Lady of Fatima. Statue of Our Lady of Fatima. Portugal. Ricardo/stock-adobe.com.

The threat of communism, together with the engagement of Mary in the struggle to defeat its atheistic ideology, dominated American Catholicism for decades. Popular devotion to Mary increased everywhere, with sodalities, novenas, processions, hymns, radio and television programs, and films—as well as Marian academic institutes and societies devoted to her and her causes.

Midcentury Mary: A New Dogma

The first of the so-called "Marian Popes," Pius XII (1876–1958; pope 1939–) was elected in 1939. Hoping to engage Catholics worldwide in prayer to defeat communism, Pius declared 1950 a "Marian Year." That year, he issued an apostolic constitution (a church document with the force of law) entitled *Munificentissimus Deus*, "Most Bountiful God," proclaiming the dogma of Mary's Assumption as a divinely revealed truth. Pius cited centuries of church "tradition" in the form of "sacred books" (their canonical status unspecified), the absence of Marian bodily relics, the proliferation of churches dedicated to the Assumption, the practice of liturgies in East and West alike, and centuries of theological writings.

Less controversial than its predecessor, the Immaculate Conception, the dogma of Mary's Assumption was less challenged, and the discussions about it less fraught, despite its extracanonical origins.

Mary the Subject of Debate in Vatican II

Who would have guessed that a 76-year-old pope would be the one to throw open the windows of tradition and bring the Catholic Church into the modern world? John XXIII (1881–1963; pope 1958–) did his best, convoking the Second Vatican Council in 1962. His work of *aggiorniamento*, or transposing the liturgy and practices of Catholicism into modern vernacular languages and local customs, would be continued beyond his death in 1963, and his initiative resulted in a rethinking of the church in the modern world.

Except, perhaps, for Mary.

Two schools of thought about Mary emerged during the church council (1962–1965). One emphasized her unique role in the salvation of humankind, deeming her a "co-redemptrix" with her son. Her special titles—Advocate, Helper, Benefactress, and Mediatrix—would "…highlight God's gifts of special graces to Mary because of her role as Mother of the Redeemer." This view was countered by those who thought that such an attitude would "…remove Mary even further from scripture and liturgy, compromising the council's emphasis on the Eucharistic liturgy as the 'source and summit' of all Christian living." In other words, this more conservative faction stoutly resisted any portrayal of Mary that did not originate in the Bible or in liturgical works. They also believed that an emphasis on Mary's active participation in salvation history would discourage efforts toward ecumenism.[4]

The council decided to base its Marian doctrine on the second school of thought. Mary was indeed to be considered an

> …advocate, helper, benefactress, and mediatrix. This, however, is understood in such a way that it neither takes away anything from, nor adds anything to, the dignity and efficacy of Christ the one Mediator…. The church

does not hesitate to profess this subordinate role of Mary, which it constantly experiences and recommends to the heartfelt attention of the faithful, so that encouraged by this maternal help they may the more closely adhere to the Mediator and Redeemer.[5]

The Dogmatic Constitution on the Church, "Lumen Gentium" ("Light of the World"), a document that emerged from Vatican II, devotes Chapter 8 to Mary. In five brief sections, it emphasizes Mary's obedience, humility, and virginity, qualities ascribed to the church itself (however euphemistically) for centuries. An effort by some prelates to emphasize Mary's partnership with God in the work of salvation was overruled; Section 56 of "Lumen Gentium" presents Mary as the quintessential handmaid, a "predestined mother, so that just as a woman had a share in bringing about death, so also a woman should contribute to life."[6] This bit of second-century wisdom (bad Eve/good Mary) echoes throughout the conciliar account of her life, bookended dogmatically with her immaculate conception and her assumption. Mary's significance in this document is that of someone who "devoted herself totally, as a handmaid of the Lord, to the person and work of her Son, under and with him, serving the mystery of redemption, by the grace of Almighty God."[7]

Although she has been called the "Mother of the Church," Mary's role in that church—even though she can be invoked as an advocate or mediatrix—became, finally, that of an abstract "Sign of True Hope and Comfort for the Pilgrim People of God," as the last heading of the Mary chapter states. This more ordinary Mary and her suitably toned-down devotions would be less likely to "lead the separated sisters and brothers or any others whatsoever into error about the true doctrine of the church."[8] (At the same time, she is effectively imprisoned on a pedestal of traditional submissive virtues, inhibiting the faithful from regarding her as a powerful helper on earth.)

In some respects, Vatican II could be viewed as a second Reformation. "The [modernizing] reformers sought not merely to reduce extreme ... expressions of Marian devotion but to 'purify' it by disallowing all perceptions of the Virgin Mary that maintain premodern recognition of diffuse presence and profound interrelatedness—such that all that would be left is what the modern mindset can respect: the literal, the objective, the concrete, and the shrinking of the sacred down to human size."[9]

In the end, Vatican II diminished and eventually erased her history of partnership with her son. Notwithstanding her altar niche and vigil lights in parishes and homes, she who was the companion of Jesus her son was all but dismissed from the larger church, to make cameo appearances on Christmas and Good Friday, with honorable mentions at the Feasts of the Annunciation in spring and the Assumption in summer.

Mary at Mid-Century: Another Denial

In addition to the evidence of Mary's ministry, from the fifth-century stone slab (in the "Mary as Minister in the Temple of Jerusalem" section in Chapter 1) and the seventh-century mosaic (in "The Revelation" section in Chapter 7) to the modern images so threatening to contemporary prelates, we have centuries of writing about Mary's participation in the ministry of her son during and after his time on earth as well as her performance of priestly duties in story, song, and drama throughout the ages. The French theologian René Laurentin compiled a massive volume of testimonies to Mary's priesthood, which he published in the mid-twentieth century. Following 600 pages of evidence from the first centuries of Christianity to the twentieth, Laurentin concluded that "[t]he coherence and the convergence of these reasons [for considering Mary a priest] are striking. We can understand very well how a Spanish [theologian], a powerful intellect, has been able to declare absolutely ... the requirement of affirming the priesthood of the Virgin." In the very next paragraph, however, Laurentin states, "However, these authors [cited throughout the book] accede only reluctantly and partially to the necessity of acknowledging [Mary's priestly dimension]. Something holds them back. Not the reasons that we find here [in the text], but a spontaneous movement of recoil, like the instinctive flight of an animal at its first encounter with an enemy of its species."[10]

In this statement, one of the church's premier Marian scholars appears to say that in the face of all the "reason" in the world, much of the Christian community draws back from admitting an uncomfortably possible truth. Nevertheless, during the course of the twentieth century and continuing into the present, reporters and scholars, women and men alike, have promoted the cause of Mary's priestly presence as an icon of women's ecclesiastical leadership. Her voice echoes in their advocacy.

Mary as Countersign: Her Presence in the Twenty-First Century

What does Mary have to say to this most contentious century, roiled with conflict in both church and state and heavy with the patriarchal governance of both? Where can we find her?

Mary is where she always has been: everywhere, available to those who look for her. On the cusp of the millennium, *Newsweek* gave her a cover story, "The Meaning of Mary: A Struggle Over Her Role Grows within the Church."[11] Summarizing Mary's history in church teachings and apparitions, the article concludes with the suggestion that Mary be honored with a new feast day or title rather than another dogma.[12] The issue features a powerful appreciation of both Eve and Mary, ending with the depiction of the two by Lorenzo Ghiberti (1378–1455) on the east doors of the Florence Baptistry in Italy.[13] The intertwined stories of Mary and Eve also wind through theologian Tina Beattie's study, *God's Mother, Eve's Advocate*. Repudiating the church fathers' designation of Eve as the mother of death, Beattie depicts her as the mother of life and Mary as "... the descendant and vindicator of the First Eve [who] crushed the head of the serpent and vanquished the Devil."[14] Refuting myths about women's bodily and spiritual lives, Beattie cites Dante's *Paradiso*, which shows Mary "at the top of descending tiers of women ... and the woman who sits nearest to her is Eve."[15]

Early in the twenty-first century (2009), the Mariological Society of America sponsored a conference, "Telling Mary's Story: The 'Life of Mary' Through the Ages."[16] Covering both Eastern and Western Christianity, encompassing canonical and extracanonical sources, conference essays also included Mary's life in film and contemporary novels. Michael Duricy noted "some important Marian content in the 1939 *Hunchback of Notre Dame*" and labeled *The Song of Bernadette* (1943) "perhaps the most famous Marian film of that era."[17] Mary featured in filmed lives of Jesus, notably Franco Zefferelli's miniseries, *Jesus of Nazareth* (1976), which began with her marriage to Joseph and included the Annunciation but otherwise showed only glimpses of her until Christ's crucifixion. One film seems to have captured the vitality of Mary's role in her son's ministry: Jean Delannoy's *Marie de Nazareth* shows her "in a leadership position with the women who followed Jesus which paralleled his role with the Apostles."[18] This seems to have been the only film—whether based only on biblical or on both biblical and extracanonical sources—to even suggest the dynamism of her life. Forthcoming in 2025, however, the film *Queen of Heaven* aims to depict Mary's activities from the time of the Crucifixion to her dormition.[19]

Mary as Messenger II

In 2015, the cover of *National Geographic* showed Mary's face as interpreted by Sandro Botticelli (c. 1445–1510). Maureen Orth's feature story, "How the Virgin Mary Became the World's Most Powerful Woman," was preceded by two pages of praises from the Litany of the Blessed Virgin.[20] Emphasizing Marian apparitions, the author begins with the series of Mary's twentieth-century appearances to six young people in Medjugorje, a village in Bosnia and Herzegovina, beginning in 1981. As the

"Queen of Peace," Mary is said to have handed down "thousands of messages admonishing the faithful to pray more often and asking sinners to repent."[21] Thousands of pilgrims flock to Medjugorje every year, as they do to Lourdes and Fatima, Paris and Mexico City to see the Madonna of their devotions.

The message of Medjugorje echoes in Kibeho, Rwanda, where Mary is said to have appeared, also in 1981, warning three girls about the genocide that would occur in 1994. In Kibeho, she called herself "Nyina wa Jambo, Mother of the Word." Her prediction came true in 1994, when more than 800,000 people were slaughtered, among them one of the girls, named Marie Claire.

The author also discusses contemporary Muslim devotion to Mary. She tells of meeting two young Muslim women at the Coptic church of Abu Serga, "...built over a cave that is said to have been used by the Holy Family." One of the women cites the *sura* in the Qur'an devoted to Mary. Another woman, "[a]long with her Koran, ... carries Christian medals of the Virgin Mary in her purse.... [S]he talks to Mary about her life and ... Mary has answered her several times by showing her visions in dreams that later came true."[22]

A two-page spread, "Seeing Mary," maps "Centuries of Miracles," beginning in the sixteenth century, when the Council of Trent first established protocols for determining the validity of visionary claims. Since that time, hundreds of Marian appearances have been recorded, in scores of locations ranging from Our Lady of Siluva in Lithuania to Our Lady of Zaytun in Egypt to Our Lady of Good Success in Ecuador. Mary has appeared on every continent but Antarctica.[23]

Gladys and the Glowing Rosary

In 1983, Mary appeared to an Argentinian woman, Gladys Quiroga de Motta, in the town of San Nicolas de los Arroyos, about 240 miles from Buenos Aires. Although not particularly religious, Gladys became devoted to Mary after recovering from a lifesaving operation. On September 24, she saw that her rosary, which was hanging in her room, was glowing. She began to pray, in the company of others in the room. The following day, she saw Mary with the Christ child; from that time on, she experienced a series of appearances, which she did not report for fear of being considered crazy.

Finally she told her local priest, who believed her. Mary continued to visit her, calling for conversion and the recitation of the rosary as well as frequent attendance at Mass and communion. In November, Mary

Chapter 9. End of Stories, End of Story? 197

identified herself as Our Lady of the Rosary, telling Gladys that a damaged and long-lost statue of Our Lady of the Rosary could be found in the bell tower of the local cathedral. The statue of Mary holding the child Jesus, with a rosary held in their right hands, was recovered; the shrine that Mary requested was built. Mary herself was said to indicate the place of its construction with a heavenly ray of light. The shrine was finished in 1989.

A strong smell of roses is associated with the shrine, along with the glowing rosaries of its visitors. In 2016, "after a long and thorough study, Bishop Hector Cardelli of San Nicolas declared the apparitions and messages to be of supernatural origin and worthy of belief."[24]

Mary's presence in modern life is more expansive, more diverse, and more subversive than accounts of her apparitions might suggest; popular enthusiasm for all things Marian has overtaken and overwhelmed clerical reserve. A remnant of the 1950s, Our Lady of the Bathtub remains enshrined throughout the U.S. Her origins lie in the years after World War II, when a building and remodeling boom made old stand-alone claw-foot tubs obsolete. Old bathtubs posed a recycling challenge, and people began to convert them (so to speak) into shrines, cutting off the claw feet, embedding the tub in their yards, and installing statues of Mary. The desired effect was that of a grotto or outdoor shrine. Often the mini-grottos were embellished with artificial or garden flowers. One area in the East boasts more than 600 bathtub Madonnas, a possible world record.[25]

The city of Encinitas, California, boasts a Surfing Madonna, "miraculously" preserved, as well as a nonprofit community organization, the Surfing Madonna Oceans Project. The Marian image is a 10-by-10-foot mosaic of Our Lady of Guadalupe on a white surfboard, created by Mark Patterson, who—assisted by his friend Bob Nichols—installed the piece on the wall of a rail bridge in 2011. The two had failed to get permission for the installation, and it was removed. Following public acclamation of the mosaic, however, the image found a permanent home in Surfing Madonna Park, across the street from its original site. The Surfing Madonna Oceans Project funds environmental efforts on land and sea and supports humanitarian causes.[26]

"Our Lady of the Underpass," an image of Mary located on a wall under the Kennedy Expressway in Chicago, was still inspiring visits and homage eighteen years after its first appearance in 2005. Although civic authorities declared it a "salt stain," visitors disagreed, leaving flowers and candles at the site. After the image was damaged, devotees not only cleaned it but installed a concrete "altar" beneath it. By 2023, as Gustavo Arellano noted in *The National Catholic Reporter*, "…the candles holding various levels of wax … attested to the fact that people still come, still believe. So did two rosaries that hung from a hook, above where the slightest outline of a head was visible."[27]

In different media, on YouTube alone there are *Lives of Mary*, daily prayers, introductions to the Litany of Loreto, meditations, sermons, songs, treatments of her Assumption, and accounts of her miracles. Gautier de Coinci, the abbot-poet-composer of the twelfth century, enjoys a robust following; as I write, four YouTube performances of his songs are available, and he has 2,913 monthly listeners on Spotify. In France, Patrice Martineau's interpretations of Marian songs have been popular for nearly thirty years; he sings ballads about Our Lady and the robber as well as Our Lady's tumbler, and he tells "The Joys of Notre Dame." There are more than 25 listings for recordings of his songs. Pop star Madonna sings "Like a Virgin," and Rihanna invokes "Mother Mary." Perhaps the most famous Marian anthem of the last 100 years is the 1970 Beatles' hit, "Let It Be," followed by their "Lady Madonna." Mary is still whispering "words of wisdom" while she somehow "manage[s] … to make ends meet."

Mary's presence on the Internet is both the subject of a scholarly book[28] and the object of countless Web searches that seek information on her interactions with visionaries throughout the world. Paul Apolito suggests that the Internet phenomenon "…has profoundly altered the very perception of religion among a substantial number of Catholics, shifting the course of the post–Vatican II transformation of the Catholic Church in a completely unexpected direction."[29] Visionaries and their followers number in the thousands; miracles are countless. Seers report messages that range from personal encouragement to announcements of impending apocalyptic events. These phenomena are available to anyone and everyone who has access to a computer, and whether one is posting or accessing, the process is democratic and free-wheeling.

The Web–based proliferation of apparitions and visionaries has been accompanied by the rise of a professional investigator of the miraculous who specializes in Marian appearances and messages. Michael O'Neill started his Web site, MiracleHunter.com, as "…a centralized spot for his research into all things miraculous, adopting a more matter-of-fact approach than the pious tone he'd found elsewhere and creating a depository of information on the topic."[30] In addition to his Web presence, O'Neill has written books on Mary and interpreted trends in the occurrence of Marian apparitions in the United States and Canada. Emphasizing that the church moves slowly to acknowledge the validity of a claimed apparition, he observes that none of eighty-three "… alleged apparition claims of the last two decades of the twentieth century in the United States and Canada was declared 'supernatural'"—and some were not deemed worthy of the church's attention.[31]

Images of Mary continue to appear, however, in countless forms in the public arena. Marian merchandise takes the form of medals, statues,

Chapter 9. End of Stories, End of Story?

plaques, candles, rosaries (and elaborate rosary cases), children's books, coloring books, journal covers, notebook sets, handbags and totes, jewelry (necklaces, rings, earrings, bracelets), jackets and hoodies, vests and T-shirts—to say nothing of tattoos. Etsy "... sells Mother Mary oracle cards and altars for charging 'reiki energized' crystals that feature Mary's likeness."[32] I remember seeing key chains and ashtrays, holy-water bottles and necklaces with Marian images in souvenir shops on two continents. At some Marian shrines and churches—the display is especially large at Lourdes—there is a collection of crutches, slings, bandages, and other health support items left in thanks for cures. Continuing an ancient tradition, other Marian churches feature *ex-votos*, miniature limbs or bodily organs such as hearts, and tiny babies representing successful births. In Mexico, *ex-votos* can depict thanksgiving for favors received in paintings that show, for example, a sick person getting out of bed.

"Mother Mary" crosses continents and artistic boundaries. Feminists depict her in the company of Frida Kahlo, Joan of Arc, and Ruth Bader Ginsburg. "Mary lends cred to high-end guitar pedals created by female gear makers.... Her story is being retold in provocative contemporary art and the theses of up-and-coming scholars."[33] Soasig Chamaillard's sculptures show Mary as Superman and Barbie; Mary appears in the designs of Jean Paul Gaultier and Alexander McQueen. "By appropriating religious iconography and celebrating not necessarily its holiness but its symbolic multitudes, artists better embrace the complexities of being a woman, which cannot be limited to maternal roles.... Mary is taken away from her (rather reductive) image as a symbol of purity and fertility, and repurposed as an emblem of strength."[34]

Latina artists are inspired, unsurprisingly, by the Virgin of Guadalupe. Yolanda Lopez's self-portrait shows her as a modern "Guadalupe," with her starry mantle swirling about her like Wonder Woman's cape, Guadalupe's rays framing her.[35] The result is both daring and endearing. A Chilean-American artist, Liliana Wilson, portrays Mary as an advocate and protector of those in borderland communities. In one painting, "El Color de la Esperanza," or "The Color of Hope," Mary hovers over a young man who is sleeping alone in "... a desert landscape marked by the barbed wire border fence at his back."[36] A portrait of Our Lady of Guadalupe on a "Wanted" poster by Ester Hernandez casts Mary in the role of outlaw protector of her people in their border crossings. "For years, apparitions of the Virgin of Guadalupe have reportedly distracted border guards to help immigrants stranded at the U.S. border slip into the country unnoticed."[37]

Mary also appears as a Black Madonna. The tradition depicting her as black and beautiful in the Song of Songs dates back to the early Middle Ages and has experienced a revival in the 20th and 21st centuries. Mark

Doox's "Our Lady of Ferguson" shows Mary "... as a Black woman with her womb in the crosshairs of a gun with a child Christ in the center.... Kelly Latimore's icon memorialized George Floyd by depicting a Black Mary holding a broken Jesus."[38]

Like the dark Madonna of Guadalupe, the Black Madonna is also a liberating force. A Haitian-American artist, Rafaella Brice, has created a 16-by-12-foot mural showing Mary as "Black Freedom, Black Madonna and the Black Child of Hope." In Haiti, "... known as the Voudoun Iwa Erzuli Dantor and the Catholic Our Lady of Czestochowa, the Black Madonna was a revolutionary force in the country." Brice attributes the overthrow of French colonizers to her support.[39]

Another artist, Ben Wildflower, has shown Mary as a revolutionary force, standing on a skull and a serpent representing death and the Devil respectively. Her fist is raised in defiance of both threats—and any others she may encounter. Surrounding the image are her words from the Magnificat: "Fill the hungry. Cast down the mighty. Lift the lowly. Send the rich away." Mary's words have been interpreted as "...so revolutionary [that] public readings of [the Magnificat] have been banned in the past."[40] Hers is the ultimate overthrow of evil in any form.

Her image might be a little raffish these days, but Mary continues to appear throughout the world in countless venues and media; as always, she's available to those who call on her. Although she may admonish, she doesn't judge; she leaves that to God, her son. Despite attempts to ignore her, diminish her, or to raise her pedestal so high that she is all but invisible, she continues to speak, particularly to the disenfranchised and the poor, words of understanding and support in every circumstance of their lives: "Am I not here, your mother? Are you not under my shadow and protection? Am I not your fountain of life? Are you not in the folds of my mantle, in the crossing of my arms? Is there anything else that you need?"[41]

Today, Our Lady asks that question of everyone, believers and skeptics, nones and devotees. She is a voice for the voiceless, a supporter of the fragile, a companion in the immigrant journey, a source of strength and hope in the struggle for dignity and for life itself: Mary, pregnant with Godhead.

Finding Mary Past and Present, There and Here

From the foundations of Christianity, Mary's life and miracles have focused the attention of church leaders and lay people alike. Besides the Gospels and the letters of Paul and others, believers could be instructed (and entertained) by the extracanonical works that featured Mary—first to reinforce the divinity of her son Jesus, then to celebrate her partnership with him in mission. Even though works such as the *Protogospel* and *Pseudo-Matthew* were influenced by the necessity to portray her as a chaste challenge to non–Christian goddesses, her power to work miracles pervaded Byzantine stories from the sixth century on. Stories of her life expanded to include detailed accounts of her death and promises to the followers of Jesus. John the Geometer and Euthymios the Athonite portrayed Mary as the close companion of her son, sharing his life until its end. Euthymios shows her celebrating the Last Supper with bread and wine as Jesus did.

In the early Middle Ages, Marian stories took the form of anecdotes, then longer narratives, about Mary's power and engagement with people of every class and degree of religious devotion. As the feudal world grew larger and more refined, Marian miracle stories spread from England to the Continent, from Sweden to Iceland. During the "long twelfth century," Mary's power and influence reached their peak as theologians and storytellers alike praised her and expanded their repertoires of miracle tales. Mary's mantle covered the world; she was a merciful countersign to a strict and judgmental ecclesiastical establishment. During the difficult fourteenth and fifteenth centuries, Marian stories were dramatized in France and England. As her speaking parts in French plays declined, her dramatized life in England kept her voice strong, if limited. Both her intimate relationship with her son and her priestly presence shone through François Villin's poetic tribute to his mother and ours.

In the wake of the Reformation and the Catholic reaction, Mary became the object of devotion and theological interpretation, and her stories evolved to meet changing public tastes and church teachings.

Magnificat, black-on-white print. Courtesy Ben Wildflower.

Accounts of her miracles became adornments of her feast days in Jacobus' ever-popular legendary; anecdotes enlivened sermons; poetry, song, and folktale carried echoes of her influence, while devotion became the focus of her cult and the discipline of Mariology grew in ecclesiastical circles. In the post–Reformation world, Mary all but disappeared from Protestant churches and seminaries. Still, in the wake of revolutions and increasing secularism, a counterintuitive interest in Mary developed during the nineteenth century as scholars, feminists, and folklorists rediscovered her stories. With the development of mass media, Mary's appearances, previously private, became public as news about the Miraculous Medal and Lourdes spread throughout the world. Marian miracle stories were adapted, translated, and printed by the dozens in the United States and abroad. Despite opposition from church authorities, the idea and image of Mary as priest persisted, only to be forbidden early in the twentieth century.

In modernity, the variety and complexity of Marian images positively dazzles: Our Lady of Fatima, ready to assume the stance of Cold War Mary; Mary of the Assumption, an affirmation of her company in the Communion of Saints and an encouragement to the rest of us; and Mary of the extraordinarily ordinary, appearing to and with everyday people, in bathtub shrines, in inner-city murals, in underpasses, in dress and personal adornment, on the Web, on YouTube, on Pinterest and Etsy. These images, and the multitude of Marian stories that continue to flood both print and internet media, pose a challenge to and contradiction of ecclesiastical insistence on humble motherhood for both Mary and contemporary women.

Modern Mary may be even more subversive than ancient or medieval Mary. Today she speaks in more languages, in more places, in more media, to more people, than ever in history. Her power and authority have changed; they haven't been taken away. She is still the woman who proclaims the Magnificat, whether through the evangelist Luke or the contemporary artist Ben Wildflower. She is still the woman who consoles the sorrowful, rejoices with the celebratory. While she remains her son's partner in the never-ending work of salvation, she still works the miracles of everyday life, offering hope and inspiration for the journey that all of us take.

And wherever she goes, she takes her son with her.

Chapter Notes

Preface

1. Charlene Spretnak, *Missing Mary: The Queen of Heaven and Her Re-Emergence in the Modern Church* (New York: Palgrave Macmillan, 2004).

Introduction

1. *Apocrypha* is the plural of the Greek *apocryphon*, which means "hidden." These early writings were not accepted into the Second Testament canon and did remain hidden for much of Christian history. I refer to those rejected writings as extracanonical to avoid the association of "apocryphal" with "untruthful" or even "heretical."
2. My interpretation of "miracle" is based on Augustine and Anselm as described in Benedicta Ward, *Miracles and the Medieval Mind*, revised ed. (Philadelphia: University of Pennsylvania Press, 1987), 3–9.
3. Elizabeth A. Johnson, *Truly Our Sister: A Theology of Mary in the Communion of Saints* (New York: Continuum, 2003), 305–325. Johnson is also author of *Friends of God and Prophets: A Feminist Theological Reading of the Communion of Saints* (New York: Continuum, 1998).

Chapter 1

1. For a comprehensive collection of biblical citations by and about Mary, see www.maryimmaculate.tripod.com/marian17.html. Accessed 4/9/24.
2. Mary Anne Case, "The Role of the Popes in the Invention of Complementarity and the Vatican's Anathematization of Gender," *Religion and Gender* 6, no. 2 (2016): 159.
3. Dorian Llewelyn, S.J., "The Life of Mary and the Festal Icons of the Eastern Church," *Marian Studies* LX (2009): 242.
4. Roberta Felker, Homily for the Wedding Feast at Cana, Holy Wisdom Monasatery, Middleton, Wisconsin, January 16, 2022.
5. J.K. Elliott, *The Apocryphal Jesus: Legends of the Early Church* (Oxford: Oxford University Press, 1996), 1.
6. Jörg Frey, "Texts About Jesus: Noncanonical Gospels and Related Literature," in Andrew Gregory and Christopher Tuckett, *The Oxford Handbook of Early Christian Apocrypha* (Oxford: Oxford University Press, 2018), 27. Quotations are taken from M.R. James, *The Apocryphal New Testament* (Oxford: Clarendon Press, 1924; rpt. 1989), 38–49.
7. Widowers were chosen on the assumption that they were too old to beget children, thus ensuring Mary's perpetual virginity.
8. Numbers 5:11–31 describes the procedure. *The New Interpreter's Study Bible: New Revised Standard Version with the Apocrypha* (Nashville: Abington Press, 2003), 198. A "Special Note" remarks on the unfairness of the procedure to women; in the *Protogospel*, however, Joseph also is accused.
9. James H. Charlesworth, *The Earliest Christian Hymnbook: The Odes of Solomon* (Cambridge: James Clark & Co., 2009), 55–56.
10. Stephen J. Shoemaker, "Epiphanius of Salamis, the Kollyridians, and the Early Dormition Narratives: The Cult of the

Virgin in the Fourth Century," *Journal of Early Christian Studies* 16, no. 3 (Fall 2008): 375.

11. Shoemaker, "Epiphanius," 376.

12. E. Chatel, "Crypte de l'Église de Saint Maximin (Var)," *Actes du Ve Congrès international d'archéologie chrétienne, Aix-en-Provence, 13–19 septembre 1954* (Citta del Vaticano Pontificio Instituto de Archeologia Cristiana, 1957): 339.

13. M. Edmond le Blant, *Les Sarcophages chrétiennes de la Gaule* (Paris: Imprimerie Nationale, 1886), 148.

14. Jan Gijsel and Rita Beyers, *Libri de nativitate Mariae* (Turnhout, Belgium: Brepols, 1997), v. *Pseudo-Matthew* also contains elements of the *Infancy Gospel of Thomas*, a second-century work.

15. Hilda Graef and Thomas A. Thompson, *Mary: A History of Doctrine and Devotion* (Notre Dame, IN: Ave Maria Press, 2008), 39–40.

16. *The Gospel of Pseudo-Matthew*, www.newadvent.org/fathers/0848.htm. Accessed 4/6/20.

17. In the Middle Ages, Titus would be renamed Dismas, the Good Thief to whom Jesus said, "This day you will be with Me in Paradise" (Luke 23:43).

18. Rita George Tvrtkovic charts the relationship among the Bible, the *Protogospel*, and the *Qur'an* in her *Christians, Muslims, and Mary: A History* (New York: Paulist Press, 2018), 5–8.

19. Hosn Abboud, *Mary in the Qur'an: A Literary Reading* (London: Routledge, 2014), 51–53.

20. I have used the text of *The Qur'an* translated by M.A.S. Abdel Haleem (New York: Oxford University Press, 2010).

21. Abboud, *Mary in the Qur'an*, 83–84.

22. Haleem, *The Qur'an*, 37–38, Sura 3, verses 35–47. Here as elsewhere, the Qur'an parallels scriptural accounts of Mary in the Bible and the *Protogospel*.

23. Haleem, *The Qur'an*, 192, Sura 19, verses 23–25.

24. Haleem, *The Qur'an*, 192, Sura 19, verses 27–34.

25. Giancarlo Finazzo, "The Virgin Mary in the Koran," *L'Osservatore Romano*, Weekly Edition in English (April 13, 1978), 4. https://www.ewtn.com/catholicism/library/virgin-mary-in-the-koran-5656. Accessed 4/22/24.

26. Haleem, *The Qur'an*, 192, verse 35.

27. Quoted in Finazzo, "Mary in the Koran," this is Hadith 102 of Book 60.

28. Tim Winter, "Mary in Islam," in *Mary: The Complete Resource*, ed. Sarah Jane Boss (New York: Oxford University Press, 2007), 484.

29. Abboud, *Mary in the Qur'an*, 116.

30. Anthony M. Buono, *The Greatest Marian Prayers: Their History, Meaning and Usage* (New York: Alba House, 1999), 21–28.

31. See E.A. Wallis Budge, *The History of the Blessed Virgin Mary and the History of the Likeness of Christ, the Syriac Texts Edited with English Translations* (London: Luzac and Co., 1899), 114. Montague James includes it in the Greek narrative of "The Discourse of St. John the Divine Concerning the Falling Asleep of the Holy Mother of God," 207.

32. *Pseudo-Matthew*, www.newadvent.org/fathers/0848.htm. Accessed 1/4/22.

33. *Arabic Infancy Gospel*, Chapter 14. www.newadvent.org/fathers/0806.htm. Retrieved 1/4/22.

Chapter 2

1. Graef, *Mary: A History*, 38.

2. Luigi Gambero, *Mary and the Fathers of the Church: The Blessed Virgin Mary in Patristic Thought*, trans. Thomas Buffer (San Francisco: Ignatius Press, 1999), 46.

3. Gambero, *Mary and the Fathers*, 115.

4. Gambero, *Mary and the Fathers*, 123.

5. Maas and Trypanis, xiv. Cited in Leena Mari Peltomaa, *The Image of the Virgin Mary in the Akathistos Hymn* (Leiden: Brill, 2001), 40.

6. Peltomaa, *Mary in the Akathistos Hymn*, 5–19.

7. Thomas Arentzen, *The Virgin in Song: Mary and the Poetry of Romanos the Melodist* (Philadelphia: University of Pennsylvania Press, 2017), 39.

8. Arentzen, *Virgin in Song*, 141.

9. R.J. Schork, *Sacred Song from the Byzantine Pulpit: Romanos the Melodist* (Gainesville: University Press of Florida, 1995), 106.

10. Schork, *Sacred Song*, 108–109.

11. Schork, *Sacred Song*, 111.

12. Schork, *Sacred Song*, 114.

13. Arentzen, *Virgin in Song*, 142.

14. Mary B. Cunningham, trans. and commentary, *Epiphanios the Monk: Life of Mary, the Theotokos, and Life and Acts of St. Andrew the Apostle* (Liverpool: Liverpool University Press, 2023), 1.

15. Cunningham, *Epiphanios*, 78.

16. Cunningham, *Epiphanios*, 78–79.

17. Cunningham, *Epiphanios*, 90. Cunningham states that the description of Jesus appears in the context of Jesus' conversation with the elders of the Temple. In note 105 of this page, she observes that "[m]any of the qualities that [Epiphanios] describes (Christ's height, hair, beard, etc.) could only apply to someone over the age of about twenty."

18. Cunningham, *Epiphanios*, 100.

19. Cunningham, *Epiphanios*, 102.

20. Cunningham, *Epiphanios*, 102–04.

21. See, for example, Mary Vincentine Gripkey, *The Blessed Virgin Mary as Mediatrix in the Latin and Old French Legend Prior to the Fourteenth Century* (Washington, D.C.: The Catholic University of America, 1938) and Mary Clayton, *The Cult of the Virgin Mary in Anglo-Saxon England* (New York: Cambridge University Press, 1990).

22. Christos Simelides discusses John Geometres and Euthymios the Athonite in "Two *Lives of the Virgin*: John Geometres, Euthymios the Athonite, and Maximos the Confessor," *Dumbarton Oaks Papers* 74 (2020), 125–60.

23. *Life of the Virgin Mary [by] John Geometres*, ed. and trans. Maximos Constas and Christos Simelidis (Cambridge: Harvard University Press, 2023), vii.

24. *Life of the Virgin Mary [by] John Geometres*, xiv.

25. *Life of the Virgin Mary [by] John Geometres*, 185, 191, 195–96.

26. Jean Galot, "La plus ancienne affirmation de la corédemption mariale. Le témoignage de Jean le Géometre," *Recherches de science religieuse* 45 (1957), 201.

27. *Life of the Virgin Mary [by] John Geometres*, 323. Mary's death and assumption are described on pages 297–343.

28. Michel-Jean Van Esbroeck, trans., *Maxime le Confesseur: Vie de la Vierge* (Leuven: E. Peeters, 1986), first published the text of the *Life*. Van Esbroeck established it as the oldest "complete set of all the episodes" in Mary's life: "Some Earlier Features in the Life of the Virgin," *Marianum* 63 (2001): 297. Stephen J. Shoemaker wrote extensively about this Marian biography, translating the Old Georgian text: *Life of the Virgin [by] Maximus the Confessor* (New Haven: Yale University Press, 2012). I have used Van Esbroeck's edition and translation of the oldest extant manuscript of the work as the basis for my retelling.

29. Simelidis, "Two *Lives*," 128.

30. Simelidis, "Two *Lives*," 138.

31. Simelidis, "Two *Lives*," 150.

32. For my own metaphrastic work, I have used Van Esbroeck's French translation (see footnote 28 above). All translations from the French are mine.

33. Maximos, *Vie*, Chapter 3, 2:3.

34. Maximos, *Vie*, Chapter 10, 2:8.

35. Maximos, *Vie*, Chapter 14, 2:11. This experience is known as a *bât qôl*, a message coming from the voice of God, making an announcement or a prophecy.

36. Maximos, *Vie*, Chapter 18, 2:13. From Chapter 16, the image of Joseph's flowering staff—usually with lilies—has become universal.

37. Maximos, *Vie*, Chapter 20, 2:14–15. Even though this dispensation appears optimistic, Sally Cuneen sees it as "a positive affirmation of humanity in relation to the divine," in "Maximus's Mary: A Minister, Not Just an Icon" *Commonweal*, December 4, 2009). https://www.commonwealmagazine.org/maximus%E2%80%99s-mary. Accessed 4/21/24.

38. Maximos, *Vie*, Chapter 35, 2:29.

39. Maximos, *Vie*, Chapter 54, 2:44. Pseudo-Maximos here draws on the *Arabic Infancy Gospel*, stating (Chapter 55, 2:46) that Jesus "annihilated every impurity of the Egyptians and drove out the snakes and scorpions of Egypt and dissipated the fog of perdition [there]."

40. Maximos, *Vie*, Chapter 63, 2:53.

41. There is not a whisper about Mary Magdalene's alleged former life as a sinner, portrayed by Pope Gregory the Great in a 591 sermon as the sinful woman of Luke 7. See Katherin Ludwig Jansen, *The Making of the Magdalen: Preaching and Popular Devotion in the Later Middle Ages* (Princeton: Princeton University Press, 2000), 32-33.

42. Maximos, *Vie*, Chapter 71, 2:61–62.

43. For background on Mary's priestly

role, see Judith M. Davis, "Virgin Mary Co-Priest or Not: The Continung Trend of Redaction and Revision in the Medieval Era," in Mary Jo Beavis and Ally Kateusz, eds., *Rediscovering the Marys: Maria, Mariamne, Miriam* (New York: T&T Clark, 2020), 141–142.

44. Maximos, *Vie*, Chapter 74, 2:64. Emphasis added.

45. Maximos, *Vie*, Chapter 80, 2:69.

46. Maximos, *Vie*, Chapter 91, 2:79.

47. Maximos, *Vie*, Chapter 91, 2:79.

48. As described in Acts 2:1–12, the action of the Holy Spirit after Christ's ascension.

49. Maximos, *Vie*, Chapter 94, 2:82.

50. Maximos, *Vie*, Chapter 98, 2:86.

51. Maximos, *Vie*, Chapter 101, 2:88.

52. Maximos, *Vie*, Chapter 118, 2:102.

53. *Life of the Virgin [by] John Geometres*, 345–47.

54. Maximos, *Vie*, Chapter 125, 2:103–09. This legendary account of a Marian relic probably originated and circulated in the sixth century: C. Mango, "The Origins of the Blachernae Shrine at Constantinople," *Actes du XIIIe Congrès International d'Archéologie chrétienne* II (Vatican City and Split, 1998): 71, 75. Shoemaker discusses the "holy theft" in "The Cult of Fashion: The Earliest *Life of the Virgin* and Constantinople's Marian Relics," *Dumbarton Oaks Papers* 62 (2008): 53–74. The tale was not unique to Pseudo-Maximos; it "probably originated in the fifth or early sixth century, 'featuring two Roman generals,'" according to Andrew S. Jacobs, "The Remains of a Jew: Imperial Christian Identity in the Holy Land," *Journal of Medieval and Early Modern Studies* 33 (2003): 34.

55. Maximos, *Vie*, Chapter 125, 2:110–12.

56. The title of his work on Mary is "A Discourse including the facts relative to the life of Our Lady, the Most Holy Mother of God, beginning with her venerable birth and upbringing, and of the divinely glorious birth of Christ our God, and all that happened up until her vivifying death, followed by the account of her precious garment showing how the Christians came to possess this great treasure." My summary is translated from the Italian of Georges Gharib, "Vita de Maria," in *Texti Mariani del Primo Millennio 2: Padri e altri autori bizentini (VI–XI sec)* (Rome: Citta Nuova Editrice, 1989), 980–1019.

57. See Sandro Sticca, *The* Planctus Mariae *in the Dramatic Tradition of the Middle Ages*, trans. Joseph R. Berrigan (Athens: University of Georgia Press, 1988).

58. Two other Marian relics were preserved in Constantinople: her sash and a likeness of her allegedly painted by Saint Luke. See Christine Angelidi and Titos Papamastorakis, "Picturing the Spiritual Protector: from Blanchernitissa to Hodegetria," in Maria Vassilaki, ed., *Images of the Mother of God: Perceptions of the Theotokos in Byzantium* (Burlington, VT: Ashgate, 2005), 209–211.

59. Angelidi and Papamastorakis, "Picturing," 211. The invaders were the Avars, a nomadic Eurasian people, who joined with the Persians (modern-day Iranians) in attempting to overthrow the Byzantine empire.

60. Averil Cameron, "The Virgin's Robe: An Episode in the History of Early Seventh-Century Constantinople," *Byzantion* 49 (1979), 42.

61. See, for example, Stephen Shoemaker, *Ancient Traditions of the Virgin Mary's Dormition and Assumption* (Oxford: Oxford University Press, 2002). My retelling draws elements from different versions, including the "Pseudo-Melito" attributed to Bishop Melito of Sardis in James, *The Apocryphal New Testament*, 209–16.

62. Most of the texts in this tradition contain references to angry Jews who attack the funeral procession, evidence of anti-Jewish polemic and prejudice that would continue up to the present.

63. James, *The Apocryphal New Testament*, "Pseudo-Melito," 216.

64. This text dates from about the seventh century or later and is attributed to Joseph of Arimathaea (James, *The Apocryphal Second Testament*, "The Assumption," 216–18).

65. Stephen J. Shoemaker, "Apocrypha and Liturgy in the Fourth Century: The Case of the 'Six Books' Dormition Apocryphon," *Jewish and Christian Scriptures: The Function of "Canonical" and "Noncanonical" Texts*, ed. James H. Charlesworth and Lee M. McDonald (London: T & T Clark International/Continuum Books, 2010), 156.

66. William Wright, trans., "The Departure of Our Lady Mary from This World," *The Journal of Sacred Literature and Biblical Record* 7 (1865), 132.
67. Wright, "Departure," 136.
68. Wright, "Departure," 141, 142, 146.
69. Wright, "Departure," 151–152. Emphasis added.
70. Wright, "Departure," 160.
71. Stephen Shoemaker observes that the Six Books tradition is "packed with nearly every sort of Marian devotion that ... has been almost completely ignored in regard to the rise of Marian devotion." *Mary in Early Christian Faith and Devotion* (New Haven: Yale University Press, 2016), 130.
72. Jane Baun, *Tales from Another Byzantium* (New York: Cambridge University Press, 2009), 273. See also Richard Bauckham, *The Fate of the Dead: Studies on the Jewish and Christian Apocalypses* (Leiden: Brill, 1998), 333–338.
73. The text can be found online as "The Apocalypse of the Virgin" [trans. Tony Burke], https://tonyburke.ca/wp-content/uploads/Apocalypse-of-the-Virgin.pdf. Accessed 2/13/22.
74. Baun, *Tales*, 273.
75. Baun, *Tales*, 400. The days of Pentecost are counted from Jesus' resurrection until the feast of the descent of the Holy Spirit on the apostles and Mary.
76. Stephen J. Shoemaker, "Between Scripture and Tradition: The Marian Apocryha of Early Christianity," in Kevork B. Bardakjian and Sergio La Parta, eds., *The Armenian Apocalyptic Tradition: A Comparative Perspective* (Leiden: Brill, 2014), 505.

Chapter 3

1. The legend of the worship of a virgin who gave birth seems to have begun in the early middle ages and was popularized in the sixteenth and seventeenth centuries. See Nicolas Balzano, *Les deux cathédrales: Mythe et histoire à Chartres* XIe–XXe siècle (Paris: Les Belles Lettres, 2012), 15–47.
2. Gregory of Tours, *Glory of the Martyrs*, trans. and intro. Raymond Van Dam (Liverpool: Liverpool University Press, 1998), 28–32.
3. Gregory, *Glory*, 28; 31–32.

4. Jaroslav Pelikan, *Mary Through the Centuries: Her Place in the History of Culture* (New Haven: Yale University Press, 1996), 94.
5. My prose translation.
6. "Hrotsvitha, *Life of Mary*," trans. William Charlton, *Maria: A Journal of Marian Studies* N.S. 1, no. 1 (July 2021): 18. This translation reflects some of the charm as well as all of the erudition of the original, replacing Sister Gonsalva Weigand, *The Non-Dramatic Works of Hrosvitha: Text, Translation and Commentary* (St. Meinrad, IN: The Abbey Press, 1937).
7. "Hrotsvitha, *Life of Mary*," 18.
8. "Hrotsvitha, *Life of Mary*," 40.
9. https:// www.udayton.edu/imri/mary/o/our-lady-of-the-pillar.php. Accessed 3/7/23.
10. Balzamo, *Les Deux Cathédrales*, traces the Chartres relic back to the story of Galbius and Candidus, 26–27.
11. Charlemagne never visited Constantinople, and there is no record of the Empress Irene's having traveled to France. For a historical approach to Chartres cathedral (which doesn't exclude the legendary), see Margot Fassler, *The Virgin of Chartres: Making History through Liturgy and the Arts* (New Haven: Yale University Press, 2010), esp. 211. Charles' gift is mentioned in Malcolm Miller, *Chartres Cathedral* (London: Pitkin Pictorials, 1985), 5, among many, many other sources.
12. Fassler, *Chartres*, 21–23; Balzano, *Deux cathédrales*, 28–31.
13. Alan Saint-Denis, "Introduction," Hériman de Tournai, *Les Miracles de Sainte Marie de Laon* (Paris: CNRS Éditions), 29. Marina Warner, *Alone of All Her Sex: The Myth and the Cult of the Virgin Mary* (New York: Random House Vintage, 1983), 294. See also Benedicta Ward, *Miracles and the Medieval Mind* (Philadelphia: University of Pennsylvania Press, 1987), 143; Miri Rubin, *Mother of God: A History of the Virgin Mary* (New Haven: Yale University Press, 2009); and Anne L. Clark, "Guardians of the Sacred: The Nuns of Soissons and the Slipper of the Virgin Mary," *Church History* 76, no. 4 (December 2007): 724–49.
14. Hériman of Tournai's collection, *Miracles of Holy Mary of Laon*, dates from the late 1140s; Hugo Farsit's work, *Little*

Book of the Miracles of the Blessed Virgin Mary in the City of Soissons, about 1132. The Miracles of Our Lady of Rocamadour is dated about 1172/73. See Saint-Denis, "Introduction," 24 and Marcus Bull, "Introduction," The Miracles of Our Lady of Rocamadour (Woodbridge, Suffolk: The Boydell Press, 1999), 3.

15. Hériman de Tournai, Les Miracles de Sainte-Marie de Laon, 150–53.

16. Recounted in Clark, 735.

17. Bull, The Miracles of Our Lady of Rocamadour, 146.

18. Second Reading from the Office for the Solemnity of the Immaculate Conception of the Virgin Mary, December 8.

19. R. M. Thompson and M. Winterbottom, ed. and trans., William of Malmesbury, The Miracles of the Blessed Virgin Mary: An English Translation (Woodbridge, Suffolk: The Boydell Press, 2015), xviii.

20. William of Malmesbury, The Miracles, 102–03.

21. William of Malmesbury, The Miracles, 55–56.

22. William of Malmesbury, The Miracles, "Prologue," 3–4. Emphasis added.

23. Bernard of Clairvaux, Homilies in Praise of the Blessed Virgin Mary, trans. Marie-Bernard Said (Kalamazoo, MI: Cistercian Publications, 1979).

24. Bernard, Homilies, 10.

25. Bernard, Homilies, 30–31.

26. Robert Thomas, La Vierge Marie: Homélies des Pères Cisterciens (Sainte-Foy, QC: Éditions Anne Sigier, 1989), 153.

27. Amadeus of Lausanne, Homilies in Praise of Blessed Mary, trans. Grace Perigo (Kalamazoo, MI: Cistercian Publications, 1979), 60.

28. Amadeus, Homilies, 72/74.

29. The Mariale sive CCXXX quaestiones super Evangelium Missus est was published as a genuine work of Albert the Great (c.1200–1280): Albert the Great, Opera Omnia, ed. August and Emil Borgnet, vol. 37 (Paris: Ludovicus Vivès, 1898), 68–246. Graef, Mary: A History, discusses the issue of authorship (213–14) and covers the Mariale itself (214–16).

30. René Laurentin, Marie, l'Église et le sacerdoce: Essai sur le développement d'une idée religieuse, vol. 1 (Paris: Nouvelles Éditions Latines, 1952), 194. My translation and interpretation.

Chapter 4

1. Jan M. Ziolkowski, "Introduction," Nigel of Canterbury, Miracles of the Virgin, ed. Jan M. Ziolkowski (Cambridge: Harvard University Press, 2022), xv.

2. Hériman de Tournai, Les Miracles de Sainte Marie de Laon, ed. and trans. Alain Saint-Denis (Paris: CNRS, 2008).

3. See Anne L. Clark, "Guardians of the Sacred: The Nuns of Soissons and the Slipper of the Virgin Mary," Church History 764 (2007): 724–49.

4. Pierre Kunstmann, ed. and trans., Adgar, Le Gracial (Ottawa: Éditions de l'Université d'Ottawa, 1982).

5. Baun observes that in the Byzantine apocalypses, Heaven was depicted in terms of an "imperial palace and bureaucracy" (Tales, 238–41). This concept is reflected in medieval depictions of the Court of Heaven.

6. Eva Vilano-Pentti, La Court de Paradis: Poème du XIIIe siècle (Helsinki: Imprimerie de la Société de Littérature Finnois, 1953).

7. See Maureen Boulton, Sacred Fictions of Medieval France: Narrative Theology in the Lives of Christ and the Virgin, 1150–1500 (Woodbridge, Suffolk: D.S. Brewer, 2015).

8. Andreas Capellanus, The Art of Courtly Love, trans. John Jay Parry (New York: Frederick Ungar, 1959).

9. See Peter Dronke, "Andreas Capellanus," The Journal of Medieval Latin, 4 (1994): 51–63, esp. 57–58.

10. Edward Järnstrom and Arthur Långfors, eds., Recueil de chansons pieuses du XIIIe siècle, vol. 1 (Helsinki: Suomalaisen Tiedeakatenian Toimituksia, 1910).

11. See Marcia Jenneth Epstein, Prions en chantant: Devotional Songs of the Trouvères (Toronto: University of Toronto Press, 1997).

12. Järnstrom, Recueil, 1:75–77.

13. Peire Cardenal, XXXVII, in René Lavaud, ed., Poésies completes du troubadour Peire Cardenal (Toulouse: Privat, 1957), 232–36.

14. Epstein, Prions, 30–31.

15. Some of the observations in this section derive from my paper, "Mediatrix, Operatrix, Redemptrix: Mary's Exercise of Power in Medieval French Literature," presented at the 39th Intenational Congress

on Medieval Studies, Kalamazoo, Michigan, May 2004.

16. Michel Tarayre, *La Vierge et le miracle: Le* Speculum historiale *de Vincent de Beauvais* (Paris: Champion, 1999).

17. Tarayre, *La Vierge*, 128–31.

18. Tarayre, *La Vierge*, 61–63.

19. Jean Blacker, Glynn S. Burgess, and Amy V. Ogden, *Wace, The Hagiographical Works: The* Concepcion Nostre Dame *and the* Lives of Saint Margaret and Saint Nicholas (Leiden: Brill, 2013), 124: Concepcion, lines 1499–1504, 1516–17.

20. Dominica Legge, *Anglo-Norman Literature and Its Background* (Oxford: Clarendon Press, 1963), 5.

21. Adgar, *Le Gracial*, publié par Pierre Kunstmann (Ottawa: Éditions de l'Université d'Ottawa, 1982), 11. This number represents a compilation from different manuscripts: see Juan Carlos Bayo's review of Jean-Louis Benoît, Le Gracial *d'Adgar: Miracles de la Vierge* (Turnhout: Brepols, 2012) in *Mediavistik* 27 (2014): 339–40.

22. Adgar, *Le Gracial*, 11.

23. Kunstmann, "Introduction," 13.

24. Adgar, *Le Gracial*, 113–21.

25. Adgar, *Le Gracial*, 265–71.

26. Jean Blacker, Glynn S. Burgess, and Amy V. Ogden, *Wace, The Hagiographical Works: The* Concepcion Nostre Dame *and the Lives of St. Margaret and St. Nicholas* (Leiden: Brill, 2013).

27. Blacker et al., *Concepcion*, "Introduction," 15.

28. Kathleen Ashley and Pamela Sheingorn, eds., *Interpreting Cultural Symbols: Saint Anne in Late Medieval Society* (Athens: University of Georga Press, 1990). The *trinubium* (three marriages) of St. Anne and the "holy kinship" are described and discussed in their introduction, 1–68.

29. Blacker et al., *Concepcion*, 124, lines 1499–1504, 1516–1517.

30. Tony Hunt, *Miraculous Rhymes: The Writing of Gautier de Coinci* (Woodbridge, Suffolk: D.S. Brewer, 2007), 4 and 18.

31. See Steven M. Taylor, "God's Queen: Chess Imagery in the Poetry of Gautier de Coinci," *Fifteenth Century Studies* (1990): 403–19. A more accessible account can be found in Marilyn Yalom, *Birth of the Chess Queen* (New York: Harper Collins, 2004, 107–21, 249–50. See also Moshe Lazar, "Satan and Notre Dame: Characters in a Popular Scenario," in Norris J. Lacy, ed., *A Medieval French Miscellany: Papers of the 1970 Kansas Conference on Medieval French Literature* (Lawrence: University of Kansas Publications, 1972), 1–14.

32. Taylor, "God's Queen," 405.

33. Yalom, *Chess Queen*, 119.

34. Frederick Koenig, ed., *Les "Miracles de Nostre Dame" par Gautier de Coinci* (Geneva: Droz, 1966), vol. 1, 197–200, 255.

35. Koenig, *Les "Miracles,"* vol. 2, 181–96.

36. Koenig, *Les "Miracles,"* vol. 3, 191–214.

37. Gautier and other writers cited the authority of other books or authors—and sometimes eyewitness accounts—to give their stories credibility.

38. David A. Flory, *Marian Representations in the Miracle Tales of Thirteenth-Century Spain and France* (Washington, D.C.: The Catholic University of America, 2000), 86.

39. Koenig, *Les "Miracles,"* vol. 2, 285–90.

40. Patrice and Roger Martineau, "Cantigas" (Paris: Kiosque d'Orfée, n.d.), Side A, No. 2.

41. Koenig, *Les "Miracles,"* vol. 3, 150–64.

42. Koenig, *Les "Miracles,"* vol. 2, 197–204.

43. Like the miracle of the little nun who left her convent, this tale has a complex history. See Arthur Langfors, "La Légende de la statue de Vénŭs," *Romania* 43 (1914): 628–29. The oldest version seems to have appeared in the *Gesta Romanorum (Deeds of the Romans)* of William of Malmesbury, written about 1125. See Paule Bétérous, *Les Collections de la Vierge en Gallo- et Ibero-Roman au XIIIe siècle* (Dayton: University of Dayton, 1983–84), 661. In this version, which originated in Rome in the 10th or 11th century, a young Roman places a ring on a statue of Venus.

44. Gautier calls them "clerçonciaus," or seminarians in minor orders (the early stages of preparation for the priesthood). Some had no aspirations to be priests but became clerics for a time in order to obtain an education.

45. Koenig, *Les "Miracles,"* vol. 1, 50–175.

46. Eva de Visscher, "Marian Devotion in the Latin West in the Later Middle Ages," in Boss, *Mary*, 185–86.
47. Grace Frank, *Rutebeuf, Le Miracle de Théophile: Miracle du XIIIe siècle* (Paris: Champion, 1925), vi; Alan Temko, *Notre-Dame of Paris* (New York: The Viking Press, 1955), 257.
48. Frank, *Rutebeuf*, vi–viii.
49. Frank, *Rutebeuf*, 23–24.
50. Frank, *Rutebeuf*.
51. Koenig, *Les "Miracles,"* vol. 2, 158–80.
52. Koenig, *Les "Miracles,"* vol. 2, 105–08.
53. Koenig, *Les "Miracles,"* vol. 4, 154–74.
54. Henry Adams and Ralph A. Cram, *Mont-Saint-Michel and Chartres* (Boston: Houghton Mifflin Company, 1904), 276. https://digitalcommons.unl.edu/etas/70. Adams had studied Old French at Yale. See Robert Mane, *Henry Adams on the Road to Chartres* (Boston: Harvard University Press, 1971).
55. Koenig, *Les "Miracles,"* vol. 4, 175–89.
56. See Marcus Bull, *The Miracles of Our Lady of Rocamadour, Analysis and Translation* (Woodbridge, Suffolk: The Boydell Press, 1999).
57. A scholarly treatment of Marian subversion appears in David Flory, "The Social Uses of Religious Literature: Challenging Authority in the Thirteenth-Century Miracle Tale," *Medieval Studies* 13 (1997): 61–69.
58. https://www.udayton.edu/imri/o/our-lady-of-loreto-and-aviation.php. Accessed 4/27/23.

Chapter 5

1. Jacobus de Voragine, *The Golden Legend: Readings on the Saints*, trans. William Granger Ryan (Princeton: Princeton University Press, 1995).
2. Jean le Marchant, *Miracles de Notre Dame de Chartres*, trans. Pierre Kunstmann (Ottawa: Éditions de L'Université d'Ottawa, 1974).
3. Le Marchant, *Miracles*, 53–60.
4. Le Marchant, *Miracles*, 162–66.
5. *Songs of Holy Mary of Alfonso X, The Wise: A translation of the* Cantigas de Santa Maria, trans. Kathleen Kulp-Hill (Tempe: Arizona Center for Medieval and Renaissance Studies, 2000).
6. Jeannie K. Bartha, Annette Grant Cash, and Richard Terry Mount, trans., *The Collected Works of Gonzalo de Berceo in English Translation* (Tempe: Arizona Center for Medieval and Renaissance Studies, 2008).
7. John E. Keller and Kathleen Kulp-Hill, "Introduction to the *Miracles of Our Lady*," 9.
8. Keller and Kulp-Hill, *Miracles*, 15.
9. Keller and Kulp-Hill, *Miracles*, 18.
10. Bartha, Cash, and Mount, *Collected Works*, 81–84.
11. Bartha, Cash, and Mount, *Collected Works*, 82–83.
12. Both Gonzalo's "Praises," 151–87, and his "Lamentations of the Virgin," 189–217, are introduced and translated by Bartha.
13. Bartha, "Lamentations," 211.
14. Alexandre de Laborde, *Les Miracles de Nostre Dame compilés par Jehan Miélot* (Paris: Société Française de Reproductions de Manuscrits à Peintures, 1928), 208–10.
15. Paul Bretel, ed. and trans., *Le Jongleur de Notre Dame* (Paris: Champion, 2011). My retelling is based on a paper, "Celebrating a Performance: Another Look at the *Tombeor Nostre Dame*," presented at the 50th International Congress on Medieval Studies, Kalamazoo, Michigan, 2015.
16. St. Benedict of Nursia (480–543) left a comfortable life of wealth and privilege to live first as a hermit and later as the founder and head of a monastic community in northern Italy. His *Rule* was written for lay people (Benedict was not a cleric) who wished to draw closer to God. Because of its practical spirituality in fostering a life balanced between prayer and work, the Benedictine Rule, and the monasteries that observed it, spread throughout Europe. For a fine translation and introduction to the Rule, see Patrick Barry, OSB, *Saint Benedict's Rule* (Mahwah, NJ: Hidden Spring [Paulist Press]), 2004. Clairvaux Abbey, founded by St. Bernard in 1115, was a huge and prosperous estate by the thirteenth century.
17. The Liturgy of the Hours has been said since the days of the early Church. It consists of prayers and song offered to God at seven times, or "hours," of the day:

Matins, or morning liturgy, celebrated about 2:00 a.m.; Lauds or praises, about 4:00 a.m.; Prime (first hour) at 6:00 a.m.; Tierce (third hour) at 9:00 a.m.; Sext (sixth hour) at noon; Nones (ninth hour) at 3:00 p.m.; Vespers, in the late afternoon; and Compline, the last service before going to bed, after sunset. The night offices were often called "vigils," the old Latin designation for a period of "vigil" or "watch" in the night. For a charming and informative introduction to cloister life, see Danièle Cybulskie, *How to Live Like a Monk* (New York: Abbeville Press, 2021).

18. A *conversus* or lay brother "is a religious brother under vows, dedicated to a life of toil, and occupying an auxiliary position in his community." James France, *Separate but Equal: Cistercian Lay Brothers 1120–1350* (Collegeville, MN: Liturgical Press, 2012), xv. "As these stories make clear, literate lay brothers were very much the exception and there is no doubt that the vast majority were and remained *illiterati*" (75). These men were assigned tasks that required physical labor, often in the fields. Literate monks, on the other hand, could read both the words and the music of the liturgy and were called "choir monks."

19. Deacons and subdeacons are members of the major orders on the way to the priesthood, and acolytes are clerical assistants in minor orders. A psalter is a book of psalms.

20. This is an echo of the oldest Marian prayer, "Sub praesidium tuum," "Under your protection."

21. Scholars have not been able to identify any of the stunts mentioned by the author. We can imagine handsprings forward and backward; cartwheels, somersaults, and back bends; back and front "walkovers"; head stands and handstands, some of which may involve dance postures, pirouettes, or more complex routines, rather like those of modern Olympic gymnasts. (Some modern techniques are known by their countries of origin, such as the German kip, the Japanese headstand, or the Czech maneuver.) Medieval illuminations and miniatures depict acrobats in different poses. One manuscript that features "Our Lady's Tumbler" shows a figure bending backward until his head touches his heels: Paul Breton, *Le Jongleur de Notre-Dame*, 121. Two acrobats, lightly clad, can be found in folio 49 of a manuscript from Moissac, French National Library Latin Collection, *côte* 52.

22. The tumbler's homage recalls King David's dance before the Ark of the Covenant in the First Testament.

23. In this sentence the tumbler calls himself a *menestrel* rather than a *jongleur*. The word *menestrel* comes from the word *ministerium* (service or office, the origin of our word *minister*) and was used to describe entertainers who entered the service of a noble house instead of wandering from court to court, town to town. *Menestrels* were attached to one master whom they served exclusively (Breton 123). The tumbler is thus literally converted into a true servant of—or minister to—the Virgin.

24. "Du Chevalier qui ooit la Messe et Nostre Dame estoit pour lui au tournoiement," in Karl Bartsch, *Chrestomathie de l'ancien Français*, 6th ed. (Leipzig: F.C.W. Vogel, 1895), 312–16.

25. Caesarius of Heisterbach, *The Dialogue on Miracles*, trans. H. von E. Scott and C.C. Swinton Bland, vol. 1 (London: George Routledge & Sons, 1929), 510–19.

26. Jacobus de Voragine, *The Golden Legend*, trans. William Granger Ryan (Princeton: Princeton University Press, 1993), vol. 1, xiii.

27. William Granger Ryan, "Introduction," xvii.

28. See the entry for the feast of St. Luke, Evangelist: "[T]his gospel was disclosed by the Virgin Mary" (Jacobus, *Golden Legend*, vol. 2, 253–54).

29. Jacobus, *Golden Legend*, vol. 1, 37–43.

30. "Brother Bartholomew" would be Bartholomew of Trent (c. 1200–1251), like Jacobus a collector of saints' lives. Like Jacobus, he was familiar with at least one version of the *Evangile de l'enfance*, or *Gospel of [Christ's] Infancy*, that appeared in the twelfth and thirteenth centuries, based on the apocryphal *Pseudo-Matthew* and the *Gospel of Thomas*.

31. Jacobus was drawing on a tradition that dated back to the eighth century at least: the three kings were named by the Venerable Bede (672/3–735) as Jaspar (gold), Balthazar (frankincense), and Melchior (myrrh). The seventh-century

Armenian Infancy Gospel identified the three as brothers Melqon, king of Persia; Balthasar, king of India; and Gaspar, king of Arabia (Jorg Frey, "Texts about Jesus," *The Oxford Handbook of Early Christian Apocrypha*, ed. Andrew Gregory and Christopher Tuckett (Oxford: Oxford University Press, 2018), 28.

32. Jacobus' source for this imaginative excursus was a little-known work by the ninth-century theologian Haymo of Auxerre. *The Golden Legend* lifted Haymo's fictive family tree from obscurity and made it the basis for an entire tradition, described in sermons and even a romance (see pp. 196–99, section on *The Romance of Saint Fanuel and Saint Anne*), and vividly depicted by artists for centuries. See Kathleen Ashley and Pamela Sheingorn, "Introduction," in *Interpreting Cultural Symbols: Saint Anne in Late Medieval Society* (Athens: University of Georgia Press, 1990), 59 (n. 34).

33. Jacobus, *Golden Legend*, vol. 2, 149–54. His account includes Mary's childhood and marriage to Joseph as well as a brief mention of the Annunciation.

34. Pamela Sheingorn, "Appropriating the Holy Kinship: Gender and Family History," in Kathleen Ashley and Pamela Sheingorn, *Interpreting Cultural Symbols*, 169–96.

35. See https://udayton.edu/imri/mary/n/nativity_of_the_blessed_virgin_mary.php. Accessed 7/15/23.

36. Jacobus, *Golden Legend*, vol. 2, 155.

37. Jacobus, *Golden Legend*, vol. 1, 201.

38. Jacobus, *Golden Legend*, vol. 2, 86–87.

39. See Catherine Oakes, *Ora Pro Nobis: The Virgin as Intercessor in Medieval Art and Devotion* (Trunhout: Brepols, 2008), 102. Chapter 5 shows the image of St. Michael weighing souls in the scales with the Virgin intervening by weighing down the balance, usually with her rosary or simply by the pressure of her hand.

40. Jacobus, *Golden Legend*, vol. 2, 85–86.

41. Mary Clayton, *The Cult of the Virgin Mary in Anglo-Saxon England* (Cambridge: Cambridge University Press, 1990), 267.

42. Mary Clayton, *The Apocryphal Gospels of Mary in Anglo-Saxon England* (Cambridge: Cambridge University Press, 1998), 101ff.

43. See Françoise Laurent, "Culte Marial et Identité Anglo-Normande: L'Exemple de Miracle de Helsin dans *La Concepcion Nostre Dame* de Wace et Deux Recueils Marials des XIIe et XIIIe Siècles," in Paul Bretel, Michel Adroher and Aymar Catafau, *La Vierge dans les arts et les littératures du moyen âge* (Paris: Champion, 2017), 69–70.

44. Adrienne Williams Boyarin, ed. and trans., "Introduction," *Miracles of the Virgin in Middle English* (Peterboro, ON: Broadview Press, 2015), 11.

45. Dates suggested by Boyarin and by Beverly Boyd, *The Middle English Miracles of the Virgin* (San Marino, CA: The Huntington Library, 1964).

46. Boyarin, *Miracles of the Virgin*, 101–02.

47. Geoffrey Chaucer, "An ABC," in *The Poetical Works of Chaucer*, ed. F. M. Robinson (Cambridge, MA: Riverside Press, 1933), 617–19. See also the editor's introduction, 612–17.

48. Boyd, *The Middle English Miracles*, 121.

49. Boyd, *The Middle English Miracles*, 50–55.

50. Karen Saupe, ed., *Middle English Marian Lyrics* (Kalamazoo, MI: Western Michigan University, 1998), 11.

51. Saupe, *Lyrics*, 147–48. My translation from Saupe's text and notes, 260–61. I disagree with Saupe's description of this poem as a *chanson d'aventure* (song about seeking a knightly challenge of adventure). The object of the speaker's quest is a "maiden," not an opponent.

52. Saupe, *Lyrics*, 61. My translation from Saupe's text and notes, 188.

53. Saupe, *Lyrics*, 71–76. My translation from Saupe's text and notes, 199–201.

54. Saupe, *Lyrics*, 113–15.

55. Saupe, *Lyrics*, 150–53.

56. François Villon, *Oeuvres*, ed. Auguste Lognon (Paris: Champion, 1967), 40–41. My translation.

57. Villon is referring to Saint Mary of Egypt, a fourth-century woman who was converted from a life of prostitution to that of a solitary penitent in the desert. She is honored in both the Eastern Orthodox and the Roman Catholic traditions.

Chapter 6

1. Camille Chabaneau, ed., *Le Romanz de Saint Fanuel et de Sainte Anne et de Nostre Dame et de Nostre Segnor et de ses apostres* (Paris: Maisonneuve et C. Leclerc, 1889).

2. The romance was edited in the twentieth century by William Musil, "Le Roman de Saint Fanuel: Édition Critique," (Ph.D. diss., University of Chicago, 1977).

3. Chabaneau, *Romanz*, 4–5.

4. Chabaneau, *Romanz*, 20–21.

5. Saint Anne as matriarch was an important figure in the fifteenth and sixteenth centuries, a period when the Holy Kinship was extremely popular as a subject for artists and craftspeople. Evidence of the popularity of Mary's mother in New France is still found in Quebec at the Shrine of Ste. Anne de Beaupré, which contains vestiges of the legend in its mosaics.

6. This section is based on Judith M. Davis, *Opening Heaven to the World: The Shrine-Madonnas of the Middle Ages* (Lakewood, OH: Future Church, 2016). Used with permission.

7. Barbara Newman, *God and the Goddesses: Vision, Poetry and Relief in the Middle Ages* (Philadelphia: University of Pennsylvania Press, 2003), 272. A recent authoritative work on shrine-madonnas is Elina Gertsman, *Worlds Within: Opening the Medieval Shrine Madonna* (University Park: Pennsylvania State University Press, 2015).

8. Newman, 269.

9. See Barbara W. Tuchman, *A Distant Mirror: The Calamitous Fourteenth Century* (New York: Alfred A. Knopf, 1978), xiii. The calamities she mentions are still with us seven centuries later.

10. Newman, *God and the Goddesses*, 284.

11. Newman, *God and the Goddesses*, 284–86, details the extravagant virtues and characteristics attributed to Joseph by Gerson.

12. Newman, *God and the Goddesses*, 287.

13. See Sarah McNamer, *Affective Meditation and the Invention of Medieval Compassion* (Philadelphia: University of Pennsylvania Press, 2010), for a description and analysis of affective piety.

14. Gaston Paris and Ulysse Robert, *Miracles de Nostre Dame par personages [Miracles of Our Lady Dramatized]* (Paris: Firmin Didot, 1876–1893; rpt. Johnson Reprint Corporation, 1996). See also Judith M. Davis, "The *Miracula Mariae* and May Festivals of the Middle Ages," *Theatre and Religion* 2 (1996): 18–27; and Donald Maddox and Sara Sturm-Maddox, *Parisian Confraternity Drama of the 14th Century: The* Miracles de Nostre Dame par personages (Turnhout: Brepols, 2008).

15. For this play, I have used the edition of Graham A. Runnalls, ed. and trans., *Le Miracle de l'enfant ressuscité. Quinzième des Miracles de Notre Dame par personnages* (Geneva: Droz, 1972).

16. *Miracles of Our Lady Dramatized*, vol. 2, 281–346. Because of her painless childbirth, Mary was invoked (as was the Roman goddess Diana before her) as the patron of fertility and birth.

17. The Fourth Lateran Council (1215) promulgated the doctrine of transubstantiation, of the transformation of bread and wine into the body and blood of Christ: the Eucharist. This play emphasizes its importance.

18. Paris and Robert, *Miracles*, vol. 1, 2–36.

19. Only the woman—Sebille—is named in the play, but for narrative purposes I have given her spouse a name also.

20. Sometime during the seventh century, according to legend, a boat bearing a luminous statue of Mary appeared near the beach at what is now Boulogne-sur-Mer. A chapel was built for it, and then a church; it became associated with miracles and remained a place of pilgrimage into the twentieth century, although the statue was destroyed during the Revolution.

21. Paris and Robert, *Miracles*, vol. 5, 89–146.

22. This child may be seen as a figure of John the Baptist, whose call to repentance is attested in Luke 3:10–18 and who may be seen as prefiguring the later Christian wild man living in the forest as a hermit. See Claude Gaignebet and Jean-Dominique Lajoux, *Art profane et religion populaire au moyen age* (Paris: Presses Universitaires de France, 1985), 132.

23. Pierre Kunstmann, "The Virgin's Mediation: Evolution and Transformation of the Motif," in Donald Maddox and Sara Sturm-Maddox, eds., *Parisian Confran-*

ternity Drama of the Fourteenth Century: The Miracles de Nostre Dame par personages (Turnhout: Brepols, 2008), 167.

24. For a translation of and more extensive commentary on this work, see Judith M. Davis and F.R.P. Akehurst, trans., *Our Lady's Lawsuits in L'Advocacie Nostre Dame and La Chapelerie Nostre Dame de Baiex* (Tempe: Arizona Center for Medieval and Renaissance Studies, 2011).

25. The "Salve Regina," or "Hail, Holy Queen," is very old, harkening back to the third-century "Under Your Protection." Its earliest forms date to the eleventh century, and it became part of monastic prayer life in the twelfth and thirteenth. See Michael O'Carroll, *Theotokos: A Theological Encyclopedia of the Blessed Virgin Mary*, rev. ed., 317–18 (Wilmington, DE: Michael Glazier, Inc., 1983).

26. The *Gospel of Nicodemus* dates from about the mid-fourth century, although the idea dates back to the second century, according to Montague James, trans., *The Apocryphal New Testament* (Oxford: Clarendon Press, 1989), 95. Zbigniew Izydorczk places the Latin translation that is the origin of "[a]ll West European versions" in the fifth century: *The Medieval Gospel of Nicodemus: Texts, Intertexts and Contexts in Western Europe* (Tempe: Arizona Center for Medieval and Renaissance Studies, 1997), 43–101. One of the manuscripts containing "Our Lady's Advocacy" also features a French translation of the *Gospel of Nicodemus*.

27. Davis and Akehurst, *Our Lady's Lawsuits*, 67.

28. Davis and Akehurst, *Our Lady's Lawsuits*, 73.

29. For an accessible presentation of the N-town plays, see Douglas Sugano, ed., *The N-Town Plays* (Kalamazoo, MI: Medieval Institute Publications, 2007).

30. Sugano, *N-Town*, 134, lines 33–44.

31. Peter Meredith, ed., "Introduction," *The Mary Play From the N-Town Manuscript* (Exeter: University of Exeter Press, 1997), 1–4.

32. Walter Harrelson, ed., *The New Interpreter's Study Bible: New Revised Standard Version with the Apocrypha* (Nashville: Abingdon Press, 2003), 827–28.

33. Hope Traver, *The Four Daughters of God: A Study of the Versions of this Allegory with Special Reference to those in Latin, French and English* (Bryn Mawr: Bryn Mawr College, 1907), 15–17.

34. *The Mary Play*, lines 1207–1210, 1239–1240, 1244–1245, 1247–1248, pages 70–72.

35. *The Mary Play*, lines 1376–1379, 1390, 1396–1398, p. 76.

36. Sugano, *N-Town*, Play 28, lines 175–178, 187–188, pp. 240–41.

37. Sugano, *N-Town*, Play 32, lines 93–95, 161–164, pp. 267 and 269.

38. Gary Waller, *The Virgin Mary in Late Medieval and Early Modern English Literature and Popular Culture* (Cambridge: Cambridge University Press, 2011), 70. The bracketed expression replaces Waller's "grotesque and fearful" as applied to women in the audiences of N-Town plays. I see no evidence for those traits except in misogynistic medieval texts, and the cited text is not one of them.

39. The Latin can be found online in many English translations. I have used "Jacopone Tudertini [da Todi], Stabat Mater" in my old book, *Medieval Latin*, ed. K.P. Harrington (Chicago: University of Chicago Press, 1962), 362–65, for my translation.

40. Gloria K. Fiero, "The *Dits*: The Historical Context," in Gloria K. Fiero, Wendy Pfeffer, and Mathé Allain, *Three Medieval Views of Women* (New Haven: Yale University Press, 1989). 64. See also Joan Young Gregg, *Devils, Women and Jews: Reflections of the Other in Medieval Sermon Stories* (Albany: SUNY Press, 1977, 83–167.

41. See Sticca, *The* Planctus Mariae.

42. Grace Frank, ed., *La Passion du Palatinus, mystère du XIVe siècle* (Paris: Champion, 1922).

43. Frank, *La Passion du Palatinus*, lines 976–989 and 1222–1225.

44. Graham A. Runnalls, *La Passion d'Auvergne* (Geneva: Droz, 1982), lines 1309–1310, 1342–1356.

45. Omer Jodogne, ed., *Le Mystère de la passion d'Arnoul Gréban*, vol. 1 (Bruxelles: Académie Royale de Belgique, 1965); Eustache Mercadé, *Le Mystère de la passion: Texte du manuscript 697 de la Bibliothèque d'Arras* (Geneva: Slatkine, 1976).

46. Sticca, *The Planctus Mariae*, 57.

47. Johannes Herolt, *Miracles of the Blessed Virgin* Mary, trans. C.C. Swinton Bland (London: George Routledge & Sons, 1928).

48. Herolt, *Miracles*, 76.
49. Herolt, *Miracles*, 22-23 (Miracle 5); 47-51 (Miracles 28 and 29).
50. Herolt, *Miracles*, 78-79.
51. Herolt, *Miracles*, 100.

Chapter 7

1. *The Colloquies of Erasmus*, trans. Craig R. Thompson (Chicago: University of Chicago Press, 1965), 631.
2. *Colloquies*, 289.
3. *Colloquies*, 290.
4. *Colloquies*, 290-91.
5. Sarah Jane Boss, "Francisco Suárez and Modern Mariology," in Boss, *Mary*, 267.
6. For a compelling overview of Marian teachings by Luther and his followers, see Beth Kretizer, *Reforming Mary: Changing Images of the Virgin Mary in Lutheran Sermons of the Sixteenth Century* (New York: Oxford University Press, 2004).
7. Eamon Duffy, *The Stripping of the Altars: Traditional Religion in England c. 1400-c. 1580*, 2nd ed. (New Haven: Yale University Press, 2005).
8. For another account of the principal Reform attitudes toward Mary, see George H. Tavard, *The Thousand Faces of the Virgin Mary* (Collegeville, MN: The Liturgical Press, 1996), 103-52.
9. Miri Rubin, *Mother of God: A History of the Virgin Mary* (New Haven: Yale University Press, 2009), 371.
10. Jaroslav Pelikan, *Mary Through the Centuries: Her Place in the History of Culture* (New Haven: Yale University Press, 1996), 163.
11. My account of the apparitions of Our Lady of Guadalupe is based on Jeanette Rodriguez, *Our Lady of Guadalupe: Faith and Empowerment Among Mexican-American Women* (Austin: University of Texas Press, 1994.)
12. Henri Leclercq, "Fourth Lateran Council (1215)," *The Catholic Encyclopedia*, vol. 9 (New York: Robert Appleton Co., 1910). https://www.newadvent.org/cathen/09018a.htm. Accessed 4/21/24.
13. Sally Cunneen, *In Search of Mary: The Woman and the Symbol* (New York: Paulist Press, 1996), 208.
14. See www.allykateusz.org/art-as-text-powerpoints/two-marys-two-traditions/, slide 5. Shawn Trive describes the significance of red as a symbol of the papacy in "The History and Symbolism of the Pope's Red Shoes," https://www.liturgicalartsjournal.com/2020/11/the-history-and-symbolism-of-popes-red.html. Accessed 1/31/24.
15. Ally Kateusz, *Mary and Early Christian Women: Hidden Leadership* (Palgrave Macmillan/Open Access, 2019), 86. She notes that "De Rossi's 1899 painting of this mosaic shows a red cross on Mary's pallium, but today the red tesserae [mosaic pieces] are almost entirely replaced with white" (214).
16. Cleo McNelly Kearns, *The Virgin Mary, Monotheism, and Sacrifice* (Cambridge: Cambridge University Press, 2008), 276-77. See also Alexei Lidov, "The Priesthood of the Virgin Mary as an Image-Paradigm of Christian Visual Culture," *Ikon* 10 (2017): 9-26, and Paul Y. Cardile, "Mary as Priest: Mary's Sacerdotal Position in the Visual Arts," *Arte Cristiana* 72, no. 703 (1984): 199-208. There are also images of Mary in priestly vestments, which may be found at https://womenpriests.org/mary-priest/gallery-gallery-of-images-of-mary-in-priestly-vestments/. Accessed 4/21/24.
17. Michael O'Carroll, *Theotokos: A Theological Encyclopedia of the Blessed Virgin Mary* (Wilmington, DE: Michael Glazier, Inc., 1983), 317.
18. Brother John M. Samaha, S.M., "Mary's Priestly Dimension," https://udayton.edu/imri/mary/p/priestly-dimension-of-mary.php. Accessed 4/21/24.
19. Graef, *Mary: A History*, 293.
20. Graef, *Mary: A History*, 295.
21. E. Pace, "Dulia," in *The Catholic Encyclopedia* (New York: Robert Appleton Company, 1909). https://www.newadvent.org/cathen/05188b.htm. Accessed 4/21/24.
22. René Laurentin, *Marie, l'Église et le sacerdoce*, vol. 1 (Paris: Nouvelles Éditions Latines, 1952), 375-82, discusses the role of the "French School" in promulgating the concept of Mary as priest.
23. Quoted in Sarah Jane Boss, "Marian Sacrifice at the Eucharist?" *Maria: A Journal of Marian Studies* 2, no. 2 (July 2022): 4. This essay is invaluable for its overview and analysis of of the "Mary Priest" motif and movement.
24. Laurentin, *Marie*, vol. 1, 249. My translation.

25. Liviana Gazzetta, "Une idée de sacerdoce féminin entre XIXe et XXe siècle: Les Filles du Coeur de Jésus et la devotion à la 'Vierge Prêtre,'" *Chrétiens et sociétés* 25 (2018): 3–4.
26. Graef, *Mary: A History*, 308.
27. Rev. Matthew R. Mauriello, "Devotion to the Immaculate Heart of Mary," https://udayton.edu/imri/mary/i/-immaculate-heart-of-mary-devotion.php. Accessed 4/21/24.
28. Quoted in Graef (*Mary: A History*), 317.
29. Graef, *Mary: A History*, 322–23.
30. Marie-Louis Grignion de Montfort, *The Secret of the Rosary*, trans. Mary Barbour, T.O.P. https://thavmapub.files.wordpress.com/2017/secret-of-the-rosary.pdf. Accessed 4/21/24. It may work best to search for "Mary Barbour Wordpress Secret of the Rosary."
31. Montfort, *Rosary*, 33–34.
32. "Maria de Agreda," https://www.newadvent.org/cathen/01229a.htm. Accessed 4/21/24.
33. Graef, *Mary: A History*, 339.
34. For a detailed outline of *The Glories of Mary*, consult https://www.ecatholic2000.com/liguori/glories.shtml. Accessed 4/21/24.
35. George Tavard, *The Thousand Faces of the Virgin Mary* (Collegeville, MN: The Liturgical Press, 1996), 178.
36. Rev. Matthew R. Mauriello, "Miraculous Medal," https://udayton.edu/imri/mary/m/miraculous-medal.php.
37. Richard McBrien, *Catholicism*, New Ed. (New York: Harper One, 1994), 187.
38. McBrien, *Catholicism*, 64.
39. https://www.papalencyclicals.net/pius09/p9ineff.htm. For additional interpretation and commentary, see Appendix 1.
40. "Immaculate Conception Dogma: Development." https://udayton.edu/imri/mary/i/immaculate-conception-dogma-development.php. Accessed 4/21/24.
41. McBrien, *Catholicism*, 1093.
42. Peter Mullen, "St. Bernadette [of] Lourdes," in *Shrines of Our Lady: A Guide to Fifty of the World's Most Famous Marian Shrines* (New York: St. Martin's Press, 1998), 81–86, here 85. I've based my retelling on his account, with additional research at https://udayton.edu/imri/mary/o/our-lady-of-lourdes.php. Accessed 4/21/24.

43. Liviana Gazzetta, "Une idée de sacerdoce feminine entre XIXe et XXe siècle: les Filles du Coeur de Jésus et la devotion à la Vierge Prêtre," *Chrétiens et sociétés* 25 (2018): 127–43, here 127. https://journals.openedition.org/chretienssocietes/4502.
44. Oswald van der Berghe, *Mary and the Priesthood* (Paris: Louis Vivès, 1875).
45. Gazzetta, "Sacerdoce feminine," 135.
46. Agnes Smith Lewis, ed. and trans., *Apocrypha Syriaca: The* Protevangelium Jacobi *and* Transitus Mariae (London: C. J. Clay & Sons, 1902). For a much-needed reappraisal of Agnes and her equally brilliant sister, see Rebecca J.W. Jefferson, "Sisters of Semitics: A Fresh Appreciation of the Scholarship of Agnes Smith Lewis and Margaret Dunlap Gibson," *Medieval Feminist Forum* 45, no. 5 (2009): 23–49.
47. Anna Brownell Jameson, *Legends of the Madonna as Represented in the Fine Arts* (London: Hutchinson & Co, 1907).
48. Jameson, *Madonna*, 357–59.
49. Jameson, *Madonna*, 34.
50. Kimberly VanEsveld Adams, *Our Lady of Victorian Feminism: The Madonna in the Work of Anna Jameson, Margaret Fuller and George Eliot* (Athens: University of Georgia Press, 2001), 8.
51. Adams, *Victorian*, 31, quoting Colleen McDannell.
52. "Angel in the House" is a phrase used to describe the "ideal" Victorian woman as described in a smarmy poem by Coventry Patmore in 1863.
53. Henry Adams and Ralph Adams Cram, *Mont-Saint-Michel and Chartres* (Boston: Houghton Mifflin Company, 1904). https://digitalcommons.unl.edu/etas/70/.
54. Adams and Cram, *Mont-Saint-Michel*, 266–269.
55. Boss, "Marian Sacrifice," 15.

Chapter 8

1. Jacobus, *Golden Legend*, vol. 2, 149–50.
2. Jacobus, *Golden Legend*, vol. 1, 197.
3. Jacobus, *Golden Legend*, vol. 1, 221.
4. Jacobus, *Golden Legend*, vol. 2, 77. He also cites Pseudo-Dionysus (79).
5. Jacobus, *Golden Legend*, vol. 2, 82–88.
6. Holy Apostles Convent, *The Life of the*

Virgin Mary, the Theotokos (Buena Vista, CO: Holy Apostles Convent and Dormition Skete), 1989.

7. Holy Apostles Convent, *Theotokos*, 272.

8. Holy Apostles Convent, *Theotokos*, 310.

9. Holy Apostles Convent, *Theotokos*, 322–23. The work could be fourth- or fifth-century, according to J.K. Elliott, *The Apocryphal New Testament* (Oxford: Clarendon Press, 1993), 111.

10. Holy Apostles Convent, *Theokotos*, 247.

11. Holy Apostles Convent, *Theotokos*, 424.

12. Holy Apostles Convent, *Theotokos*, 427.

13. Holy Apostles Convent, *Theotokos*, 432–39. The sources for this adventure include liturgical elements of the feast of St. Lazarus, a pilgrimage book, and accounts of Mount Athos by resident monks.

14. *The Life of the Virgin Mary [Attributed to Maximus the Confessor]*, trans. Timothy Fisher (Virgin Mary and Oceania [Australia]: St. George Monastery/Monaxi Agapi, 2022).

15. Maximos, *Life*, 73–74.

16. Grace Frank, *Le Miracle de Théophile: Miracle du XIIIe siècle* (Paris: Champion, 1967), xiii–xiv.

17. See Jerry Root, *The Theophilus Legend in Medieval Text and Image* (Cambridge: D.S. Brewer, 2017), for a history of the legend and its depiction throughout Europe.

18. See Robert Guiette, *La Légende de la sacristine: Étude de littérature comparé* (Paris: Champion, 1927); also Hilding Kjellman, "Le miracle de la sacristine," in M. Johan Melander, *Mélanges de philologie offerts à Johan Melander* (Uppsala: A.B. Lundequistska Bokhandeln, 1943), 47–81.

19. Legrand D'Aussy, *Fabliaux et contes, fables et romans, du XIIe et du XIIIe siècle*, 3rd ed., vol. 5 (Paris: Jules Renouard. 1829), 79–85; M. Méon, *Nouveau recueil de fabliaux et contes inédites des poètes français des XIIe, XIIIe, XIVe et XVe siècles*, vol. 2 (Paris: Chasseriau, 1823), 154–72.

20. Charles Nodier, *Contes*, ed. Pierre-Georges Castex (Paris: Garnier Frères, 1961).

21. Auguste Villiers de l'Isle-Adam, *Contes cruels, suivis des Noveaux contes cruels*, ed. Pierre-Georges Castex and Pierre Glaudes (Paris: Garner Frères, 2012), 354–58.

22. For an analysis of Nodier, Villiers and Maeterlinck, see Christina Ferree Chabrier, "Béatrix Gets a Makeover: Modern Rewritings of a Medieval Legend," *Romance Notes* 42, No. 3 (Spring 2002): 273–81.

23. For a comprehensive description of this extravaganza, see https://en.wikipedia.org/wiki/The_Miracle_(1912_film). Accessed 2/21/24.

24. "Saints and Spinners," Monday, March 28, 2005. www.saintsandspinners.blogspot.com/2005/03/keeper-of-keys-legend-of-beatrix-nun.html. Accessed 10/20/23.

25. Stith-Thompson, *Motif-Index of Folk Literature*, rev. and enlarged ed. (Bloomington Indiana University Press, 1955–58), vol. 5, 465–76, and vol. 6, 163. Vol. 5 lists 90 legends and miracle stories; vol. 6 contains an additional 19.

26. https://sites.pitt.edu/~dash/grimm 003.html. Accessed 4/21/24.

27. Pamela Berger cites this story as a grain-goddess tale adapted for medieval audiences: "Metamorphosis from Goddess to Virgin Mary," Chapter VI of *The Goddess Obscured: Transformation of the Grain Protectress from Goddess to Saint* (Boston: Beacon Press, 1985).

28. See William Wright, "The Departure of My Lady Mary From This World," *The Journal of Sacred Literature and Biblical Record* 7 (April 1865): 151.

29. See Ruth Whittredge, *La Nativité et Le Geu des trois rois, Two Plays from Manuscript 1131 of the Bibliothèque Sainte Geneviève, Paris* (Bryn Mawr: The William Byrd Press, 1944).

30. Francis James Child, *The English and Scottish Popular Ballads*, vol. 2 (New York: Dover, 1965), 7. The ballad is reproduced on pages 8–10.

31. Henri Pourrat, *Le Trésor des contes*, vol. 4 (Paris: Gallimard, 1953), 56–60. My translation.

32. Robert J. Voigt, *The Story of Mary and the Grasshoppers* (Cold Spring, MN: n.p., 1991), 10–11.

33. Gaston Paris, *La Littérature française au moyen âge*, 1st ed. (Paris: Hachette, 1888), 208.

34. Anatole France, "Le Jongleur de Notre-Dame/Conte pour le mois de Mai," *Le Gaulois*, 10 mai 1890, according to the notes for the tale: Anatole France, *Oeuvres*, vol. 1 (Paris: Gallimard, 1984), 1421. The tale itself is reprinted on pages 918–23. France also published it in *L'Étui de nacre* (Paris: Colmann Lévy, 1899), 92–105.

35. My translation of "Le Jongleur de Notre-Dame" in Anatole France, *Oeuvres*, 918–23, here 919.

36. Except for the Disney/Paulist film, most adaptations of the Anatole France story can be found—in addition to many others—in Jan Kiolskowski, "Juggling the Middle Ages: The Reception of Our Lady's Tumbler and Le Jongleur de Notre-Dame," *Studies in Medievalism* 15 (2006), 157–97.

37. Jan M. Ziokowski, *The Juggler of Notre Dame and the Medievalizing of Modernity* (Cambridge: Open Book Publishers, 2018).

38. Sugano, *N-Town*, 134, Play 15, lines 32–52. My translation.

39. Francis James Child, ed., *The English and Scottish Popular Ballads*, vol. 2 (New York: Houghton Mifflin and Company, 1886); rpt. Dover, 1965, 1–2.

Chapter 9

1. My account of the Fatima visions is based on Mullen, *Shrines*, 139–43.

2. For comprehensive coverage of the political and religious depictions of Mary in the twentieth century, see Peter Margry, ed., *Cold War Mary: Ideologies, Politics and Marian Devotional Culture* (Leuven: University Press, 2020). See also Dorian Llewelyn, "The Patriotic Virgin: How Mary's Been Marshaled for Religious Nationalism and Military Campaigns," *The Conversation*, July 7, 2022. https://theconversation.com/the-patriotic-virgin-how-marys-been-marshaled-for-religious-nationalism-and-military-campaigns-183220.

3. My account of Mary's importance in this era is based on Peter Margry, "Envisioning and Exploring Mary's Theater of War," in Margry, *Cold War Mary*, 7–56.

4. This summary can be found in Biaggio Mazza, "The Blessed Virgin Mary—Vatican II Asked: Is She Truly Our Sister?" *National Catholic Reporter*, January 16, 2015, 1. https://www.ncronline.org/blessed-virgin-mary-vatican-II-asked-she-truly-our-sister. Accessed 4/21/24.

5. "Lumen Gentium," Chapter VIII, #62, in *Vatican Council II: Constitution, Decrees, Declarations*, ed. and trans. Austin Flannery, O.P. (Northport, NY: Costello Publishing Company, 1996), 86.

6. "Lumen Gentium," Chapter VIII, #56, "The Role of the Blessed Virgin in the Plan of Salvation," 82.

7. "Lumen Gentium," Chapter VIII, "Our Lady," 82–83.

8. "Lumen Gentium," Chapter VIII, "The Cult of The Blessed Virgin in the Church," 89.

9. Charlene Spretnak, "Mary and Modernity," in *The Oxford Handbook of Mary*, ed. Chris Maunder (New York: Oxford University Press, 2019), 543.

10. René Laurentin, *Marie, L'Église et le sacerdoce* (Paris: Nouvelles Éditions Latines, 1952), 632.

11. Andrew Murr, Christopher Dickey, Eric Larson, Sarah Van Boven and Hersch Doby, "Hail Mary," in *Newsweek*, August 25, 1997, 49–55.

12. Murr et al., 55, quoting Fr. Johan Roten of the International Marian Institute, University of Dayton.

13. Grizutti Harrison, "My Eve, My Mary." *Newsweek*, August 25, 1997, 56.

14. Tina Beattie, quoting Jaroslav Pelikan, in *God's Mother, Eve's Advocate: A Marian Narrative of Women's Salvation* (London: Continuum, 2002), 106.

15. Beattie, *God's Mother*, 154.

16. See Thomas A. Thompson, S.M., ed, *Marian Studies* LX (2009). Published by the Mariological Society of America, University of Dayton (Ohio).

17. Michael Duricy, "*The Life of Mary* in Film: Marian Films in the Twentieth Century," *Marian Studies* 60 (2009), 278.

18. Duricy, "Mary in Film," 184.

19. https://www.imdb.com/title/tt2504 9058. Accessed 12/8/23.

20. Maureen Orth, "How the Virgin Mary Became the World's Most Powerful Woman." *National Geographic* (December 2015), 30–59. The story is available online by subscription.

21. Orth, "Powerful Woman," 34.

22. Orth, "Powerful Woman," 54–55.

23. Orth, "Powerful Woman," 40–41 "Seeing Mary" chart. For a reported Marian

appearance in Australia, see Carol M. Cusack, "The Virgin Mary at Coogee: A Preliminary Investigation," *Australian Religion Studies Review* 16, No. 1 (2003): 116–29. Statistics are available at https://udayton.edu/imri/mary/a/apparitions-statistics-modern.php. Accessed 4/21/24.

24. Father John Flader, "Gladys Quiroga de Motta and the apparitions of Our Lady of San Nicolas," *Catholic Weekly*, July 30, 2016. https://www.catholicweekly.com.au/gladys-quiroga-de-motta-and-the-apparitions-of-our-lady-of-san-nicolas/ Accessed 12/11/23.

25. https://dustyoldthing.com/bathtub-madonnas-history/ Accessed 3/6/24.

26. https://en.wikipedia.org/wiki/Surfing_Madonna and www.coolsandiegosights.com/2020/05/24/the-miracle-of-the-surfing-madonna. Accessed 3/6/24.

27. Gustavo Arellano, "Chicago's Downtrodden, Magnificent Our Lady of the Underpass Still Inspires," National Catholic Reporter, June 21, 2023. https://www.ncronline.org/opinion/chicagos-downtrodden-magnificent-our-lady-underpass-still-inspires. Accessed 3/1/24.

28. Paolo Apolito, *The Internet and the Madonna: Religious Visionary Experience on the Web,* trans. Antony Shugaar (Chicago: University of Chicago Press, 2005). For a condensed account of the book, see Eugene Hynes, rev. of Paulo Apolito, *The Internet and the Madonna: Religious Visionary Experience on the Web,* H-Catholic, H-Net Reviews, October 2009. https://networks.h-net.org/node/3595/reviews/4400/hynes-apolito-internet-and-madonna-religious-visionary-experience-web. Accessed 4/20/24.

29. Apolito, *Internet Madonna*, 2.

30. Sam Scott, "Michael O'Neill Explains and Explores the Miraculous: The Virgin Mary's 'Number Cruncher,'" *Stanford Magazine*, December 2018, 5. https://stanfordmag.org/contents/michael-o-neill-explains-and-explores-the-miraculous. Accessed 1/18/24.

31. Michael O'Neill, "Marian Apparition Claims in the United States and Canada in the Twentieth Century," *Marian Studies* 63 (2012): 270. https://ecommons.udayton.edu/marian_studies/vol63/iss1/13.

32. Whitney Bauck, "The Virgin Mary Returns as an Icon for Pop Stars and Social Justice Warriors." *America Magazine*, July 27, 2021. https://www.americamagazine.org/faith/2021/07/27/mary-pop-icon-social-justice-culture-trend-241123. Accessed 4/20/24.

33. Bauck, "The Virgin Mary returns."

34. David Mouriquand, "The Assumption: The Virgin Mary as a Powerful Icon of Pop Culture?" https://www.euronews.com/culture/2023/08/15/the-assumption-the-virgin-mary-as-a-powerful-icon-of-pop-culture. Accessed 4/20/24.

35. Judith Huacuja, "Chicana Women Artists Draw Inspiration from the Virgin of Guadalupe," *National Catholic Reporter.* December 8–21, 2023, 13.

36. Huacuja, "Chicana Artists," 16.

37. Bauck, "The Virgin Mary returns."

38. Bauck, "The Virgin Mary returns."

39. Damian Costello, "The Black Madonna Makes Her Mark in the Least Religious State in the U.S.," *National Catholic Reporter*, November 10–23, 2023, 14.

40. Bauck, "The Virgin Mary returns."

41. Quoted in Jeanette Rodriguez and Ted Fortier, *Cultural Memory: Resistance, Faith and Identity* (Austin: University of Texas Press, 2007), 22.

Bibliography

Primary Sources

Adgar. *Le Gracial*. Publié par Pierre Kunstmann. Ottawa: Éditions de l'Université d'Ottawa, 1982.

[Alfonxo X of Spain]. *Songs of Holy Mary of Alfonso X the Wise*. Translated by Kathleen Kulp-Hill, with an introduction by Connie L. Scarborough. Tempe: Arizona Center for Medieval and Renaissance Studies, 2000.

Amadeus of Lausanne. *Homilies in Praise of Blessed Mary*. Translated by Grace Perigo. Kalamazoo, MI: Cistercian Publications, 1979.

Andreas Capellanus. *The Art of Courtly Love*. Translated with an introduction and notes by John J. Parry. New York: Frederick Ungar, 1959.

Apocalypse of the Virgin. Translated by Tony Burke. https://tonyburke.ca/wp-content/uploads/Apocalypse-of-the-Virgin.pdf. Retrieved 2/13/22.

Arabic Infancy Gospel. www.newadvent.org/fathers/0806.htm. Retrieved 2/14/22.

Bartha, Jeannie K., Annette Grant Cash, and Richard Terry Mount, trans. *The Collected Works of Gonzalo de Berceo in English Translation*. Tempe: Arizona Center for Medieval and Renaissance Studies, 2008.

Bernard of Clairvaux. *Homilies in Praise of the Virgin Mary*. Translated by Marie-Bernard Said. Kalamazoo, MI: Cistercian Publications, 1979.

Boyarin, Adrienne Williams, ed. and trans. *Miracles of the Virgin in Middle English*. Peterboro, ON: Broadview Press, 2015.

Boyarin, Adrienne Williams, and Beverly Boyd. *The Middle English Miracles of the Virgin*. San Francisco: The Huntington Library, 1964.

Bretel, Paul, ed. and trans. *Le Jongleur de Notre Dame*. Paris: Champion, 2011.

Bull, Marcus, trans. *The Miracles of Our Lady of Rocamadour, Analysis and Translation*. Woodbridge, Suffolk: The Boydell Press, 1999.

Caesarius of Heisterbach. Vol. 1 of *The Dialogue on Miracles*. Translated by H. von E. Scott and C.C. Swinton Bland. London: George Routledge & Sons, 1929.

Chabaneau, Camille, ed. *Le Romanz de Saint Fanuel et de Sainte Anne et de Nostre Dame et de Nostre Segnor et de ses apostres*. Paris: Maisonneuve et Leclerc, 1889.

Child, Francis James. Vol. 2 of *The English and Scottish Popular Ballads*. New York: Dover, 1965.

Davis, Judith M., and F.R.P. Akehurst, trans. *Our Lady's Lawsuits in* L'Advocacie Nostre Dame *and* La Chapelerie Nostre Dame de Baiex. Tempe: Arizona Center for Medieval and Renaissance Studies, 2011.

De Laborde, Alexandre. *Les Miracles de Nostre Dame compilés par Jehan Miélot*. Paris: Société Française de Réproductions de Manuscrits à Peintures, 1928.

Dominic of Evesham. *De Miraculis Sanctae Mariae*, edited by J.M. Canal. Léon: Studium Legionense, 1998.

Erasmus. *The Colloquies of Erasmus*. Translated by Craig R. Thompson. Chicago: University of Chicago Press, 1965.

France, Anatole. "Le Jongleur de Notre-Dame/Conte pour le mois de mai." In Vol. 1 of *Oeuvres*, 918–23. Paris: Gallimard, 1984.

Frank, Grace. *Rutebeuf, Le Miracle de*

Théophile: Miracle du XIIIe siècle. Paris: Champion, 1967.

———, ed. *La Passion du Palatinus, Mystère du XIVe Siècle.* Paris: Champion, 1922.

Gonzalo de Berceo. "The Miracles of Our Lady." Translated by Annette Grant Cash and Richard Terry Mount. In *The Collected Works of Gonzalo de Berceo in English Translation*, translated by Jeannie K. Bartha, Annette Grant Cash, and Richard Terry Mount. Tempe: Arizona Center for Medieval and Renaissance Studies, 2008, 3–150.

Gospel of Pseudo-Matthew. www.newadvent.org/fathers/0848.htm. Retrieved 3/2/22.

Gregory of Tours. *Glory of the Martyrs.* Translated and with an introduction by Raymond Van Dam. Liverpool: Liverpool University Press, 1998.

Grignion de Montfort, Marie-Louis. *The Secret of the Rosary.* Translated by Mary Barbour, T.O.P. https://thavmapub.files.wordpress.com/2017/03/secret-of-the-rosary.pdf. Retrieved 9/24/23. Also available at https://www.ecatholic2000.com/montfort/rosary/rosary.shtml. Accessed 4/22/24.

Hériman de Tournai. *Les Miracles de Sainte Marie de Laon.* Translated and edited by Alain Saint-Denis. Paris: CNRS Editions, 2008.

Herolt, Johannes. *Miracles of the Blessed Virgin Mary.* Translated by C. Swinton Bland. London: George Routledge & Sons, 1928.

Holy Apostles Convent. *The Life of the Virgin Mary, Theotokos.* Buena Vista, CO: Holy Apostles Convent and Dormition Skete, 1993.

Jacobus de Voragine. *The Golden Legend.* 2 vols. Translated by William Granger Ryan. Princeton: Princeton University Press, 1993.

Jacques de Vitry. The *Exempla or Illustrative Stories of Jacques de Vitry.* Edited and with an introduction by Thomas Frederick Crane. London: David Nutt, 1890.

James, Montague Rhodes, trans. *The Apocryphal New Testament.* Oxford: Clarendon Press, 1989.

Järnstrom, Edward, and Arthur Järnstrom, eds. *Recueil de chansons pieuses du XIIIe siècle.* Helsinki: Suomalaisen Tiedeakatenian Toimituksia, 1914.

Jodogne, Omer, ed. *Le Mystère de la Passion d'Arnoul Gréban.* Brussels: Académie Royale de Belgique, 1965.

John Geometres. *Life of the Virgin Mary.* Translated and edited by Maximos Constas and Christos Simelidis. Cambridge: Harvard University Press, 2023.

Koenig, Frederick, ed. *Les Miracles de Nostre Dame par Gautier de Coinci.* Geneva: Droz, 1966.

Kreitzer, Beth. *Reforming Mary: Changing Images of the Virgin Mary in Lutheran Sermons of the Sixteenth Century.* New York: Oxford University Press, 2004.

Kulp-Hill, Kathleen, trans. *Songs of Holy Mary of Alfonso the Wise: A Translation of the* Cantigas de Santa Maria. Tempe: Arizona Center for Medieval and Renaissance Studies, 2000.

Kunstmann, Pierre, trans. and comp. *Vierge et merveille: Les Miracles de Notre-Dame narratifs au moyen âge.* Paris: Union Générale d'Éditions, 1981.

Lavaud, René, ed. *Poésies complètes du troubadour Peire Cardenal.* Toulouse: Privat, 1957.

Legrand d'Aussy, Pierre Jean-Baptiste. Vol. 5 of *Fabliaux et contes, fables et romans du XIIe et du XIIIe siècle*, 3rd ed. Paris: Jules Renouard, 1829.

Le Marchant, Jean. *Miracles de Notre-Dame de Chartres.* Publiés par Pierre Kunstmann. Ottawa: Éditions de l'Université d'Ottawa, 1973.

Lewis, Agnes Smith, ed. and trans. *Apocrypha Syriaca: The* Protevangelium Jacobi *and* Transitus Mariae. London: C.J. Clay & Sons, 1902.

Maximus the Confessor [Saint]. *The Life of the Virgin Mary.* Translated by Timothy Fisher. Virgin Mary and Oceania [Australia]: St. George Monastery/Monaxi Agapi, 2022.

Méon, [Dominique] Martin. Vol. 2 of *Nouveau recueil de fabliaux et contes inédits des poètes français des XIIIe, XIVe et XVe siècles.* Paris: Chasseriau, 1823.

Mercadé, Eustache, and Jules-Marie Richard. *Le Mystère de la passion: Texte du manuscrit 697 de La Bibliothèque d'Arras.* Geneva: Slatkine, 1976.

Meredith, Peter, ed. *The Mary Play from the N-Town Manuscript.* Exeter: University of Exeter Pres, 1997.

Nigel of Canterbury. *Miracles of the Virgin.* Translated and edited by Jan M.

Ziolkowski. Cambridge: Harvard University Press, 2022.

Paris, Gaston, and Ulysse Robert. *Miracles de Nostre Dame par personnages*. 8 vols. Paris: Firmin Didot, 1876–93; rpt. Johnson Reprint Corporation, 1996.

Pourrat, Henri. Vol. 4 of *Le Trésor des Contes*. Paris: Gallimard, 1953.

The Qur'an. Translated by M.A.S. Abdul Haleem. New York: Oxford University Press, 2010.

Runnals, Graham A., ed. *La Passion d'Auvergne*. Geneva: Droz, 1982.

_____, ed. and trans. *Le Miracle de l'enfant ressuscité: Quinzième des Miracles de Nostre-Dame par personnages*. Geneva: Droz, 1972.

Saupe, Karen, ed. *Middle English Marian Lyrics*. Kalamazoo: Western Michigan University, 1998.

Shoemaker, Stephen, trans. *The Life of the Virgin by Maximus the Confessor*. New Haven: Yale University Press, 2012.

Sugano, Douglas, ed. *The N-Town Plays*. Kalamazoo, MI: Medieval Institute Publications, 2007.

Symeon Metaphrastes. *Vita de Maria* [*Life of Mary*]. Translated by George Gharib. In *Testi Mariani del Primo Millennio 2: Padri e altri autori bizantini (VI–XI sec.)*. Roma: Citta Nuova Editrice, 1989. 980–1019.

Van Esbroeck, Michel-Jean, *Maxime le Confesseur: Vie de la Vierge*. 2 vols. Leuven: E. Peeters, 1986.

Vatican Council II: Constitution, Decrees, Declarations. Translated and edited by Austin Flannery, O.P. Northport, NY: Costello Publishing Company, 1996.

Villiers de l'Isle-Adam, Auguste. *Nouveaux contes cruels suivis de l'Amour suprême*. Paris: Librairie José Corti, 1862.

Villon, François. *Oeuvres*. Edited by Auguste Longnon. Paris: Champion, 1967.

Wace. *The Hagiographical Works: The Concepcion Nostre Dame and the Lives of St. Margaret and St. Nicholas*. Translated and with an introduction and notes by Jean Blacker, Glyn S. Burgess, and Amy V. Ogden. Leiden: Brill, 2013.

William of Malmesbury. *The Miracles of the Blessed Virgin Mary*. Translated and edited by R.M. Thomson and M. Winterbottom. Woodbridge, Suffolk: The Boydell Press, 2017.

Secondary Sources

Abboud, Hosn. *Mary in the Qur'an: A Literary Reading*. London: Routledge, 2014.

Adams, Henry, and Ralph Adams Cram. "Mont-Saint-Michel and Chartres" (1904). *Electronic Texts in American Studies*, 70. https://digitalcommons.unl.edu/etas/70/.

Adams, Kimberly Van Esveld. *Our Lady of Victorian Feminism: The Madonna in the Work of Anna Jameson, Margaret Fuller and George Eliot*. Athens: University of Georgia Press, 2001.

Angelidi, Christine, and Titos Papamastorakis. "Picturing the Spiritual Protector: from Blanchernitissa to Hodegetria." In *Images of the Mother of God: Perceptions of the Theotokos in Byzantium*, edited by Maria Vassilaki, 209–17. Burlington, VT: Ashgate, 2005.

Apolito, Paolo. *The Internet and the Madonna: Religious Visionary Experience on the Web*. Translated by Antony Shuggar. Chicago: University of Chicago Press, 2005.

Arellano, Gustavo. "Chicago's Downtrodden, Magnificent Our Lady of the Underpass Still Inspires." https://www.ncronline.org/opinion/chicagos-downtrodden-magnificent-our-lady-underpass-still-inspires. Retrieved 4/22/24.

Arentzson, Thomas. *The Virgin in Song: Mary and the Poetry of Romanos the Melodist*. Philadelphia: University of Pennsylvania Press, 2019.

Ashley, Kathleen, and Pamela Sheingorn, eds. *Interpreting Cultural Symbols: Saint Anne in Late Medieval Society*. Athens: University of Georgia Press, 1990.

Balzano, Nicolas. *Les Deux Cathédrales: Mythes et histoire à Chartres, XIe–XXe siècle*. Paris: Les Belles Lettres, 2012.

Barry, Patrick, OSB. *Saint Benedict's Rule*. Mahwah, NJ: Hidden Spring [Paulist Press], 2004.

Bartsch, Karl. *Chrestomathie de l'ancien français*, 6th ed. Leipzig: F.C.W. Vogel, 1895.

Bauck, Whitney. "The Virgin Mary Returns as an Icon for Pop Stars and Social Justice Warriors." *America Magazine*, July 27, 2021. https://www.americamagazine.org/faith/2021/07/27/mary-pop-icon-social-justice-culture-trend-241123. Retrieved 4/22/24.

Bauckham, Richard. *The Fate of the Dead: Studies on the Jewish and Christian Apocalypses*. Leiden: Brill, 1998.

Bauer, Judith A. *The Essential Mary Handbook: A Summary of Beliefs, Practices and Prayers*. Liguori, MO: Liguori Publications, 1999.

Baun, Jane. *Tales from Another Byzantium*. New York: Cambridge University Press, 2009.

Bayo, Juan Carlos. Review of *Le Gracial d'Adgar. Miracles de la Vierge. Témoins de notre histoire* by Jean-Louis Benoit. *Mediaevistik* 27 (2014): 338–43.

Beattie, Tina. *God's Mother, Eve's Advocate: A Marian Narrative of Women's Salvation*. London: Continuum, 2002.

Benoit, Jean-Louis. *Le Gracial d'Adgar. Miracles de la Vierge: Dulce chose est de Deu cunter*. Turnhout: Brepols, 2012.

Berger, Pamela. *The Goddess Obscured: Transformation of the Grain Protectress from Goddess to Saint*. Boston: Beacon Press, 1985.

Bététous, Paule. *Les Collections de la Vierge en Gallo- et Ibéro-Roman au XIIIe siècle*. Marian Library Studies N.S. 15–16. Dayton: University of Dayton, 1983–84.

Boase, Roger. *The Origin and Meaning of Courtly Love: A Critical Study of European Scholarship*. Totawa, NJ: Rowman and Littlefield, 1977.

Boss, Sarah Jane, ed. "Francisco Suarez and Modern Mariology." In *Mary: The Complete Resource*, edited by Sarah Jane Boss, 256–78. New York: Oxford University Press, 2007.

———. "Marian Sacrifice at the Eucharist?" *Maria: A Journal of Marian Studies* 1, no. 2 (July 2022): 1–17.

———. *Mary: The Complete Resource*. New York: Oxford University Press, 2007.

Boulton, Maureen Barry McCann. *The Old French Evangile de l'Enfance*. Toronto: PIMS, 1984.

———. *Sacred Fictions of Medieval France: Narrative Theology in the Lives of Christ and the Virgin, 1150–1500*. Cambridge: D.S. Brewer, 2015.

Boureau, Alain. *Satan the Heretic: The Birth of Demonology in the Medieval West*. Translated by Teresa Lavender Fagan. Chicago: University of Chicago Press, 2006.

Boyarin, Adrienne Williams. *Miracles of the Virgin in Middle English*. Peterborough, CA: Broadview Press, 2015.

Boyd, Beverly. *The Middle English Miracles of the Virgin*. San Marino, CA: The Huntington Library, 1964.

Boys, Mary C. *Has God Only One Blessing?: Judaism as a Source of Christian Self-Understanding*. Mahwah, NJ: Paulist Press, 2000.

Bretel, Paul, Michel Adroher, and Aymat Catafau, eds. *La Vierge dans les arts et les littératures du moyen âge*. Paris: Champion, 2017.

Brock, Sebastian. "The Genealogy of the Virgin Mary in Sinai Syr. 16." In *Universum Hagiographicum: Mémorial R.P. Michel van Esbroeck, S.J. (1934–2003)*, edited by Sevir Broriscovic Cernov, 58–71. Saint Petersberg: Bzantinorossica, 2006.

Brown, Rachel Fulton. *Mary and the Art of Prayer: The Hours of the Virgin in Medieval Christian Life and Thought*. New York: Columbia University Press, 2018.

Budge, E.A. Wallis. *The History of the Blessed Virgin Mary and the Likeness of Christ, the Syriac Texts Edited with English Translations*. London: Luzac and Co., 1899.

———, trans. *Legends of Our Lady Mary the Perpetual Virgin and Her Mother Hanna*. London: Martin Hopkinson and Company, 1922.

Buono, Anthony M. *The Greatest Marian Prayers: Their History, Meaning and Usage*. New York: Alba House, 1999.

Cameron, Averil. "The Virgin's Robe: An Episode in the History of Early Seventh-Century Constantinople." *Byzantion* 49 (1979): 42–56.

Cardile, Paul Y. "Mary as Priest: Mary's Sacerdotal Position in the Visual Arts." *Arte Cristiana* 72/73 (1984): 199–208.

Carroll, Michael. *The Cult of the Virgin Mary: Psychological Origins*. Princeton: Princeton University Press, 1986.

Cartlidge, David R., and J. Keith Elliott. *Art and the Christian Apocrypha*. London: Routledge, 2001.

Case, Mary Ann. "The Role of the Popes in the Invention of Complementarity and the Anathematization of Gender." *Religion and Gender* 6, no. 2 (2016): 155–72.

Cash, Annete Grant, and Richard Terry Mount. "The Miracles of Our Lady/Los Milagros de Nuestra Señora." In *The*

Collected Works of Gonzales de Berceo in English Translation. Translated by Jeannie K. Bartha, Annette Grant Cash and Richard Terry Mount. Tempe: Arizona Center for Medieval and Renaissance Studies, 2008.

Chabrier, Christine Ferree. "Béatrix Gets a Makeover: Modern Rewritings of a Medieval Legend." *Romance Notes* 42, no. 3 (Spring 2002): 273–81.

Clark, Anne C. "Guardians of the Sacred: The Nuns of Soissons and the Slipper of the Virgin Mary." *Church History* 76, no. 4 (December 2007): 724–49.

Clayton, Mary. *The Apocryphal Gospels of Mary in Anglo-Saxon England*. Cambridge: Cambridge University Press, 1998.

———. *The Cult of the Virgin Mary in Anglo-Saxon England*. Cambridge: Cambridge University Press, 1990.

Cooke, Thomas. "Pious Tales: Miracles of the Virgin." In vol. 9 of Albert E. Hartung et al., *A Manual of the Writings in Middle English 1050–1500*, 3177–258. New Haven: The Connecticut Academy of Arts and Sciences, 1993.

Costello, Damian. "The Black Madonna Makes Her Mark in the Least Religious State in the United States." *National Catholic Reporter*, 11/10/23, 13–14.

Cunneen, Sally. "Maximus's Mary: A Minister, Not Just an Icon." *Commonweal*, December 4, 2009. https://www.commonwealmagazine.org/maximus%E2%80%99s-mary. Retrieved 4/22/24.

———. *Searching for Mary: The Woman and the Symbol*. New York: Ballantine Books, 1996.

Cunningham, Mary B. "Apocryphal and Hagiographical Influences on Epiphanios of Kallistratou's Life of the Virgin Mary." In *Presbeia Theotokou, The Intercessory Role of Mary Across Times and Places in Byzantium (4th to 9th Century)*, edited by Leen Marie Peltomaa, Andres Külzer, and Pauline Allen, 147–52. Vienna: Austrian Academy of Sciences Press, 2015.

———. "The Life of the Theotokos by Epiphanius of Kallistratos: A Monastic Approach to an Apocryphal Story." In *The Reception of the Virgin in Byzantium: Marian Narratives in Texts and Images*, edited by Thomas Arentzen and Mary B. Cunningham, 309–23. Cambridge: Cambridge University Press, 2019.

———. *The Virgin Mary in Byzantium, c. 400–1000: Hymns, Homilies and Hagiography*. Cambridge, UK: Cambridge University Press, 2021.

Cusack, Carol M. "How the Virgin Mary Became the World's Most Powerful Woman." *National Geographic* (December 2015), 30–59.

Cybulski, Danièle. *How to Live Like a Monk: Medieval Wisdom for Modern Life*. New York: Abbeville Press, 2021.

Davis, Judith M. "Mediatrix, Operatrix, Redemptrix: Mary's Exercise of Power in Medieval French Literature." Paper presented at the 39th International Congress on Medieval Studies, Kalamazoo, Michigan, May 2004.

———. "The *Miracula Mariae* and May Festivals of the Middle Ages." *Theatre and Religion* 2 (1998): 18–27.

———. "Virgin Mary Co-Priest or Not." In *Rediscovering the Marys: Maria, Mariamne, Miriam*, edited by Mary Ann Beavis and Ally Kateuz, 131–44. New York: T & T Clark, 2020.

Degl'Innocenti, Martina, and Stella Marinone. *Mary*. Translated by Rosanna M. Giammanco Frongia. New York: Abrams, 2009.

DeVisscher, Eva. "Marian Devotion in the Latin West in the Later Middle Ages." In *Mary: The Complete Resource*, edited by Sarah Jane Boss, 177–201. New York: Oxford University Press, 2007.

Duffy, Eamon. *The Stripping of the Altars: Traditional Religion in England c. 1400–c. 1580*. 2nd ed. New Haven: Yale University Press, 2005.

Duricy, Michael. "The Life of Mary in Film in the Twentieth Century." *Marian Studies* LX (2009), 275–86.

Ebertshauser, Caroline, Herbert Haag, Joe H. Kerchberger, and Dorothee Solle. *Mary: Art, Culture and Religion Through the Ages*. New York: The Crossroad Publishing Company, 2007.

Ellington, Donna Spivey. *From Sacred Body to Angelic Soul: Understanding Mary in Late Medieval and Early Modern Europe*. Washington, D.C.: The Catholic University of America Press, 2001.

Elliott, J.K. *The Apocryphal Jesus: Legends of the Early Church*. Oxford: Oxford University Press, 1996.

Epstein, Marcia Jenneth. *Prions en Chantant: Devotional Songs of the Trouvères*.

Toronto: University of Toronto Press, 1997.
Fassler, Margot E. *The Virgin of Chartres: Making History through Liturgy and the Arts.* New Haven: Yale University Press, 2011.
Fastiggi, Robert L., and Michael O'Neill. *Virgin, Mother, Queen: Encountering Mary in Time and Tradition.* Notre Dame, IN: Ave Maria Press, 2019.
Faulkner, Mark. *A New Literary History of the Long Twelfth Century.* Cambridge: Cambridge University Press, 2022.
Felker, Roberta. "Homily for the Wedding Feast at Cana." Unpublished sermon, Holy Wisdom Monastery (Middleton, WI), January 16, 2022.
Fiero, Gloria. "The *Dits*: The Historical Context." In *Three Medieval Views of Women*, edited by Gloria K. Fiero, Wendy Pfeffer, and Mathe Allainm 28–83. New Haven: Yale University Press, 1989.
Finazzo, Giancarlo. "The Virgin Mary in the Koran." *L'Osservatore Romano*, Weekly Edition in English. April 13, 1978. https://www.ewtn.com/catholicism/library/virgin-mary-in-the-koran-5656. Retrieved 4/22/24.
Flader, Father John. "Gladys Quiroga de Motta and the Apparitions of Our Lady of San Nicolas." *Catholic Weekly*, July 30, 2016. https://www.catholicweekly.com.au/gladys-quiroga-de-motta-and-the-apparitions-of-our-lady-of-san-nicolas/. Retrieved 4/22/24.
Flory, David A. *Marian Representations in the Miracle Tales of Thirteenth-Century Spain and France.* Washington, D.C.: The Catholic University of America Press, 2000.
———. "The Social Uses of Religious Literature: Challenging Authority in the Thirteenth-Century Marian Miracle Tale." *Essays in Medieval Studies* 13 (1997): 61–69.
France, James. *Separate but Equal: Cistercian Lay Brothers 1120–1350.* Collegeville, MN: Liturgical Press, 2012.
Frey, Jörg. "Texts About Jesus: Noncanonical Gospels and Related Literature." In *The Oxford Handbook of Early Christian Apocrypha*, edited by Andrew Gregory and Christopher Tuckett, 13–47. Oxford University Press, 2018.
Friedan, Betty. *The Feminine Mystique: Annotated Text, Contexts, Scholarship.* Edited by Kirsten Fermaglich and Lisa M. Fine. New York: W.W. Norton, 2013.
Gaignebet, Claude, and Jean-Dominique Lajoux. *Art Profane et Religion Populaire au Moyen Âge.* Paris: Presses Universitaires de France, 1985.
Gambero, Luigi. *Mary and the Fathers of the Church: The Blessed Virgin Mary in Patristic Thought.* Translated by Thomas Buffer. San Francisco: Ignatius Press, 1999.
———. *Mary in the Middle Ages: The Blessed Virgin Mary in the Thought of the Medieval Latin Theologians.* Translated by Thomas Buffer. San Francisco: Ignatius Press, 2005.
Gazzetta, Liviana. "Une Idée de sacerdoce feminine entre XIXe et XXe siècle: les Filles du Coeur de Jésus et la dévotion à la Vierge Prêtre." *Chrétiens et Société* 25 (2018): 127–43.
Gertsman, Elina. *Worlds Within: Opening the Medieval Shrine Madonna.* University Park: Pennsylvania State University Press, 2015.
Gibson, Gail McMurray. *The Theater of Devotion: East Anglian Drama and Society in the Late Middle Ages.* Chicago: University of Chicago Press, 1989.
Gijsel, Jan, and Rita Beyers, *Libri de Nativitate Mariae.* Turnhout, Belgium: Brepols, 1997.
Graef, Hilda, and Thomas A. Thompson. *Mary: A History of Doctrine and Devotion.* Notre Dame, IN: Ave Maria Press, 2008.
Gregg, Joan Young. *Devils, Women and Jews: Reflections on the Other in Medieval Sermon Stories.* Albany: SUNY Press, 1977.
Gregory, Andrew, and Christopher Tuckett, eds. *The Oxford Handbook of Early Christian Apocrypha.* Oxford: Oxford University Press, 2018.
Guiette, Robert. *La Légende de la sacristine: Étude de littérature comparée.* Paris: Champion, 1927.
Harrelson, Walter, ed. *The New Interpreter's Study Bible: New Revised Standard Version with the Apocrypha.* Nashville: Abingdon Press, 2003.
Harrington, K.P., ed. *Medieval Latin.* Chicago: University of Chicago Press, 1962.
Harrison, Grizutti. "My Eve, My Mary." *Newsweek*, August 25, 1997, 56.
Hopkins, Gerard Manley. *Poems.* Edited by

Robert Bridges and W.H. Gardner. 3rd ed. New York: Oxford University Press, 1948.

Huacuja, Judith. "Chicana Women Artists Draw Inspiration from Our Lady of Guadalupe." *National Catholic Reporter*, December 8–21, 2023, 13–15.

Hunt, Tony. *Miraculous Rhymes: The Writing of Gautier de Coinci*. Woodbridge, Suffolk: D.S. Brewer, 2007.

Hynes, Eugene. *Review of Paulo*, The Internet and the Madonna: Religious Visionary Experiences of the Web. H-Catholic, October 2009. https://networks.h-net.org/node/3595/reviews/4400/hynes-apolito-internet-and-madonna-religious-visionary-experience-web. Retrieved 1/17/24.

Ihnat, Kati. "Marian Miracles and Marian Liturgies in the Benedictine Tradition of Post-Conquest England." In *Contextualizing Miracles in the Christian West, 1100–1150*, edited by Matthew M. Mesley and Louise Wilson, 63–97. Oxford: The Society for the Study of Medieval Language and Literature, 2014.

———. *Mother of Mercy, Bane of the Jews: Devotion to the Virgin Mary in Anglo-Saxon England*. Princeton: Princeton University Press, 2016.

Iogna-Prat, Dominique, Éric Palazzo, and Daniel Russo. *Marie: Le Culte de la Vierge dans la société médiévale*. Paris: Beauchesne, 1996.

Izydorczk, Zbigniew S. *The Medieval Gospel of Nicodemus: Texts, Intertexts and Contexts in Western Europe*. Tempe: Arizona Center for Medieval and Renaissance Studies, 1997.

Jacobs, Andrew S. "The Remains of a Jew: Imperial Christian Identity in the Holy Land." *Journal of Medieval and Early Modern Studies* 33 (2003): 23–45.

James, M.R. *The Apocryphal New Testament*. Oxford: Clarendon Press, 1924; repr. 1989.

Jameson, Anna Brownell. *Legends of the Madonna as Represented in the Fine Arts*. London: Hutchinson & Co., 1907.

Jansen, Katherine Ludwig. *The Making of the Magdalen: Preaching and Popular Devotion in the Later Middle Ages*. Princeton: Princeton University Press, 2000.

Jefferson, Rebecca J.W. "Sisters of Semitics: A Fresh Appreciation of the Scholarship of Agnes Smith Lewis and Margaret Dunlap Gibson." *Medieval Feminist Forum* 45, no. 5 (2009): 23–49.

Johnson, Elizabeth A. *Friends of God and Prophets: A Feminist Theological Reading of the Communion of Saints*. New York: Continuum, 1998.

———. *Truly Our Sister: A Theology of Mary in the Communion of Saints*. New York: Continuum, 2003.

Kateusz, Ally. "Collyridian Déjà Vu: The Trajectory of Redaction of the Markers of Mary's Liturgical Leadership." *Journal of Feminist Studies in Religion* 29, no. 2 (2013): 75–92.

———. *Mary and Early Christian Women: Hidden Leadership*. Palgrave Macmillan/Open Access, 2019.

———. "'She Sacrificed Herself as the Priest': Early Christian Female and Male Co-Priests." *Journal of Feminist Studies in Religion* 33, no. 1 (2017): 45–67.

Kearns, Cleo McNelly. *The Virgin Mary, Monotheism and Sacrifice*. Cambridge: Cambridge University Press, 2008.

Kiolskowski, Jan. *The Juggler of Notre Dame and the Medievalizing of Modernity*. 6 vols. Cambridge: Open Book Publishers, 2018.

———. "Juggling the Middle Ages: The Reception of *Our Lady's Tumbler* and *Le Jongleur de Notre Dame*." *Studies in Medievalism* 15 (2006): 57–97.

Kjellman, Hilding. "Le Miracle de la sacristine: Étude sur les versions métriques de l'ancien français." In *Mélanges de philologie offerts à Johan Melander*, 47–81. Geneva: Slatkine Reprints, 1977.

Kreitzer, Beth. *Reforming Mary: Changing Images of the Virgin Mary in Lutheran Sermons of the Sixteenth Century*. Oxford: Oxford University Press, 2004.

Kunstmann, Pierre, trans. and comp. *Vierge et merveille: Les miracles de Notre Dame narratifs au moyen âge*. Paris: Union Générale des Éditions, 1981.

———. "The Virgin's Mediation: Evolution and Transformation of the Motif." In *Parisian Confraternity Drama of the Fourteenth Century: The* Miracles de Nostre Dame par personnages, edited by Donald Maddox and Sara Sturm Maddox, 163–78. Turnhout: Brepols, 2008.

Långfors, Arthur. "La Légende de la statue de Venus." *Romania* 43 (1914): 628–29.

Laurent, Françoise. "Culte Marial et identité normande: L'Exemple de Helsin dans *La Concepcion Nostre Dame* de Wace et deux recueils Marials des XIIe et XIIIe siècles." In *La Vierge dans les arts et les littératures du moyen âge*, edited by Paul Bretel, Michel Adroher and Aymar Catafau, 63–78. Paris: Champion, 2017.

Laurentin, René. *Marie, l'Église et le Sacerdoce*. 2 vols. Paris: Nouvelles Éditions Latines, 1952.

Lazar, Moshe. "Satan and Notre Dame: Characters in a Popular Scenario." In *A Medieval French Miscellany: Papers of the 1970 Kansas Conference on Medieval French Literature*, edited by Norris J. Lacy, 1–14. Lawrence: University of Kansas Press, 1972.

Leclercq, Henri. "Fourth Lateran Council (1215)." In Vol. 9 of *The Catholic Encyclopedia*. https://www.newadvent.org/cathen/09018a.htm. Retrieved 4/21/24.

Legge, Dominica. *Anglo-Norman Literature and Its Background*. Oxford: Clarendon Press, 1963.

Lidov, Alexei J. "The Priesthood of the Virgin Mary as an Image-Paradigm of Christian Visual Culture." *Ikon* 10 (2017): 19–26.

Llewelyn, Dorian, S.J. "The Life of Mary and the Festal Icons of the Eastern Church." *Marian Studies* LX (2009): 231–52.

Maddox, Donald, and Sara Sturm Maddox, eds. *Parisian Confraternity Drama of the Fourteenth Century: The Miracles de Nostre Dame par personnages*. Turnhout: Brepols, 2008.

Mâle, Émile. *L'Art religieux du XIIIe siècle en France.: Étude sur l'iconographie du moyen âge et sur les sources d'inspiration*. Paris: Librairie Armand Colin, 1948.

Mane, Robert. *Henry Adams on the Road to Chartres*. Boston: Harvard University Press, 1971.

Mango, C. "The Origins of the Blachernae Shrine at Constantinople." *Actes du XIIIe congrès international d'archéologie chrétienne II*, 61–76. Split, Croatia: Archeoloski Muzej; Rome: Pontifico Instituto de Archeologica Cristiana, 1998.

Margry, Peter, ed. *Cold War Mary: Ideologies, Politics, Marian Devotional Culture*. Leuven: Leuven University Press, 2020.

Martineau, Patrice. *Légendes Mariales d'après les Cantigas de Santa Maria d'Alphonse le Sage*. Paris: Médiaspaul, 1995.

Martineau, Patrice and Roger. "Cantigas." Paris: Kiosque d'Orfée, n.d. Side A, no. 2.

Matthews, David. *Medievalism: A Critical History*. Woodbridge, Suffolk: D.S. Brewer, 2015.

Maunder, Chris. *Mary, Founder of Christianity*. London: Oneworld Publications, 2022.

———, ed. *The Origins of the Cult of the Virgin Mary*. London: Burns & Oates, 2008.

———. "Why Did Rome Try to Ban This Image that Portrays Mary as a Priest?" https://www.godgossip.org/article/why-did-rome-try-to-ban-this-image-that-portrays-mary-as-a-priest#:~:text=A%20decree%20of%2029%20March%201916%2C%20during%20the,rapidly%20at%20the%20turn%20of%20the%20twentieth%20century. Retrieved 4/22/24.

Mauriello, Rev. Matthew R. "Devotion to the Immaculate Heart of Mary." https://udayton.edu/imri/mary/i/immaculate-heart-of-mary-devotion.php. Retrieved 4/22/24.

Mazza, Biaggio. "The Blessed Virgin Mary—Vatican II Asked: Is She Truly Our Sister?" *National Catholic Reporter*, January 16, 2015, 1. https://www.ncronline.org/blessed-virgin-mary-vatican-II-asked-she-truly-our-sister. Retrieved 11/4/2023.

McBrien, Richard. *Catholicism*, New Ed. New York: Harper One, 1994.

Mesley, Matthew M., and Louise E. Wilson. *Contextualizing Miracles in the Christian West. 1100–1500: New Historical Approaches*. Oxford: The Society for the Study of Medieval Languages and Literatures, 2014.

Milhoc, Justin A., and Leonard Aldea, eds. *A Celebration of Living Theology: A Festschrift in Honour of Andrew Louth*. London: Bloomsbury Academic, 2014.

Miller, Malcolm. *Chartres Cathedral*. London: Pitkin Pictorials, 1985.

Mouriquand, David. "The Assumption: The Virgin Mary as a Powerful Icon of Pop Culture." https://www.euronews.

com/culture/2023/08/15/the-assumption-the-virgin-mary-as-a-powerful-icon-of-pop-culture. Retrieved 4/22/24.

Mullen, Peter. *Shrines of Our Lady: A Guide to Fifty of the World's Most Famous Marian Shrines*. New York: St. Martin's Press, 1998.

Murr, Andrew, Christopher Dickey, Eric Larson, Sarah Van Boven, and Hersch Doby. "Hail Mary." *Newsweek*, August 25, 1997, 48–56.

Najork, Daniel C. *Reading the Old Norse-Icelandic* Maríú saga *in Its Manuscript Contexts*. Berlin: Walter de Gruyter, 2021.

Newman, Barbara. *God and the Goddesses: Vision, Poetry and Belief in the Middle Ages*. Philadelphia: University of Pennsylvania Press, 2003.

Oakes, Catherine. *Ora Pro Nobis: The Virgin as Intercessor in Medieval Art and Devotion*. Turnhout: Brepols, 2008.

O'Carroll, Michael. *Theotokos: A Theological Encyclopedia of the Blessed Virgin Mary*. Rev. ed. Wilmington, DE: Michael Glazier, Inc., 1983.

O'Neill, Michael. "Marian Apparition Claims in the United States and Canada in the Twentieth Century." *Marian Studies* 63 (2012): 256–79.

Orth, Maureen. "How the Virgin Mary Became the Most Powerful Woman in the World." *National Geographic*, December 2015. 30–59.

O'Sullivan, Daniel. *Marian Devotion in Thirteenth-Century French Lyric*. Toronto: University of Toronto Press, 2005.

Pelikan, Jaroslav. *Mary Through the Ages: Her Place in the History of Culture*. New Haven: Yale University Press, 1996.

Pentcheva, Bissera V. *Icons and Power: The Mother of God in Byzantium*. University Park: Pennsylvania State University Press, 2006.

Pons Pons, Guillermo, ed. and trans. *Vida de Maria*. Montevideo-Santiago: Editorial Ciudad Nueva, 1990.

Pourrat, Henri. Vol. 4 of *Le Trésor des contes*. Paris: Gallimard, 1853.

Reynolds, Brian K. *Gateway to Heaven: Marian Doctrine and Devotion, Image and Typology in the Patristic and Medieval Periods. Vol. 1: Doctrine and Devotion*. Hyde Park, New York: New City Press, 2012.

Rodriguez, Jeannette, and Ted Fortier. *Cultural Memory: Resistance, Faith and Identity*. Austin: University of Texas Press, 2007.

_____. *Our Lady of Guadalupe: Faith and Empowerment Among Mexican-American Women*. Austin: University of Texas Press, 1994.

Root, Jerry. *The Theophilus Legend in Medieval Text and Image*. Cambridge: D.S. Brewer, 2017.

Rubin, Miri. *Mother of God: A History of the Virgin Mary*. New Haven: Yale University Press, 2009.

Runnalls, Graham A., ed. and trans. *Le Miracle de l'enfant ressuscité. Quinzième des* Miracles de Nostre Dame par personnages. Geneva: Droz, 1972.

Samaha, Brother John M. "Mary's Priestly Dimension." https://udayton.edu/imri/mary/p/priestly-dimension-of-mary.php. Retrieved 4/22/24.

Saupe, Karen. *Middle English Marian Lyrics*. Kalamazoo, MI: Medieval Institute Publications, Western Michigan University, 1998.

Schork, R.J. *Sacred Song from the Byzantine Pulpit: Romanos the Melodist*. Gainesville: University Press of Florida, 1994.

Scott, Sam. "Michael O'Neill Explains and Explores the Miraculous: The Virgin Mary's Number Cruncher." *Stanford Magazine* (December 2018): 1–7.

Sheingorn, Pamela. "Appropriating the Holy Kinship: Gender and Family History." In Kathleen Ashley and Pamela Sheingorn, *Interpreting Cultural Symbols: Saint Anne And Late Medieval Society*, 169–96. Athens: University of Georgia Press, 1990.

Shoemaker, Stephen J. *Ancient Traditions of the Virgin Mary's Dormition and Assumption*. Oxford: Oxford University Press, 2002.

_____. "Apocrypha and Liturgy in the Fourth Century: The Case of the 'Six Books' Dormition Apocryphon." In *Jewish and Christian Scriptures: The Function of "Canonical" and "Non-canonical" Texts*, edited by James H. Charlesworth and Lee M. McDonald, 153–72. London: T & T Clark International Continuum Books, 2010.

_____. "Between Scripture and Tradition: The Marian Apocrypha of Early Christianity." In *The Armenian Apocalyptic*

Tradition: A Comparative Perspective, edited by Kvork B. Bardakjian and Sergio La Parta, 491–510. Leiden: Brill, 2014.

———. "The Cult of Fashion: The Earliest Life of the Virgin and Constantinople's Marian Relics." *Dumbarton Oaks Papers* 62 (2008): 53–74.

———. "Epiphanius of Salamis, the Kollyridians and the Early Dormition Narratives: The Cult of the Virgin in the Fourth Century." *Journal of Early Christian Studies* 16:3 (Fall 2008): 371–401.

———. *Mary in Early Christian Faith and Devotion*. New Haven and London: Yale University Press, 2009.

Simeldis, Christos. "Two Lives of the Virgin: John Geometres, Euthymios the Athonite, and Maximos the Confessor." *Dumbarton Oaks Papers* 73 (2020): 235–60.

Solberg, Emma Maggie. *Virgin Whore*. Ithaca: Cornell University Press, 2018.

Spretnak, Charlene. "Mary and Modernity." In *The Oxford Handbook of Mary*, edited by Chris Maunder. 531–45. New York: Oxford University Press, 2019.

———. *Missing Mary: The Queen of Heaven and Her Re-Emergence in the Modern Church*. New York: Macmillan, 2004.

Sticcca, Sandro. *The Planctus Mariae in the Dramatic Tradition of the Middle Ages*, translated by Joseph R. Berrigan. Athens: University of Georgia Press, 1988.

Tarayre, Michel. *La Vierge et le miracle: Le* Speculum historiale *de Vincent de Beauvais*. Paris: Champion, 1999.

Tavard, George H. *The Thousand Faces of the Virgin Mary*. Collegeville, MN: The Liturgical Press, 1996.

Taylor, Steven M. "God's Queen: Chess Imagery in the Poetry of Gautier de Coinci." *Fifteenth Century Studies* (1990): 403–19.

Temko, Alan. *Notre-Dame of Paris*. New York: The Viking Press, 1955.

Thomas, Robert. *La Vierge Marie: Homélies des pères Cisterciens*. Sainte-Foi [Québec]: Éditions Anne Sigier, 1989.

Thompson, Stith. Vols. 5 and 6 of *Motif Index of Folk Literature*. Rev. and enl. ed. Bloomington: Indiana University Press, 1955–58.

Thompson, Thomas, S.M., ed. *Telling Mary's Story: The "Life of Mary" Through the Ages*. Marian Studies 60 (2009).

Thurlkill, Mary F. *Chosen Among Women: Mary and Fatima in Medieval Christianity and Shi'ite Islam*. Notre Dame: University of Notre Dame Press, 2007.

Traver, Hope. "The Four Daughters of God: A Mirror of Changing Doctrine." *PMLA* 40 (1925): 44–92.

———. *The Four Daughters of God: A Study of the Versions of This Allegory with Special Reference to Those in Latin, French and English*. Bryn Mawr: Bryn Mawr College, 1907.

Tubach, Frederic C. *Index Exemplorum: A Handbook of Medieval Religious Tales*. Helsinki: Academia Scientarum Fennica, 1981.

Tuchman, Barbara. *A Distant Mirror: The Calamitous Fourteenth Century*. New York: Alfred Knopf, 1978.

Tvrtkovic, Rita George. *Christians, Muslims, and Mary: A History*. New York: Paulist Press, 2018.

———. "Some Earlier Features in the Life of the Virgin." *Marianum* 63 (2003): 97–308.

Van Esbroeck, Jean-Michel. "Généalogie de la Vierge en Georgien." *Analecta Bollandiana* 91 (1973): 347–56.

Vassilaki, Maria, ed. *Images of the Mother of God: Perceptions of the Theotokos in Byzantium*. Burlington, VT: Ashgate, 2004.

Vilano-Pentti, Eva. *La Court de Paradis: Poème du XIIIe siècle*. Helsinki: Imprimerie de la Société de Littérature Finnoise, 1953.

Villiers de l'Isle d'Adam, Auguste. *Contes cruels, suivis des nouveaux contes cruels*. Edited by Pierre-Georges Castex and Pierre Glaudes. Paris: Garnier Frères, 2012.

Voigt, Robert J. *The Story of Mary and the Grasshoppers*. Cold Spring, MN: n.p., 1991.

Waller, Gary. *The Virgin Mary in Late Medieval and Early Modern English Literature and Popular Culture*. Cambridge: Cambridge University Press, 2011.

Ward, Benedicta. *Miracles and the Medieval Mind*. Philadelphia: University of Pennsylvania Press, 1987.

Warner, Marina. *Alone of All Her Sex: The Myth and the Cult of the Virgin Mary*. New York: Random House Vintage, 1983.

Weigand, Sister M. Gonsalva. "History of the Nativity and of the Praiseworthy

Conversation of the Immaculate Mother of God, Which I have Found in the Works of Saint James, the Kinsman of the Lord." With notes. In *The Non-Dramatic Works of Hrosvitha: Text, Translation, and Commentary*, 15–73. St. Meinrad, IN: The Abbey Press, 1937.

Whiteford, Peter, ed., from Wynkyn de Worde's edition. *The Myracles of Oure Lady*. Heidelberg: Carl Winter, 1990.

Whittredge, Ruth. *La Nativité et le Geu des trois rois, Two Plays from Manuscript 1131 of the Bibliothèque Sainte Geneviève, Paris*. Bryn Mawr: William Byrd Press, 1944.

Wills, Garry. *Papal Sin: Structures of Deceit*. New York: Doubleday Image, 1990.

Wilson, Evelyn F. *The Stella Maris of John of Garland*. Cambridge: The Medieval Academy of America, 1946.

Winston-Allen, Anne. *Stories of the Rose: The Making of the Rosary in the Middle Ages*. University Park: Pennsylvania State University Press, 1997.

Winter, Tim. "Mary in Islam." In *Mary, The Complete Resource*, edited by Sarah Jane Boss, 429–502. New York: Oxford University Press, 2007.

Wright, William, trans. "The Departure of Our Lady Mary From This World." *The Journal of Sacred Literature and Biblical Record* 7 (1865): 129–60.

Yalom, Marilyn. *Birth of the Chess Queen*. New York: HarperCollins, 2004.

Ziolkowski, Jan M. *A Commentary on Nigel of Canterbury's* Miracles of the Virgin. Cambridge: Harvard University Press, 2022.

———. *The Juggler of Notre Dame and the Medievalizing of Modernity*. 6 vols. Cambridge: Open Access Publications, 2018.

Index

Abboud, Hosn 18
Abraham 128, 130
Abu Serga (church) 196
Acts 11
Adam 53, 128, 166
Adams, Henry: *Mont-Saint-Michel and Chartres* 89–90, 171–72
Adgar 53, 60–61; "Cleric Cured in a Field of Flowers" (miracle) 61–62; "Enlarging a Country Church" (miracle) 62–63; *Le Graciale* 61
Advocacie Nostre Dame 144
affective piety 133–34, 146, 170
aggiornamento (updating of the church) 192
Akathistos Hymn 23, 32
Alfonso X of Spain, El Sabio, "The Wise" 98; *Cantigas de Santa Maria* ("Songs of Holy Mary") 98; "Insult to Mary Punished" (miracle) 99; "Miracles of the Bees" 98–99; "Miraculous Cures" 99
Alpheus 69
Amadeus of Lausanne 49–50
Andreas Capellanus (Andrew the Chaplain): *De Arte Honeste Amandi* ("The Art of Loving Nobly," 55Amse. Saomt 47, 52
Anglo-Norman (language) 53, 60–61
Anglo-Saxon (language) 119
Anna (Mary's mother) 13, 25, 63–64, 114, 129–30, 143
Annas (scribe) 13, 30
Anne, Saint 114, 128, 130
Annunciation (feast) 40, 167, 193
Annunciation (Luke) 9, 10
Annunciation (N-Town *Play of Mary*) 144–45
Annunciation (Passion plays) 148, 195
Anselm, Saint 47, 52
anti-Judaism 4
antisemitism 4, 82, 206n62

apocalypse 37–38
The Apocalypse of the Theotokos 38
apocryphon (apocrypha) 5, 12, 13, 26, 38; *see also* extracanonical
Apolito, Paul 198
Arabic Infancy Gospel 20, 180, 205n39
Arellano, Gustavo 197
Armenian Infancy Gospel 212n31
The Art of Loving Nobly see Andreas Capellanus
Assumption (dogma) 192, 202
Assumption (extracanonical account) 37
Assumption (feast) 193
Athans, Mary Christine xiv, 3
Athos, Mount 18, 28
Auden, W.H.: "The Ballad of Barnaby" 186
Augustine, Saint: *City of God* 162; Original Sin 166
Ave (prayer, abbreviation of the "Hail Mary") 78, 122
Ave Maris Stella ("Hail, Star of the Sea"), hymn 42, 52

Bader Ginsburg, Ruth 199
ballade (poem) 48; "Ballade of Prayer to Notre Dame" 126–27
Barnaby 186; *see also* Auden, W.H.; France, Anatole
Baroque 158
Beatles: "Lady Madonna"; "Let It Be"
Beatrice (*Divine Comedy*) 118–19
Beatrice, Sister (miracle) 112; *see also* "Sister Beatrice, Perennial Penitent"
Beattie, Tina: *God's Mother, Eve's Advocate* 195
Bede, Saint 175
Benedict, Saint 49, 210n16, 216n16
Benedict XV (pope) 161
Bernard of Clairvaux, Saint 49, 101, 144, 170

Index

Black Madonna 46, 199–200
Blechman, R.O.: "The Juggler of Our Lady" 186
Blue Army of Our Lady 191
Book of the Infancy of the Savior 174
Botticelli, Sandro 195
Brice, Rafaella 199
Brothers Grimm 180
Brown, Rachel Fulton 3
Brownell Jameson, Anna 169–70
Byzantium (Eastern empire) 22–23, 26, 32, 43; Byzantine 174–77

Caesarius of Heisterbach 70, 149, 111, 152; *Dialogus Miraculorum* (*Dialogue on Miracles*): "Beatrice, the Nun Who Left the Convent" (miracle) 112; "The Knight Whose Place Our Lady Took at the Tournament" (miracle) 111–12; "Mary as Mother of Mercy" 113; "Sir Walter of Birbeck, Tardy Knight and Saintly1 Monk" (miracle) 111–12
Caiaphas 30
Calvin, John 155
Canisius, Peter: *On the Incomparable Virgin Mary* 161
canon (of accepted biblical books) 12
Cardelli, Bishop Hector 197
"The Carnal and the Crane" (ballad) 181–82
Case, Mary Ann 9
Chamaillard, Soasig 199
Chartres 2, 43–44, 95–97
Chaucer, Geoffrey: *Canterbury Tales*, "A Marian ABC" 121–22
Cherry Tree Carol 187–88
chess as metaphor for life; Mary as Chess Queen 65–66; *see also* Gautier de Coinci
Child, Francis James 181, 187
Chrétien de Troyes 60
Church Militant 191
Clairvaux (abbey) 49, 210n16
Cleophas 64
Cluny (monastery) 186
"Cold War Mary" 191, 202
Collyridians 14–15, 22
Concepcion Nostre Dame 63–64; *see also* Wace
Confraternity of the Most Holy Rosary 162–63
Constantine I 12
Constantinople 12, 34, 152–53, 207n11
converso, conversus (lay member of a monastery) 109, 211n16
Council of Ephesus 12, 16, 170

Council of Nicaea 12
Council of Rome 12
Council of Trent 158, 166, 196
Counter-Reformation 190
Court de Paradis 55
Cova da Iria 190
Crasset, Jean: *True Devotion to the Holy Virgin Established and Defended*; *True Devotion to the Blessed Virgin* 163
Cyril, Saint 20

Dante Alighieri: *The Divine Comedy* 38, 118–19; *Paradiso* 195
Daude de Pradas 57
Daughters of the Sacred Heart 68
David (King, ancestor of Mary) 10, 25
De Arte Honeste Amandi (*The Art of Loving Nobly*) *see* Andreas Cappellanus
"Demure Mother Mary" (painting) **159**
dePaola, Tomie: *The Little Jester* 186
de Salazar, Quirino 160–62
The Devil (devils) 19, 53, **54**, 67, 71, 75, 81–83, 85, 87, 89, 116–118; *see also* Satan
Dismas 175
The Divine Comedy see Dante Alighieri
The Dogmatic Constitution on the Church, "Lumen Gentium" 193
Dominic de Guzmán, Saint 95, 131
Dominic of Evesham 46, 52
Doox, Mark 199–200
The Dormition (passing) of Mary (feast) 40
The Dormition of the Theotokos 34–35
dos Santos, Lucia and Francisco 180
dulia (form of veneration) 162
Dumachus 18
Duricy, Michael 195

Eadmer 47
Ecclesia (Church) 4
Eliud 64
Elizabeth (Mary's cousin) 14, 64, 146
Eminen (Saint Eminen Servatius) 64
Encinitas, California 197
Enlightenment 165
Ephesus (city) 35, 177
Ephrem of Syria 22
Epiphanios the Monk 25–26
Epiphanius of Salamis 15–16, 22
Erasmus 152; "A Pilgrimage for Religion's Sake" 153–154
Etsy 202
Eudes, Jean 162
Euthymios the Athonite 26, 28–29, 31, 39, 160, 172, 174, 176, 210; *Life of Mary* 29–33

Index

Evans, Marian (George Eliot) 170–71
Eve 5, 22, 29, 53, 118, 128, 166, 195
Extracanonical 5, 7- 8, 12–13, 21, 26, 39
ex-voto 46, 199

Fanuel, "Saint" *see Romance of Saint Fanuel and Saint Anne*
Farsit, Hugh 53, 207n14
Fatima, Portugal 190, 196; *see also* Our Lady of Fatima
Fatima, spouse of Muhammad 19
Faust 178
Festial see Mirk, John
Feudalism 54–55, 66–67
Fourth Lateran Council 95, 100, 149, 213n7
France, Anatole: "The Juggler of Notre Dame" 185
Francis (pope) 5
Francis, Saint 131
Fulbert, Bishop of Chartres (Saint) 44, 61
Fuller, Margaret 170–71

Gabriel (angel) 6, 9, 10, 29, 35, 136–37, 144–46, 175–77
Gamaliel 148
Gantelmus, Bishop of Chartres 44
Gaultier, Jean-Paul 198
Gautier de Coinci 65–92, 96, 140; "Candle That Came Down to the Jongleur" (miracle) 90–92; "Hanged Thief" (miracle) 75, **76**, 77; " Knight of 150 Hail Marys" (miracle) 77–79; "Misplaced Engagement Ring" (miracle) 80–81; "Peasant Who Could Learn Only Half of the Hail Mary" (miracle) 89–90; "Pregnant Abbess" (miracle) 66–70; "Priest Who Knew Only One Mass" (miracle) 88–89; "Rich Man and the Widow" (miracle) 86–88; "Théophile, or The Devil's Charter" (miracle) 81–86; "Young Nun Who Left the Convent" (miracle) 70–74
Gehenna 37
Gerson, Jean 122
Gestas 175; *see also* Dumachus
Ghiberti, Lorenzo 195
Glory of the Martyrs see Gregory of Tours
Goethe 178
The Golden Legend 95, 113–18, 143; *see also* Jacobus of Voragine
Gonzalo de Berceo 100–101; "Image Miraculously Saved from the Flames" (miracle) 100–101; "Pregnant Woman Saved by the Virgin" miracle 101–102

The Gospel of Nicodemus 214n36
The Gospel of the Birth of Mary 114
Gounod, Charles 178
Le Graciale see Adgar
Grain Miracle (medieval) 180; *see also The Play of the Three Kings*
Grain Miracle as Folk Tale 182–84
Grain Miracle in the Upper Midwest 184–85, 189
grant mariale 58
Great Schism (1054) 44
Gregory of Tours 41, 98; *Glory of the Martyrs* 41; "Mary, Provider" (miracle) 41
Grignion de Monfort, Marie-Louis 163, 191; *The Secret of the Rosary* 163

hadith 19
Harold, king of England 63
Haymo of Auxerre 64, 212n32
Helsin, Abbot of Ramsey 63
Hemmerode (abbey) 112
Henry VIII 156
Hériman de Tournai 53, 207–8n14
Hernandez, Esther 199
Herod 29, 181–82, 184
Herolt, Johannes 149; "A Dead Man Revives" (miracle) 150; "A Deaf-Mute Able to Confess" (miracle) 150; "A Man Who Was Religious in Name Only" (miracle) 149; "A Sinful Woman" (miracle) 150
Hismeria (Esmeria) 64
History of Joseph the Carpenter 176
Hoccleve, Thomas: "Miracle of the Monk and Our Lady's Sleeves" 122–23
Holy House of Loreto 99
Holy Kinship 64, 114, 128, 155
Holy League 158
Holy Reliquary [of Chartres] 197
"Holy Theft" 32
Hrotsvitha of Gandersheim: "Life of Mary," Theophilus story 42–43
Hunchback of Notre Dame (film) 195
Hundred Years' War 152
Hypapante (Encounter) *see* Presentation of Jesus
Hyperdulia (form of veneration) 162

icons 10, 12, 26
Immaculate Conception 63, 163, 168 170; dogma ("Ineffabilis Deus" ("Ineffable God"), papal pronouncement 166
Immaculate Heart of Mary (devotion) 162, 191
Imram (Joachim) 18

Index

The Infancy Gospel of Thomas 204n14, 211n30

Jacobus of Voragine 95, 113–18, 174–75, 194, 202; "The Knight Who Sold His Wife to the Devil" (miracle) 117–18; Marian Genealogies and Holy Kinship 114; "Mary's Hand on the Scale" (miracle) 116; "The Monk Who Could Only Learn Two Words of the Ave Maria" (miracle) 115; "A Son Restored to His Mother" (miracle) 114
Jacopone da Todi 146
Jacques de Vitry 74, 152
James, Saint 43; shrine in Compostela, Spain 153
Jaufre Rudel 56
Jerome, Saint 42, 64, 114, 174
Jesus of Nazareth (film) 195
Joachim (Mary's father) 13, 63–64, 114, 129, 143
Joan of Arc 199
Jo(h)anna 26, 29
John (apostle, saint) 26, 31, 35–36, 64, 148, 177
John (baptist, saint) 14, 213n22
John (evangelist, saint) 11, 31, 174, 178
John Geometres 26; *Life of Mary* 27–28, 30, 32, 34, 160, 172, 201
John the Hermit (saint) 139–140
John XXIII (pope) 192
Johnson, Elizabeth A. xiv, 3
jongleur (performer) 90
Josaphat (Valley) 35
Joseph, saint 13–14, 27, 29, 113–14, 132, 144, 148, 155, 175–77, 181–82, 189, 195
Juan Diego Cuauhtlaoatzin 156
"The Juggler of Notre Dame" *see* Anatole France
"Juggling the Middle Ages" (exhibition) 186; *see also* Ziolkowski, Jan

Kahlo, Frieda 199
Kallistratos (monastery) 25
Kateusz, Ally 3
kathisma 40
"The Keeper of the Keys: The Legend of Beatrix the Nun and the Virgin Mary" (blog) 179
Kibeho, Rwanda 196
kontakia 23, 123

Labouré, Catherine 165–66
Laon 44, 95; *see also* Notre Dame de Laon
Last Supper 7, 176
Latimore, Kelly 199

latria (form of veneration) 161
Laurentin, René 194
Lazarus 177, 217n13
Legenda Aurea (*The Golden Legend*) *see* Jacobus of Voragine
legendaries 45
Legion of Mary 191
le Marchant, Jean 95; "About Gondrée" (miracle) 95–97; "Knight Saved from Death by the Undergarments That Touched the Chemise of Chartres" (miracle) 97–98
Leo I (Byzantine emperor) 32
Lepanto, Battle of 158
Life of Mary. Epiphanios the Monk 25–26
A "Life of Mary" in *The Middle English N-Town Plays* 143–46
The Life of the Blessed Virgin Mary Attributed to Maximus the Confessor 177
The Life of the Virgin, Epiphanios the Athonite 28–33
The Life of the Virgin Mary, the Theotokos (modern Greek Orthodox text) 9, 175–77
Liguori, Alphonsus: *Glories of Mary* 164, 170
Litany of the Blessed Virgin (Litany of Loreto) 198
Little Office of the Blessed Virgin 60
Liturgy of the Hours 60, 105–6, 210–11n17
Llewelyn, Dorian 10, 218n2
Lopez, Yolanda 199
Lourdes 167, 190, 196, 202; apparitions of Mary 167–68; *see also* Soubirous, Bernadette
Luke, saint 9, 10, 20, 23, 113–14
Luther, Martin 153, 155, 161

Madonna (singer): "Like a Virgin" 198
Maeterlinck, Maurice: *Soeur Beatrice* (*Sister Beatrice*) 179
Magi 14, 25, 29, 114, 180, 211–212n31
"Magnificat" (Mary's proclamation in Luke) 143, 200, **202**
Maria of Agreda: *Mystical City of God* 163–65
Mariale or 230 Questions on the Annunciation (Pseudo-Albert) 50, 208n29
Mariales 44, 45, 47
A Marian Lament/Lament for Mary 34, 146–47
Marian Lyrics in Middle English 123–25
Marie de France 60
Marie de Nazareth (film) 195

Mariological Society of America 195
Marlowe, Christopher: *The Tragical History of Doctor* Faustus 178
Martineau, Patrice 75, 198
Marto, Francisco 190
Marto, Jacinta 190
Mary as bishop or pope **159–60**
Mary in the Passion Plays of France 147–49
Mary Magdalene 26, 29–31
The Mary Play 143
Mary Tales and Poems in Middle English 119–21
Maximos (Maximus) the Confessor 28
McQueen, Alexander 198
Medjugorje, Bosnia-Herzegovina 195–96
Megeldis 179
menestrel (minister) 211n23
Merry del Val, Rafael (Cardinal) 169
Metalogion see Symeon Metaphrastes
Michael, archangel, saint 35–36, 38, 53, 101, 136–37, 146
Middle English (language) 119
Miélot, Jehan 102; "The Artisan Monk and the Ugly Devil" (miracle) 102–5
The Miracle (film) 179
Le Miracle de Théophile (Rutebeuf) 82, 86, 178
miracle, defined 6
The Miracle of Our Lady at the Tournament" (anonymous) 109–11
Miracle of Our Lady's Tumbler (anonymous) 105–9
Miracles of Our Lady Performed 134–40; "A Baby Restored to Life" 134; "The Child Promised to the Devil" 135; "The Devil in Disguise" 135–39; "The Miracle of Saint John the Hermit" 139–40
Miraculous medal 202
Mirk, John 120; *Festial*, "The Widow's Candle for the Feast" (miracle) 120–21
Mirror of History (*Speculum historiale*) *see* Vincent of Beauvais
Mont Saint-Michel and Chartres *see* Adams, Henry
Muhammad 18–19
"Munificentissimus Deus" ("Most Bountiful God") 192; *see also* Assumption, feast

N-Town plays of Mary's Life 143–46
narrative theology (definition) 6; Century II 125–26; of Subversion 92, **93**, 94; of the Early Middle Ages 50–51; of the Gospels 20–21; of the *Lives of Mary* 38–39; of the Long Twelfth of the Waning Middle Ages, 150–51; of the Post-Reform Era 172–72
Narratives and Theologies Across the Centuries 188–89
National Catholic Reporter 197
National Geographic 195
Nativity of the Virgin (feast) 40
Newsweek 194
Nichols, Bob 197
Nicodemus *see Gospel of Nicodemus*
Nigel of Canterbury 52–53, 58
Nodier, Charles: "La Légende de Soeur Béatrix" 179
Norman Conquest 60, 119
The North English Homily Collection 119–20
Notre Dame (Paris cathedral) 44, 52
Notre Dame de Laon (church) 44–45
Notre Dame de Soissons (church, shrine) 44, 46

"O Intemerata" ("O Spotless One"), hymn 52
Occitan (language) 167
Odes of Solomon 15
Olier, Jean-Jacques 162
O'Neill, Michael ("Miracle Hunter") 198
Original Sin 166
Orth, Maureen 195
Ottoman Turks 152, 158
Our Lady of Czestochowa 199
Our Lady of Fatima 190–**91**
"Our Lady of Ferguson" (art work) 200
Our Lady of Good Success (Ecuador) 196
Our Lady of Guadalupe 156–**57**, 199–200, **201**
Our Lady of Siluva (Lithuania) 196
Our Lady of the Bathtub 199
Our Lady of the Rosary 197
Our Lady of the Underpass 197
Our Lady of Victory 158
Our Lady of Zaytun (Egypt) 196
"Our Lady's Advocacy" (*Our Lady's Day in Court, or Why She Is Called Our Advocate*) 141–43, 151

Palm Tradition [of Mary's passing] 34–35, 174
Panarion 25
Paradiso see Dante, *The Divine Comedy*
Paris, Gaston 185
Passion d'Auvergne (Passion play) 148
Passion de Palatinus (Passion play) 147
Patterson, Mark 197
Paul, saint 26, 200

238   Index

Paul the Deacon 42, 178 see also Theophilus
Peire Cardenal 57
Pelikan, Jaroslav 3
Peter, saint 30, 35–36, 154
Peyramale, Father 168
Picardy (region of France) 95
Pierre de Siglars 90–92
Pilate 48
"A Pilgrimage for Religion's Sake" see Erasmus
Pius V (pope) 258
Pius IX (pope) 166, 168, 170
Pius XI (pope) 164
Pius XII (pope) 191
The Play of the Three Kings 180
The Praise of Folly 63; see also Erasmus
Presentation of Jesus 22, 40; feast 162; see also *hypapante* (Encounter)
Presentation of Mary (feast) 40
"Priesthood of the Virgin" (painting) 160
Protogospel of James 13–15, **17**, 20, 25, 33, 38, 40, 64, 114, 129, 143, 169, 174, 200–1
psalter, defined 106, 123, 211*n*19
Pseudo-Albert [the Great]: *Mariale or 230 Questions on the Annunciation* 50, 161
Pseudo-Matthew (*Gospel of Pseudo-Matthew*) 16–18, 20, 64, 114, 143, 174–75, 180, 187, 201, 211*n*201
Pseudo-Melito (*Gospel of Pseudo-Melito*) 64
Purgatory 149

Queen of Heaven (film) 195
Quiroga da Matta, Gladys 196
The Qu'ran 18–19, 21, 196

Reformation 188–89, 193, 201, 202
Reformers 7, 155–56
Relics defined 6; Marian relics: hair, milk, etc. 54; *maphorion* (veil) 34; sash 34; slipper 44; tunic ("chemise") 32–34, 175
Renaissance 152–54
Rhianna 198
Rocamadour 2, 44, 46, 58, 90, 207–8*n*14
Rollo (Viking) 43
The Romance of Saint Fanuel and Saint Anne 128–30, 212*n*32
Romanos the Melodist 23–25, 27, 133, 147
Rosary 153, 163, 190–91
Rubin, Miri 3
Rutebeuf 82, 86, 177

Sainte Chapelle (Paris chapel) 44
Salome, husband of Anna 69
Salome. midwife 14, 114
Salome, mother of the sons of Zebedee 26
"Salve Regina" ("Hail, Holy Queen"), hymn 52, 143
"Salve Sancta Parens" ("Hail, Holy Parent") Mass 88, 146
San Nicolas de los Arroyos (city) 196–97
Santa Maria Maggiore (church) 40
Satan 53, **54**, 67, 71, 75, 81–82, 85, 87, 89, 116–18, 135–43, 150, 178–200; see also Devil
Schism, papal (1378–1417) 152
Second Vatican Council 192–93
Shoemaker, Stephen 3, 16
shrine-madonna 128, 130–31, ***132–33***
Simeon 14, 22, 148
Six Books Tradition [of Mary's passing] 35–37, 174, 180, 201*n*71
Smith Lewis, Agnes 169
Soissons 58, 95–97; see also Notre Dame de Soissons
"*sola scriptura, sola fide, sola gratia*" ("only Scripture, only faith, only grace") 155
"*solus Christus, soli Dei gloria*" ("only Christ, to the glory of God alone") 155
The Song of Bernadette (film) 195
Soubirous, Bernadette 167–68, 290
The South English Legendary 119
Spotify 198
Spretnak, Charlene 2, 218*n*9
"Stabat Mater" (hymn) 146
The Story of Mary and the Grasshoppers 184
story theology see narrative theology
Suarez, Francisco 161–62
"*Sub Tuum Praesidium*" ("Under Your Protection") 214*n*25
sura 18, 19, 196
Surfing Madonna 197
Symeon Metaphrastes 26, 33–34, 133
Synagoga (Synagogue) 4

Tavard, George 165
"Telling Mary's Story: The 'Life of Mary' Through the Ages" 195
The Tragical History of Dr. Faustus see Marlowe, Christopher
Theophilus 42; later history of the story 178; see also Gautier de Coinci; Goethe; Gounod, Charles; Hrotswitha of Gandersheim; Marlowe, Christopher; Rutebeuf; William of Malmsbury
Theotokos (Mother of God) 22, 39–40, 155
Thomas, saint 36

Index

Titus 18; *see also* Dumachus
Transitus Mariae (Mary's Passing) 35–36, 159; *see also The Dormition of the Theotokos*
Tree of Paradise 128, 130

Van den Berght, Oswald: *Mary and the Priesthood* 168
Vatican II 2, 293–93
Venantius, saint (chapel) 159, 172
Vernon Manuscript 119
Villiers de l'Isle d'Adam, Auguste: "Soeur Natalia" 179
Villon, François: "Ballade of Prayer to Notre Dame" 125–27
Vincent of Beauvais: "The Monk of Chartres Whom Mary Saved from Demonic Attack" (miracle) 58–59, 96, 149
Virgin Priest, devotion 168; *see also Virgo Sacerdos*
Virgo Sacerdos ("Virgin Priest") 161–62

Wace 63; *Concepcion Nostre Dame* 63–65; "Seafarers Menaced by a Storm" 59–60
Warner, Marina 3, 207n5
Wildflower, Ben 200, 202
William of Malmesbury: "Ebbo the Thief" (miracle) 47–48, 52
William the Conquerer 63
William IX of Aquitaine 55–56
Wilson, Liliana 199

"The Young Juggler" (film) 186
YouTube 198

Zacharias (Zaccarius, Zachary) 13–15, 18, 145
Zebedee 64
Zebel (midwife) 114
Zelomy 144; *see also* Salome
Ziolkowski, Jan M.: *The Juggler of Notre Dame and the Medievalizing of Modernity* 186
Zumárraga, Bishop 156
Zwingli, Ulrich 155

www.ingramcontent.com/pod-product-compliance
Ingram Content Group UK Ltd.
Pitfield, Milton Keynes, MK11 3LW, UK
UKHW010808100625
2148IPUK00007B/40